A Lotus Trail

Tara Gardiner

Copyright © 2021
Tara Gardiner
A LOTUS TRAIL
All rights reserved.

No part of this publication may be reproduced, distributed, or transmitted in any form or by any means, including photocopying, recording, or other electronic or mechanical methods, without the prior written permission of the publisher, except in the case of brief quotations embodied in critical reviews and certain other non-commercial uses permitted by copyright law.

Tara Gardiner

Printed in the United States of America
First Printing 2021
First Edition 2021

ISBN: 979-8543979877

10 9 8 7 6 5 4 3 2 1

Edited By: *Rachel Papworth*

Reviewed By: *Fran Linares*

To every being, that came into my life.

Table Of Contents

PROLOGUE 1
PART ONE 2
INTRODUCTION 3
    1. CRACKING UP: 1984 9
    2. SPECULATE TO ACCUMULATE: 1988-90 30
    3. WODKA DAZE: 1992-1995 120
    4. LIFT LIFE: 1996 172
    5. DOWN UNDER: 1997 189
    6. INSTITUTIONALISED CONCRETE JUNGLE: 1998 204
    7. MZUNGU: 1999 216
    8. BLOWN AWAY: 2001 259
    9. NOTHING BUT HASSLE: 2002 290
    10. BUCKET POWER: 2002 304
PART TWO 324
INTRODUCTION 325
    1. OM SWEET OM 2004 326
    2. TOP OF THE WORLD: 2004 361
    3. A DEVASTATING LOSS: 2005 369
    4. THE CENTER OF THE UNIVERSE: 2007 379
    5. DOGS AND GODS: 2004-2020 391
    6. LOCKDOWN: 2020 409
EPILOGUE 425
DEDICATION 427
GLOSSARY 428
ABOUT THE AUTHOR 439

Prologue

This is the true story of 20 years of my life, wandering around the world with a backpack; sex, drugs and rock 'n' roll: an outward journey...

...then discovering yoga, meditation, and gurus, and studying and practicing for 16 years; celibacy, abstinence, and self-reflection: an inner journey.

It has taken me 20 years to write this book, which is based on my personal experiences, my perspectives and what I was sober enough to remember.

All the characters mentioned herein are real but their names have been changed though, if you recognise yourself in this, it's probably you.

I want to thank all the people I have met. You made my life what it is.

PART ONE

Introduction

I woke in my hut, naked, surrounded by empty beer bottles, five naked Thai men—and no recollection of how I got there or who the men were.

I was born into a working-class family in the slums of Notting Hill, West London in 1962.

My father was a big, strong, singing Welshman with two jobs: an insurance salesperson by day, which provided him with a car; a singer and compere by night. He was at his happiest on stage, belting out Al Jolson songs, waving his hands and kicking his legs. He worked in the local pub until he eventually got his own, a rough dive in Notting Hill—where the frequent violence, and accessibility of drink at any time of day, accelerated his death.

My mumma, a beautiful, petite Londoner, also had two jobs: cleaning offices in the early mornings; selling fruit and vegetables on her father's Portobello Road stall at weekends.

They met in their teens, at the local pub where my father was singing, and fell in love. They were soon to marry and move into one room, in a shared house in the slums of Notting Hill, and they had four children: two boys and two girls.

I am the youngest by 20 minutes to my twin brother. My other brother is seven years older than us: my sister five years older than us.

With six mouths to feed, money was scarce. But we always had plenty of fruit and veg from my grandad's stall, and plenty of hand-me-downs, tots, and opportunities to buy something for half price because it had 'fallen off the back of a lorry'. We were the first in our street to have a video recorder, and the first to have a telephone.

When the slums got demolished, the council rehoused us in a small, three-bedroom house, which my father eventually bought. It had a front and back garden and was on a peaceful, tree-lined street. The neighbourhood was poor but vibrant. It was a happy community where everyone looked out for each other, sharing whatever they had.

I am the only member of my family who has backpacked around the world. It's a life I would not change for anything. I have never been married, though I've refused a few proposals, and never had children. If something didn't fit in my backpack, I didn't want or need it.

The earliest memory I have is from when I was seven years old. I managed to crush my right leg under a cast iron rocking horse in the park. I crushed both my tibia and my fibula: six breaks in total.

Because my parents were at work, my twin and his friend tried to carry me home, which moved the shattered pieces of bone. So when my leg healed it was deformed. I had eight operations in as many years to try to rectify this; resetting, staples, pins, plates. Part of my right hip was even moved into my leg.

So I spent most of my childhood and teenage years in hospital, in a wheelchair, on crutches or with a walking stick.

The doctors told my parents I would always have problems with my leg and would never have much mobility, or be able to play sports or lead a 'normal life'. Which was true; the leg never became straight. It bent to the side and was an inch shorter than the left one, so I had to wear a raised shoe.

I missed a lot of school because I was either in hospital or recovering at home using walking aids. And when I did go, I found it hard to catch up with the others in my class and could not understand what the teachers were teaching. Plus I was dyslexic—and the teachers didn't know what dyslexia was. They thought I was simply 'backward' so they used to leave me gazing out the window, daydreaming.

Most kids nicknamed me 'Spastic' or 'Hop-A-Long' and, at home, I was called 'Dopey girl' or 'Burkie'.

I accepted my status, and the blows to my already damaged confidence, becoming something of a hermit.

I could not play sports or run around with the other kids because my leg didn't bend properly and would drag behind, and I never got invited out because most kids didn't want to play out with a 'spastic'. So I didn't have many friends or outside activities and spent most of my earlier years alone, just watching.

I watched other girls my age get dressed up to go out, and fall in and out of love, get drunk, take drugs, and become pregnant and then single mothers—while I was still a virgin on crutches at home, making crafts, drawing and painting.

I still have a few problems with my leg now, arthritis being the main one. It's why I prefer to live in a hot climate.

In 1999, the doctors told me I needed a knee replacement. The thought of another operation, and the time it would take to recover, without even being certain it would work, terrified me. An arthroscopic knee washout bought me time but it was yoga that eventually saved me, at the same time as turning my whole life around for the better. Eventually, I came to realise that my disability, my lack of education, and having been bullied were among my greatest blessings and, in fact, among my greatest gurus. But I had a long journey to travel, both literally and metaphorically, before I reached that point.

I left school at 16, uneducated, with no qualifications, when the UK was in a severe recession. Finding a job, let alone a career, wasn't easy so my father employed me in his pub in Notting Hill. I worked and lived there for three years.

At first, I was timid and found it challenging to add up the rounds of drinks in my head, using my fingers or bits of paper instead. But as I got to know the customers and gained confidence behind the bar, I came out of my shell, joined in the banter and had a lot of fun. It wasn't long before I knew what everyone liked to drink, and could serve and add up three or four rounds at a time.

There was live music every night so the pub was always buzzing. It was frequented mainly by tough street boys, gangsters, hooligans and Hells Angels, all fighting to keep their reputations while drinking themselves into oblivion, taking whatever drugs were on offer and fucking around. I was getting an education no school could offer and also starting to make a few friends. My dad would give me the evenings off to enjoy the entertainment, and I started getting a social life and enjoying a completely different lifestyle.

I didn't drink alcohol then. I was probably the only sober one in the pub. So I spent some more time just watching.

I watched people turn into idiots after a few drinks, addicts after a few hits. I watched discussions turn into fights and marriages into battlefields, all fuelled by lying and cheating. Fights could start at any time with a "Who are you looking at?!" Then everything in the pub that wasn't screwed down would be used as a weapon. Bar stools, tables, glasses, bottles and ashtrays would take flight across the smoke-filled room, until there was no glass left unbroken or window left unsmashed.

Then you had the protection rackets. "Pay me 50 quid a week or I'll smash the pub up." If there was anything left to smash!

Once, our whole family needed police protection from a mob of gangsters. My father had thrown them out for troublemaking and they were out to get any one of us.

My father was a strong man but having to fight four or five men several times a week sometimes became too much for him, and then a quick push of the optic would give him the whiskey shot he needed to calm his nerves. I watched a powerful man turn into a nervous wreck and alcoholic seemingly overnight. My mumma decided she had had enough and moved out, back to our house. But then she too found solace—a companion to replace my father—in whiskey.

When the shell of my Father retired from the pub, he moved back in with my mumma. And I moved into a flat with my handsome, hippy boyfriend, Dickey, who had been living with me above the pub for the previous two years.

Dickey brought puff into my life and I enjoyed its relaxing feeling and the rose-tinted glass it put over my eyes and the world.

We were both on unemployment benefit and we lived hand-to-mouth, spending all our time together getting stoned, playing music, watching TV and going to the many free concerts that were happening in response to the recession and the miners' strike.

Often we would talk about all the things we were going to do and all the places we were going to travel to.

Two years later, we were still in London, puffing day and night, talking the same bullshit, living in a fantasy.

One day, I had had enough talk and decided that I wanted to get out into the world. I'd already spent so much of my life disabled. Now I was disabling myself voluntarily!

I kissed Dickey goodbye, moved into a bedsit and started to do casual work in an exhibition centre. That was when my life began.

Read on to find out what happened to the dopey girl who would never lead a 'normal life'.

1. Cracking Up: 1984

I met crazy Molly when we both worked at the exhibition centre in London. She sold hotdogs—and various other things, like ups, downs, in the middle, hash, weed and LSD. She had long, curly, black air that flowed down her back, with a fringe that almost covered her big, brown eyes, a wide, plump mouth and an overbite that could eat an apple through a letterbox. Molly used to say that her mouth was like a plunger!

I worked in a restaurant selling teas and coffees, standing behind a big, metallic machine for ten to twelve hours a day.

If a customer wanted tea, I had to press the green button: for coffee, the red one. It was easy—and dull—and the perfect job to enable me to get stoned all day. I soon became one of Molly's regular customers and, of course, it wasn't hot dogs I wanted.

"A few of us are going to the pub tonight to celebrate the last day. You fancy it?" she asked, at the close of an exhibition, her husky voice escaping that throat burnt by too many spliffs.

"Sounds good to me. Which one?"

"The Thorny around the corner."

"Can you puff in there?" I wasn't going if you couldn't.

"Does a bear shit in the woods?"

"Great, I'll see you later."

I wasn't sure where it was but, after four weeks of us working long hours without days off, I was up for a night out. When I finished my shift, I went to the toilet to pack myself tightly into my size eight drainpipe jeans, tuck in my low-cut, red shirt that showed off my 40-inch bust, re-spike my multi-coloured hair and put on some makeup.

My big blue eyes checked me over. I was looking good and ready to party.

When I arrived, the jukebox was blaring and the atmosphere was alive and exciting. People were already dancing around the back by the pool table and I couldn't wait to join in. I got myself a large vodka and coke and cruised over, accepting the spliff some guy passed me.

"Go on! Go on! Argh, you bastard!" Molly shouted at the pool balls. I walked over and passed her the spliff.

"Cheers. I got lots of supplies," Molly tapped her jeans' pockets.

"Good to know. What do you plan to do with your cash?" We had just been paid for the whole show: an entire month's wages. She shrugged her petite frame. "I don't wanna spend mine in the pub," I continued. "I want to go travelling. I've heard there's work in France, in tourist places or picking fruit."

"France! That's a shit 'ole. They don't even speak English," she said, pulling hard on the spliff.

"I want to get out. I'm 21 and haven't done anything with my life. For the last four years, I've just been getting stoned with my boyfriend. I need some adventure."

"If you go to New York, I'll come with you."

"New York? I'm not even sure I know where that is," I laughed.

"It's America. They have liquid acid there that you put in your eyes. And I've just split up with me bird as well and could do with a change of scene. I heard there are women all over Manhattan begging for it." Molly's description of her mouth came to my mind and suddenly I was picturing a plunger over a plughole!

"Oi! Carpet muncher! It's your shot," some Aussie guy shouted across the table.

BANG! She whacked him around the head with her pool cue and he was down, "Get some respect, you wanker!" she yelled over his semi-conscious body, while the other guys removed him from the pub and I took over his game.

I liked this girl.

"Yeah, let's do it!" I said as the spot ball rolled gently into the pocket.

We celebrated our new friendship by dropping acid and singing *New York, New York*.

Two days later we had our tickets and nothing could stop us. We packed our clothes and headed to the airport.

"Fuck, I forgot about these," Molly said as we arrived at the entrance to the airport.

"What is it?" I was looking at the piece of cling film she was holding.

"It's a couple of acid tabs. Well, the best place for these is our mouths." Her massive smile took over her whole face as she popped one into her mouth and the other into mine. After 20 minutes, we were both hallucinating and enjoying a psychedelic ride to New York City.

We arrived in the land of giants, where everything seemed bigger than in London, at six pm, looking like something that the cat brought in. "Fuck! He's huge," I said to Molly as a beefy immigration man, with a black buckled belt and gun, towered over me. His eyes stared into mine and I froze.

"Passport, ma'am." The drawl of his accent was loud and scary as he zoomed in and out of my drug-hazed vision.

My brain was complete mush from the acid but I managed to find his hand to give him my passport. Molly was standing close beside me, staring into space, working her jaw so fast it made her foam at the mouth.

"Are you together?"

"No, we're just friends," I said and we both burst out laughing.

The immigration guy realised we were off our tits and split us up, putting us into separate interrogation rooms, where we were searched and asked many questions regarding our visit. Finally, after three hours, they let us through with six-week visas. We ripped those out of our passports because we were staying as long as we wanted. We were in New York and it was playtime!

Still too mashed to work out the subway system, I hailed a yellow and black cab. "Taxi!" I hollered. (That in itself was so exciting). One pulled up to the sidewalk and we jumped in.

"Where to, pretty ladies?" we were asked in a gum-chewing drawl.

"The Holiday Inn bar in the East Village, please." It was the only place we knew of and we needed a drink.

"You're going to the city?" We were soon to learn that that was what most people called it.

"We sure are," I said. Hardly able to believe I had got out of London, I was so excited. Sitting back in the safety of the cab, I took in my first sights of New York as we slotted into the mass of traffic. "Oh man! I can't wait to be part of this," I said to Molly, who was still staring into space.

On either side of our taxi, the sidewalks were an abundance of bright, colourful clothes wrapped around overweight bodies moving at high speed in trainers, skateboards or rollerblades. It was a whole new world of fashion —baseball jackets and caps, short dresses and crop tops—against a backdrop of neon-flashing concrete that reached the grey skies, all wrapped up in the smell of piss and Chinese food.

"The end is nigh!" shouted a grey, old man, with a billboard around his neck, into my window.

"Oh my! Am I in an open-air lunatic asylum?" My mind raced around in a mixture of fear and excitement.

"Oh, it's a lunatic asylum ma'am. Yes indeed," the cab driver replied.

I am sure my mouth was gaping when we stopped at the traffic lights as I gazed at a woman, trying to work out where her body was. Apart from her eyes, she seemed to be nothing but a mass of hanging blubber while another, with a body like a rake, ate out of the bin.

"Oh my! Look up, Molly. It's the Empire State Building."

She was still staring in shock.

We finally arrived at the Holiday Inn and, for the first time, I felt the touch of Manhattan under my feet.

So this is New York! I was ecstatic as I walked the ten steps down into a basement bar and entered the small room. It was dimly lit and scattered with neon Budweiser and Miller Lite signs, and a jukebox blaring out the Rolling Stones' *I Can't Get No Satisfaction*. I went to the counter on the right, while Molly staggered to the back, past four booths and the pool table, to use the toilet. "Only bottled beer," the bartender told me as I stuffed our bags into a corner.

"Then two of those, my lovely." It was cold and refreshing but piss-weak. We were gonna need something more potent than that to get through this jet lag and acid come down. "Two vodka and cokes, please."

The bars were open from four pm until two am. There was usually only one counter and one bartender in charge of everything: money; stock-check; cleaning; and customers. There was no optic on the bottles, so it was up to the bartender to decide how much they put in your glass. Plus every fourth drink was a 'bar back', which meant the bar bought you a drink; in other words, buy-three-get-one-free. Which also meant the more you tipped the bartender, the more alcohol you got.

Molly was now bouncing around the pool table, still tripping off her tits, trying to sort out a game of pool, and I sat on the only available bar stool next to a gentle giant with short-cropped ginger hair and freckles to match. "New to town?" he said.

"Just arrived from London. I think I'm still in shock."

"I know what you mean. I'm from upstate New York. Angus is my name".

"Nice to meet you." I shook his proffered hand.

"My lady just left me, but I'm glad she's gone 'cause now I can go rock climbing with my buddies for the summer," he drawled.

"We're looking for somewhere to stay. Maybe we could work something out with your apartment, if it's available, when you go rock climbing?"

"Sure. If you clean it up and keep it clean, you can move in tomorrow and stay for free."

"Deal!" And we high-fived.

"When we going to go to New York, then?" Molly had come to join me at the bar.

"We're here, you dope! This is Angus, and we're moving in with him tomorrow." I smiled, well chuffed with myself.

"Are we really here?" Molly surveyed the bar with her bulging eyes.

"You sure are, ma'am," Angus told her.

She ran out to the street, then rushed back in, her huge smile lighting up her face.

"Fuck! We did it!"

"Yes, we fucking did it." I laughed, and we hugged and jumped up and down.

Amazement written on her face, she went back to the pool table, and I continued to listen to Angus' story.

"What you on about, 'high and low'?! They're spots and stripes!" Molly bellowed her response to the American style of pool, over the din of the bar. I enjoyed watching her beat everyone hands down, while I chatted with anyone who would listen.

"Do you want to come to my place for a party? My folks are away," Mickey, who lived in Brooklyn, asked me.

"That'd be great!" The bar was closing and we had nowhere else to go.

The party was a private affair, with Mickey playing the guitar, me singing and Molly rolling the spliffs. After a few songs, I raided the massive, double-doored, metallic fridge. It was full of food that was wrapped and wrapped again. There was so much packaging on everything. But I managed to get it all off and at the goods, while Mickey and Molly played backgammon.

With a belly full of home-cooked pasta, New York biscuits and ice cream, I crashed out on the sofa until, a few hours later the sound of Molly's voice, dragged me from sleep. "I don't care if you've cleaned your teeth. I'm not sleeping with you." Molly was trying to fit on the sofa with me, while Mickey was standing in the doorway, holding a toothbrush. Reluctantly Mickey went to bed, leaving us puzzled as to how often he cleaned his teeth.

In the morning, still not sober enough to work out the subway, we hailed a cab. "Taxi!" It was Molly's turn to call it.

"Second Avenue between First and Second," I told the driver when he pulled over and popped his head out of the window. We jumped in the back with our bags and he headed over the Brooklyn Bridge back to Manhattan.

We got out in front of a tall, brown building, between two delicatessens, and entered through heavy metal doors. In front of us was a stone staircase and we climbed to the second floor and knocked on the door. "Morning, Angus. Your cleaners are here," I sang out as he opened the door. He just grunted and nodded for us to enter.

"Late night, was it?" Molly croaked.

"Mmmmm, I sure got a hell of a steam train riding through my head." He looked rough and in need of a shower. "I'm going to get out of here and leave you girls to it, OK?" wiping the sleep out of his eyes.

"Sure, Angus," we chorused.

Patting down his hair and adjusting his dirty baggy jeans, he left the apartment.

It was a small, one-bedroom place that looked like someone had just emptied a whole garbage truck inside. It took us all day and many trash bags just to make it liveable.

"Wow! You girls have done a great job. You take the bedroom and I'll sleep in the hammock in the lounge," Angus said on his return. "I haven't paid the rent or electricity bills so you can't cook, and by four pm you need to use candles."

"That's fine by us." We only planned to sleep there anyway.

The first day, once the sun went down, I understood why Angus slept in the hammock. Cockroaches! And not normal cockroaches: they were New Yorkers with attitude, the size of your thumb, and would fight you over a piece of candle wax. I would often feel them crawling around the bed at night but, hey, a free apartment in the city. I wasn't complaining.

We celebrated our first night in a clean kitchen with a Chinese takeaway. All three of us tucked in, getting our stomachs ready for a 'family' night at the Holiday.

"I love these little boxes the food comes in and all these condiments."

"Yeah, they're a meal in itself," Molly said, her mouth full of rice.

After we had finished the food in the boxes, not leaving even one crumb for the cockroaches, we moved into the lounge to let it all digest. All of a sudden, I had to rush to the toilet to vomit. "I need to lie down," I told the others once I was finally able to leave the bathroom. I headed to the bedroom, feeling dizzy and weak.

"What about the bar?" Molly shouted to my back.

"Go ahead, I'll join you when I feel better," and I lay down and didn't get up again until morning.

I had just experienced my first case of Monosodium Glutamate (MSG) poisoning. Most of the food seemed to include this flavour enhancer and we both got bouts of sickness in reaction, but Molly would get them the worst and couldn't eat much more than a pizza slice or crisps. She lost so much weight that her mouth stood out even more against her thin face.

It was summertime and the smell from the subways, traffic and MSG food, combined with the heat, was overpowering and suffocating. But the parks provided welcome opportunities for traffic-free breaks. Most were concrete squares, with a tree or two, that served as open stages for free entertainment. They were always packed with a mishmash of people, each of whom had a show to perform.

Out-of-work actors, comedians, and singers who worked in bars or restaurants, would turn up and perform. Self-expression was in abundance, especially with fashion. You could get away with anything and everything. It was so exciting: you never knew what craziness you were going to come across next.

I had been walking around, looking in the windows of restaurants and bars for job advertisements, when I took a break on a park bench to watch the never-ending entertainment. "Hi, how's it going? Wanna do a line?" a cute guy offered. He had come to sit next to me.

"Sure." I had never tried coke, so I was up for giving it a whirl.

Anthony, who had fashioned himself like Jim Morrison, had a tiny spoon on a chain around his neck with which he spooned white powder up my nose. My nose and throat went numb as it slipped down them into my body, and I felt the need to dance, walk or run.

"Let's go and check out the music," I said with a mouth that was moving faster than the words. We headed over to a three-piece band, and I danced away with the rest of the freaks.

"You got 20 bucks?" Anthony asked. "I'll get us some more." That was his scam: get me high and fleece me.

"I don't have any money, dude. I'm looking for a job." I moved away.

Mashed as I was, I was glad that the streets and avenues were gridded with either numbers or letters, so I could mechanically drift along. Otherwise, I would have got completely lost.

Nearing home, I noticed a sign in the window of a restaurant indicating they were looking for bartenders and went in to check it out.

"Hi, I'm interested in the job advertised on the window." The girl behind the counter was sporting a purple Mohawk.

"Just a minute." She went out the back and yelled "Cory!"

A short Korean guy in a Hawaiian shirt came over. "Hello. You can work bar?"

"Yes, I have excellent bar experience."

"Ooh, you no from here?"

"Yes, I am. I've just been living in England a while and picked up the accent." It was worth a try.

"You need pay tax?" he whispered. Not knowing how best to answer, I just shrugged. "You no need pay tax. You start tomorrow." He nodded at me.

"Great. I have a friend that no need pay tax also." I smiled to let him know I understood.

"OK. You and friend come here tonight and we talk." And with that, he walked off.

I ran to the Holiday Inn to tell Molly the good news and, a few hours later, we returned to the bar together.

"Fill application forms. OK?" He handed each of us a form. "You have green card?" He pointed to the boxed line on the form.

"Of course we do," I replied as I wrote any ol' number.

"If you need, you buy in Times Square. Fifty dollars." He smiled.

"OK. Thank you." That was good to know.

"You start tomorrow. Meet me outside The Blue Bird at four pm." He took our filled-out forms and shuffled off.

The Blue Bird, a long bar, with a pool table and jukebox at the back next to the toilets, became Molly's. In the centre of the wall facing the counter was a stage that hosted live music a few nights a week. The bar was rarely busy so Molly would hustle pool, drink, enjoy her choice of begging-for-it women and pop over to my bar, directly opposite, in her free time.

The Boom Boom was where all the action was. It was small, dark and dingy, illuminated only by the usual Budweiser and Miller neon lights. The counter, on the left as you entered, had a couple of bar stools and, at the back by the toilets, was a jukebox and pool table.

"You no sell to prostitutes, OK?" Cory said to me when we entered my bar.

"Oh, OK." I had never met a prostitute before, so I was wondering how I'd be able to recognise one. Maybe they wore badges around here?

I'd just gone behind the bar to familiarise myself with the setup when my first customer walked in.

"I need the bathroom," she told me as she walked past in a tight red skirt so short it was little more than a thick belt, with a gold crop top. Her long, muscular, light coffee-coloured legs ended in gold stilettos.

"Excuse me, miss? You want to have a bath?" I called after her, baffled, as she went into the toilet. Oh, *that's* a bathroom. I had a whole new language to learn.

"Hi, I'm Starlight. Can I get a glass of water, please?" she asked on her return, in a soft southern accent that had a hint of maleness. Her pretty face was somewhat masculine despite her big black eyes, surrounded by gold glitter, and long false eyelashes. Her bright red lipstick gave her mouth a sensual look and enhanced her white teeth. "What's a pretty girl like you doing in hell?" she asked as I put the glass of water in front of her.

"Working," I answered.

"Oh my! Listen to that voice. Say something more," she teased.

"What's a pretty girl like you doing in hell?"

"Working." And we both laughed.

She was hanging around, looking for business, like the rest of the people that came in.

The door opened. "Lordy Lordy," I breathed while Starlight eyed the newcomer with a chuckle. A bright silver-besuited man was entering, with the classic Swagger of 1980s New York, dragging one leg and swinging one arm. Tilted on the side of his jet-black face was a silver fedora with a zebra-skin band.

"Gimme a screwdriver." His psychedelic shirt was louder than his voice. He threw five bucks on the counter.

"A screwdriver?" I looked at Starlight for guidance.

"It's vodka and orange. You worked in a bar before, right?"

"Yes, but I never heard it called that."

As I fixed his drink, I watched girls flock around him to receive snorts from the gold spoon that, like Anthony, he wore on a chain around his neck. "Now, get to work," he told them, and they left the bar to flaunt their miniskirted legs at the passing traffic.

"You're new to town?" he observed, giving me a once-over. I nodded and smiled.

"Welcome to Manhattan." He offered me a spoonful of powder and I gladly accepted. As numbness rolled down my throat, I grabbed a Bud and took a seat on the flat fridge next to the counter, opposite Starlight.

"My name's Bingo. If you need any more of this, just let me know." He winked, then loped over to the jukebox. The sound of *Sexual Healing,* by Marvin Gaye, filled the room while he made love to himself in the reflection of the glass.

"He's the number one pimp around here," Starlight whispered, "but I don't work for him. I work for myself. He beats them girls up if they don't bring in enough cash, and you don't wanna be taking any blow off him again, you hear me? I'll get it for you if you need it. That nigga will have you hooked and on the streets in no time. Yes ma'am." She nodded decisively. I was happy she was in the bar to teach me the drinks' names and the ways of the new world I'd entered.

Soon the bar became a mass of excitement as it filled up with prostitutes, pimps, johns and dealers. I got busy making their drinks and Starlight got busy informing me on who was who, between taking johns outside for 20 minutes at a time. I kept my mouth shut as I watched johns come in, take their pick of the beauties and leave, lines of coke getting cut up on the bar counter, the spliffs and crack pipes being passed around.

Then the night was over. I checked my tips bowl next to the register and was surprised to find fifty-seven bucks, some weed, a few wraps of coke. "Wow! I have a party right in my hands," I said to Starlight, who was still propping up the counter.

"You wanna hang out?" she smiled.

"Sure, if there's something open?"

"Honey, this ain't called the 24-hour city, for nuffing."

"Let's do it!" I cut us up a line each and took two beers from the fridge.

"First, I need to make you into arm candy," she said, and set about piling makeup over my face. "Now you look so hot them niggas will be screaming! I'm gonna call you Twinkle."

I looked like a clown.

Starlight hailed a cab and we were off.

The after-hours bar was dark and dingy, with blacked-out windows. Starlight guided me towards the bar. "Yo bro'. This is my sister, Twinkle. You take care of her, OK?" she said to the bartender, who looked like a black version of The Hulk. "I'll be back soon," she told me as she went off with a john. No time off for that girl.

A few people from The Boom Boom were shaking up a storm on the dance floor, so I joined them, trying to learn the new funky moves.

"Inhale it in one, girl, and then hold it for as long as you can," Bingo said, handing me a test tube pipe.

"Ooh man!" was all I could say as I returned it, feeling energised and numb.

"That, my sweet child, is crack cocaine," and he handed me a little glass bottle with a white rock in it. "This one's on me," and he Funky Chickened away to the middle of the dance floor.

I was soon to find another pipe to smoke up that baby. It was a fantastic sensation that finished too quickly, leaving you wanting more.

My life became The Boom Boom bar, after-hour bars and crack cocaine. I was on full power 24 hours a day, in the 24-hour city.

One day, I was in my apartment swinging in the hammock and checking out the uninteresting life of a cockroach, when there was a ring of the bell. It was Cory. "You go work. Problem there. I pay you." He was rubbing his head to ease his stress.

"Sure, I'll just get my stuff." Anything was better than watching cockroaches; they don't get up to much.

I could hear music blasting out of the bar from a few blocks away and was curious about what I would find inside. "Look out! The Brit's here," someone shouted as I entered the cage of chimps on acid.

"What the fuck happened here?" I said to anyone who would listen as I put the liquor bottles back on the shelf, and closed the empty fridges and register. Most people were dancing around the bar, and one fat lady was sitting on the pool table with dollar bills sticking out from her cleavage, swigging from a bottle, singing at the top of her voice.

"Go home, you Brit," bounced off the walls as I turned the jukebox down and went over to Starlight, who was occupying her regular spot at the bar.

"What's happened?" I asked her.

"Well Twinkle, this guy came in shooting a gun, and that army-type bartender ran out."

"Oh, that's Grets. Was she hurt?"

"No, ma'am. She ran like her arse was on fire, straight out that door." Starlight was laughing so much she nearly fell off her stool.

Grets grew up in a small village in Iceland, which wasn't accepting of her as a gay woman. She had moved to New York with, her lover, Yana, so that they could be together. They did not drink much alcohol and never touched drugs.

Molly heard about the shootout and came over to my bar when her shift finished. "Let's go over there when you've finished. I bet Grets is in a right state," she suggested as I made us each a Long Island Iced Tea.

Grets and Yana had a one-bed apartment two blocks away. We rode the elevator to the third floor and knocked on their door. "Just came to see if you're OK," I said as we entered the spotless, modern apartment.

"That focking bastard give me a gun and told me to sort the problem out," Grets replied, running her hands through her cropped white hair. "I no touch guns." I watched her slim body shaking as she walked up and down the lounge.

"Don't stress out, man," Molly offered. "Let's go and have a drink." Her answer to everything.

"Yeah, let's. Yana, no tea, we go out." Yana entered from the kitchen, elegant in a long, flowing dress that fitted perfectly over her tall, slim body. Her long, blonde hair framed her pretty face, with its big blue eyes. She was stunning.

We went to a quiet restaurant next door and sat in a booth. "I no go back. It's good if you no go back," Grets told us.

"Yeah, we need to stick together." Molly agreed. She was fed up with her job anyway.

"What?!!! I love my job. I don't want to no go back!" I said in shock.

The three women were looking at me in disbelief. I had no choice. "OK, I no go back either."

Molly and I became tourists for a few days, checking out high rise after high rise, sitting at the Statue of Liberty and taking all the drugs on offer at the park. But I wanted some fresh air. "Let's check out the beach, Molly. Coney Island is just a train ride away," I proposed one sunny morning.

"Yeah. I get a great tan. My skin goes black in hours."

She got third-degree burns. Her skin was one big blister, and she could not walk or be touched.

We got the train back, straight to the free hospital, where she was given a nice room for the night and put on a drip to bring her fluids up. I went back to the apartment, happy for an early night.

While I was sleeping, I felt something touch me and thought it was a cockroach. Oh, it was a cock all right, but no roach. "What are you doing?" I screamed at Angus as I punched him in the face. He was trying to slip his uncontrollable friend inside me.

"Sorry, sorry. I just thought... ," he stuttered as he scurried back to his hammock like a cockroach that had just had candle wax tipped on it.

The next day, I went to get Molly to bring her home and told her what had happened. "What you been doing to my bitch?" she barked at Angus when she entered the apartment. I was not her bitch but we let Angus think I was to keep him from hitting on us.

"I'm sorry. I was drunk and didn't realise what I was doing." He was such a soft giant. He quickly left—and did not come home that night.

The next morning, I went to the Holiday Inn to check if anyone had seen him. As I approached the bar, I saw a hammock hanging from two lamp posts with a bedraggled Angus lying in it. "What are you doing, man?" I asked.

"I thought I'd stay here a few days to give you some space."

"What? I've forgotten all about it. Come home."

"No. Honest, I want to stay here." And he closed his eyes.

Angus camped outside the Holiday Inn, leaving the whole apartment to Molly and me. But a man sleeping in a hammock outside a bar caused such a stir in the Village that even the local newspaper came to do a report. We needed to resolve the situation, so Grets let us move in with her and Angus moved back in with the cockroaches.

Grets' place was clean, with electricity, hot water, and no cockroaches. It was heaven. She made us a camp bed in the lounge and a hot meal.

Chilling out on the sofa, she noticed I was limping and that my knee was red and swollen. "What happen you?"

"Too many sleepless nights and too much dancing," I confessed.

"Tomorrow, I take you hospital," Grets said sternly. I had no choice but to obey.

I left the hospital in a brace and on crutches, and had to rest while Molly hit the streets to see what job she could find. "No jobs for me out there today," she told me when she came home.

I wasn't surprised. Unable to eat the MSG food and with all the partying, she now looked like a thin stick, with bulging eyes and that wide mouth from which her voice issued in a croak. Looking more like a bullfrog than a human, her chances of getting work serving the public were slim.

"Let's go out to see what's happening on the streets," she croaked. So the stick insect and the cripple headed off to hang out outside The Boom Boom bar.

The corner was buzzing, with hookers walking up and down, swinging their skirts up to expose their gender, pimps collecting their money and dealers selling their wares. "Wanna good time, handsome?" If he did, the car door would open, and off they would go.

"Ooh Twinkle, what happened to you?" Starlight said when she saw me approaching on my crutches.

"Old injury, Starlight. I'm used to it." And I leaned against the wall outside the bar.

"I miss you. The new guy doesn't let us in," she sighed.

"We quit over the gun thing," I said as I hobbled over to the window to take a look inside. It was empty save for a bored Asian guy, playing cards with himself.

"You look like a piece of shit, girl," she told me and started to apply makeup all over my face. "You been fucking with that blow. Hell, that shit is bad. You'll be on these streets next if Bingo sees you." And she went off to flash her cock at a passing car and get inside.

"Oh wow! He was so good, I wanted to give him his money back!" Starlight told me on her return.

"Haha. I've missed you too, Starlight."

"Oh, the British Empire is here." It was Jamaican Joe, a local crack dealer, in a black suit and trilby hat—worn on the side, the trademark style of the pimps and dealers. Like Bingo, he walked with the Swagger. All the black men in The East Village had special walks. It was something to see—especially when they were high.

"What's happening, girls?" Joe glided towards us.

"We're cool, Joe. Just checking out being on the other side of the bar," I said, pointing over to Molly, who was sitting down, rolling a spliff.

"Yo! Joe!" Molly got up to come over. "What's up?"

"I'm hanging. Let's go shoot some pool over at The Bluebird. There's a band playing, and I think we can hustle us some money." And we set off for the Bluebird, Joe dragging his leg behind him in the Swagger.

As we entered, he handed me a plastic bag of crack capsules. "Put that in your brace. Dirty Babylon everywhere. You better take one: you look like you need it." And he was off to make bets on the game.

I sat at the bar, smoking my crack cigarette, enjoying the live music and watching the game. Molly was on a winning streak, and Joe was making money. When he needed a capsule, he would stand next to me, and I would fish him one out.

"You girls worked good tonight! Let's go out and party." Joe said, and we headed to the after-hours bar.

We met Joe every night, and this became our new job.

After a month, I was starting to get confused about whether I was asleep or awake. Everything was blending into one big haze, and I was becoming paranoid, thinking someone was following me. Molly was becoming agitated, anxious, and fighting over the games.

"Molly, I think we're losing the plot, mate, and smoking way too much crack. It was just a bit of fun, and now look at us chasing that pipe."

"Yeah, you're right. I was thinking only yesterday that I want to go home. I'm starving."

"Yeah, I'm starving too."

And the next day, we booked tickets, said our goodbyes and flew back to London—a little shabbier and a little thinner, but a lot more streetwise.

2. Speculate To Accumulate: 1988-90

Molly answered the door to our one-bedroom squat on a council estate in London.

"You got a quarter of hash?" Mick stood just inside the door with 15 quid in his hand.

"Yeah. I've also got tenner bags of the best weed I've ever smoked, if you want."

"Go on then," he smiled.

We'd been back a few months, had broken into an empty flat and had made it home. It wasn't long before our New York skills came into play, and we were cooking up cocaine into crack rocks to satisfy our naughty little pleasure, while selling bits of puff, weed, and coke to support it.

"Ready?" Molly asked me as she put on her jean jacket with the secret pockets, where she stashed the stuff she would sell tonight.

"I'm coming," I said, hobbling behind her, stuffing my pipe and a rock into my jeans pocket for later.

I was still waiting for knee surgery to repair the torn cartilage and ligament. The operation day finally came and, as soon as I recovered and was back on my feet, I got a job with an airline company.

It was an easy job; sending out tickets for people going on holiday. With this income and our other business, I was able to take occasional advantage of this job's perks; employees could buy any unsold flight tickets for the next day at half price.

But weekend jaunts to Europe did not satisfy my yearning to explore the world. Molly was content as long as she could be pissed and stoned—unfortunately, she's still in that condition today—but numbing my urge to travel, with drugs and booze, wasn't enough for me.

On one of our weekend breaks, I met Dolphin, a handsome, 24-year-old estate agent. He was clean and polite in a middle-class public schoolboy sort of way; with big brown eyes that had eyelashes so long they reached his eyebrows, and a beautifully-chiselled chin that held a big smile with a dolphin-sounding laugh.

I was upgrading from small-time gangsters and drug dealers, and he enjoyed a fascinating bit of rough. They say 'opposites attract'.

We continued dating when we got back to London and started to get closer, maybe even falling in love.

"I've just made a big deal on a property sale. Let's go on holiday," he said to me excitedly one night in the pub.

"Where d'ya wanna go? I've got savings." I'd been waiting for someone to travel with for a long time.

"Greece? Spain?"

"Boring! I can go there with work. Why don't we get an around-the-world ticket?"

"What? I said 'holiday!'" He was horrified at the thought.

"It *will* be a holiday; just a long one! Come on, Dolphin! We're young, and we can do all this other stuff when we're old." I didn't want to leave him, and I didn't want to go alone, but I needed to get out. Life in London was becoming a drug and booze-filled haze.

That night I gave him the dirtiest, naughtiest sex of his life, and he realised he didn't want to lose me, so he agreed. In the morning, we went to a travel agent. Still sore from the night before, I just about managed to sit down and we booked two tickets to India, Thailand, Indonesia, Bali, Australia, New Zealand, Fiji and Los Angeles, leaving in one week.

I was excited and shitting myself at the same time. I had only just heard of these countries and now I was going to them.

~ ~ ~

We finished the last of our puff outside Heathrow airport and then went to check in. Sitting around waiting to board, I could feel Dolphin was thinking to back out.

"You OK?"

"Yeah, of course," he lied, clutching his guidebook like it was a ventilation machine.

"You're just stoned. We have each other. We're going to have the best time of our lives," I tried to reassure my baby. Underneath, I wasn't sure either. I just knew I had to get away.

I felt great relief once we had boarded the plane and took off to the unknown. "No running away now," I told him as I kissed him and relaxed into my seat and into my new life with the man I loved.

As we landed in Bombay, reality hit us: we were in a completely new world—one that felt like being inside an oven. With Dolphin holding onto his guidebook like a life vest, we left the airport to get a taxi to a hotel.

The air was heavy, still and hot, under a smoggy, grey, pollution-shaded sky. Sweat dripped down my face and onto my clothes, which were starting to stick to my body. I gathered my thick long hair and tied it into a bun on top of my wet head.

After a push and shove at the prepaid taxi counter, we got a ticket for our car. Having found it, we quickly threw our bags in the boot and jumped into the back. "Put on the A-C," Dolphin shouted to the driver, over the sound of a Bollywood song screeching from tiny, rusty speakers on the dashboard, which also held a burning incense stick, a crumpled photo of some Hindu gods, and a statue of Ganesh, the jolly, potbellied, elephant-headed god who brings good luck.

"What was that smell?" he asked me, fanning himself with his guidebook.

"Probably piss and shit," I said, looking out the window in shock at people pissing and shitting in the parched street. Every patch was cramped with dirty, ragged people snorting and spitting over the empty plastic bottles and rubbish spilling out alongside tin huts, stray dogs, and sacred cows.

At the traffic lights, deformed beggars, some without limbs, filthy children carrying babies, some sniffing glue from paper bags, were tapping on our window insistently, with their hands out, trying to get our attention.

"It's like a horror movie! What's all the noise?" Firecrackers were sounding off everywhere.

"Deafening, that's what it is," I said, holding his hand.

When the taxi pulled up at our hotel, we ran inside like scared kids and breathed deeply in the grubby foyer. A greasy, unkempt man showed us our passable room, and I locked the door and relaxed. "What the fuck was that?" I laughed so loud that Dolphin just had to join in, and we flopped onto the floral blanket.

"I found this restaurant in the guidebook. Let's shower and go eat," Dolphin said, once we had calmed down and started to peel off my soggy, sweaty clothes.

We were not brave enough to walk, so we got a taxi to the upmarket restaurant. "Now this is more like it," Dolphin said as a man open the restaurant door, and a smartly-dressed waiter walked us across a clean marble floor to a table covered in a starched white tablecloth, sparkling cutlery and a vase of plastic flowers. The aromatic smells of spice had my mouth watering, and I couldn't wait to eat.

"What do you suggest?" Dolphin asked the waiter who was smiling down on us.

"First time in India?" he asked.

"Yes." Was it that obvious?

"I think that you would be liking to try the thali." And he pointed at the table to the side of us.

I could see several small dishes, rice and bread all on a tin plate. "There is veg or non-veg option," he said, with a wobble of his head. I'd never seen that gesture and found myself smiling in surprise.

The guidebook said we shouldn't eat meat in this country." Dolphin whispered in my ear.

"Then I'll have a veg one."

"Two veg thalis and one big bottle of Kingfisher beer, please."

The waiter was back almost instantly, opening the bottle in front of us and filling two glasses with amber liquid and foam. "Cheers." Clinking our glasses, we washed down the dust with the refreshing cold beer, finally relaxing into our new life of adventure.

The waiter returned and put two big plates down in front of us. "Ooh, this is delicious," I said between bites, shoving it in, and Dolphin nodded in agreement.

With full bellies, we got a taxi back to the hotel and flopped onto the bed to check the guidebook. "There's a beach not too far away from here," Dolphin told me as I lay on his chest.

"Yay! A tropical ocean!" I nearly wet myself at the thought.

"Yeah. Let's go to acclimatise and get over the culture shock."

I was already off the bed, dragging Dolphin to the reception desk to ask the hotel manager the best way to get there. "I will try to get you tickets for a train, but they may be full because people are travelling for the start of Diwali tomorrow," he told us.

"What's that?" I asked.

"It's the festival of light, when we pray to Ganesha to remove obstacles and we clean the house and fill it with light to welcome Lakshmi, the goddess who brings luck and prosperity." He told us proudly.

"Ooh, is that why everyone's setting off firecrackers?" Dolphin asked.

"Yes, this is the light for Lakshmi." He pointed to a plaster statue dressed in bright clothes.

"So cute," I said as we headed back to our room.

But before we could even get the key in the door, the hotel manager was hovering beside us. "I can get you two tickets in first class for 10 pm tomorrow, but an extra charge because of Diwali."

"We'll take them," Dolphin said, nodding at me.

"Yep. I'm cool with that." I was excited to get out of this stifling furnace and see a tropical beach.

The next evening, we got a taxi through traffic-choked streets and filthy alleyways to the railway station. "It's a fucking freak show," Dolphin said as we got out of the taxi. The station looked like an overcrowded home for the desolate and insane.

"Just look ahead and keep moving," I told him as we moved through the nightmare of half-dead bodies.

"I can taste the piss. It's so strong," he choked at me, his eyes watering.

"Breathe through your nose, baby," I said as we tried to dodge through what felt like some kinda war zone, with hands grabbing at us.

"Ooh, the smell! I'm gonna be sick." His long legs strode faster, stepping over the bodies that were scattered over the floor, either waiting for a train or taking shelter.

We walked the length of the train—a long, rusty, metal contraption with people hanging from the doors and sitting on the roof—and were relieved to find our carriage was empty and self-contained, with only two sets of bunk beds. "All ours," I said as I locked the door.

"That cheating fucker at the hotel, saying all the trains were booked! These other beds are empty!" He was fuming.

"Yes, so it's all ours." I sat next to him and started to remove his clothes. I had to chill him out somehow.

~ ~ ~

Margao railway station, in Goa, smelt fresh and was clean and organised. We stepped outside onto a paved road, lined with palm trees stretching up into a clear blue sky. "Whoopee!" We grabbed each other and starting dancing before jumping into a taxi.

There was no traffic noise, deformed people or begging kids; just blue, blue skies meeting the blue, blue sea and soft yellow sand with palm trees everywhere. We were both speechless, staring out the window at an incredible tropical paradise.

"My friend has a good room. I take you?" asked the taxi driver.

"Yes, my friend, you take us." Dolphin was happy.

It was a small attached room with a rusty ceiling fan over a rusty bed, smack on the sandy beach. "We'll take it"—unison.

After a quick shower, I was in my bikini, ready to roll. "The last one in does the washing," I said, running across the softest yellow sand to reach the immense, still ocean in front of me. The water was clear and warm, and I could see multi-coloured fish all around me. "It's heaven!" I shouted to Dolphin, who was sitting outside the room, as I did handstands and backflips in the water.

"I'm going back to bed. I feel a bit sick," he shouted to me and disappeared into the room.

Looking back along the beach, I noticed a wooden shack with a palm-leaf roof and a few plastic tables and chairs inside, so I went to check it out. A guy in just a pair of shorts, showing his all-over golden tan, was sitting at the front table staring out to sea, looking chilled. "Hey hey, a newbie." His English voice greeted me as I walked in. "Welcome to paradise," and he passed me a spliff.

"You're smoking that in here?" I said, looking around as I sat at his table.

"Chill out. This is Goa. Everything is possible here."

"What's in this?" I asked, as I took the offered spliff.

"Weed. It's strong, so go easy. I'm Scott. I've been here for a few weeks and I'm planning to move on soon, but it's so easy here," he told me as he pushed a loose strand of his long, brown hair into his ponytail.

"I could be happily stranded here for a while with my boyfriend. He's in the room with an upset stomach at the moment," I told Scott, to make sure he wouldn't hit on me, and I inhaled deeply.

"Ooh, Delhi belly! That's normal around here," he said, laughing.

"Fuck, that's strong! I can hardly move," I said, blowing out a thick haze of blue smoke and passing the spliff back.

"Then don't." I could see why Scott was still here.

We sat in stoned silence, staring out to sea, until my fresh fruit salad arrived, and I enjoyed every morsel of the tropical fruit.

"Phew! It's so hot. I'm getting back in the water." I paid the waiter and left.

I pushed through the knee-high waves to calmer water and floated on its soft, warm surface, looking up at the cloudless blue sky, while gentle ripples bobbed around me. Once the stoned feeling was washed away from my head, I walked barefoot along the warm sand, as the palm trees bowed to the mighty ocean, collecting pretty seashells.

Heading back to the room to check on Dolphin, I waved to Scot, still sitting at the same table.

"You can't just lie in bed, Dolphin. It would help if you ate something. We can go to that shack and sit near the toilet." His long legs were hanging over the bottom of the small bed, and he looked uncomfortable, sweaty and tired.

"I can't move. The whole of the Thames is coming out of my arse, and these toilets are a nightmare. I need a sitting-down one." He looked like he was going to cry.

"Did you take the Imodium?" I asked as I mixed rehydration salts into a litre of water.

"Yeah, hours ago. Some toilet paper would be nice. Fuck washing my arse with my hand!" He tried to prop himself up against the wall.

"I don't think India has them. You're just gonna have to get used to squatting over a hole, and I've not seen any toilet paper since we arrived." I passed him the bottle of diluted rehydration salts, and he gulped it down then ran back to the loo.

"I hope that's the last of it," he said on his return, and we slowly walked over to the shack. Scott was still at the same table, so we joined him.

"Did you move yet?" I asked as we sat down.

"No need," he smiled before turning to an off-white Dolphin. "So I hear you got the shits mate. A lassi will sort you out."

"What's that?" I asked.

"It's a tasty yoghurt drink."

It sounded good, so I ordered one of them for my shit factory, and curry veg with rice for me.

The sun had just set, and the sky was a beautiful orange and red glow, with black palm-tree silhouettes dancing to the sounds of the waves. I couldn't believe I was there.

"That feels good," Dolphin said as he sipped his lassi. "But I don't think it's gonna stay down." I could hear his stomach growling as he jumped up to run to the toilet.

"Looks like he's got it bad. It could be dysentery or giardia. Either way, it will last a few days," Scott informed me.

Dolphin returned, now looking green and exhausted. "I gotta go," and he walked off, hunched up holding his stomach.

"I'll come after I've eaten," I shouted after him as he disappeared against a star-studded sky.

~ ~ ~

"What the fuck is that noise?" It was early morning, and something had woken me up.

"Sounds like someone being sick or choking." Dolphin rolled over into my arms. I gave him a quick hug then went out to see what was going on. A short, potbellied Indian man in worn-out, brown pants ran a piece of metal over his tongue and spat goo onto the floor.

"I clean throat," he smiled at me. It was disgusting—and became our alarm clock every morning.

A few days later, as I sat in the shack with Scott, my heart skipped a beat when I saw my handsome man finally coming to join me for breakfast. "I'm starving," he said, and he picked up the menu.

"And I'm Scott, the guy that's been looking after your missus while you've been shitting for England." We all laughed. "I managed to get a ticket before the Krishna puja starts, so I'll be hitting the road tomorrow," he told us as we searched the menu.

"What? Another puja? No wonder nothing gets done in this country. They always have days off for pujas," Dolphin joked.

"India is a very spiritual place," Scott told him.

"Where are you going?" I asked Scot, before Dolphin could add his views.

"To Pune. There's an ashram there where you can learn how to meditate."

"I wouldn't mind doing that. What d'ya think?" I asked Dolphin as he slowly nibbled his eggs on toast.

"A loada nonsense, that's what I think."

"Bet it's in your guidebook," I said as I kissed him and went for a swim.

I managed to talk Dolphin into it and, a week later, after another life-in-our-own-hands train journey, we arrived in Pune. Dodging through the spitting and snorting people with staring eyes on the dirty platform, we finally made it to the dusty street.

There were no taxis on the roadside, so that meant taking a rickshaw. There are three types of rickshaws: pulled by a man on foot; attached to a bicycle; or attached to a motorbike. Either way, up to three passengers are pulled along in a door-less chair, like a carriage.

About 15 people were already hanging off a motorbike one whose driver enthusiastically encouraged us to join. "You're alright, mate," Dolphin said and got us another one. "Just us two," he insisted, pushing away the people that were trying to jump in to join us

We rattled and bumped along the dusty, potholed roads, with our backpacks under our feet and the hot air swimming in, almost choking us. "It's better than Bombay," was the only positive thing I could say.

"It's still a shit 'ole," Dolphin said, pointing at a man shitting on the side of the road.

Our room was like a nature reserve, given how many unidentifiable insects and lizards there were inside. It was a square enclosure, with dirty walls and a grey, stained sheet over a wafer-thin mattress on a metal bed frame.

I switched on the greasy, black fan above the bed, opened the cracked-glass window, and peeled off my sweat-stuck clothes to hang them over the plastic chair. "At least we're opposite the ashram," I said as I wrapped myself in a towel and went to look for the shared bathroom, which turned out to consist of a hole in the floor, a tap, and a bucket with a plastic jug.

"I can't do more than one night here," Dolphin called, shaking the sheet out the door.

Wait until he sees the bathroom! I thought.

After a cold bucket shower, dressed in baggy pants and shirts bought from a roadside stall, we walked to the ashram, which we found behind a high iron fence with an enormous gate for its entrance.

The smiling woman behind the desk of the small reception handed us application forms, telling us to submit them along with two passport-size photographs each. "You'll need a negative HIV test, which you can take at the office on that corner." We picked up our application forms and went to get our tests.

"I am responsible for my mental health," I read out loud as we filled in the application forms while we waited for our results. "No perfume or strong smells. I agree to a sniff test before entry." I was laughing. "This is gonna be some trip," I said to a silent Dolphin, who was not buying it.

We got our negative HIV results and walked along the road, past a few dusty trees and lots of traffic going in all directions. "I'm never gonna get used to this noise," my baby said, clearly not enjoying this town at all.

"Let's get lunch." Maybe he's hungry. "Look, that place is full. It must be good," I said encouragingly, leading him into a tin shack. "There's an empty table there," and I rushed past the other five full tables to get it.

"Thali?" A little Indian man in a grubby shirt put a banana leaf in front of us.

"Yes, please." It smelt so good, my mouth was watering.

A second man, as grubby as the first, came over with a big pot and spooned a generous helping of rice on the banana leaf, before returning to add dal, vegetable curry and chickpea curry.

"There's no cutlery," Dolphin said.

"Look, everyone's eating with their hands."

"Fuck that." Dolphin got up to look for a spoon.

I watched the other diners mould their food into balls with the tips of their fingers, turning their hands around to pop the food into their mouths with their thumbs. "It's a little tricky but try it," I said to Dolphin as I put some dal-soaked rice into my mouth.

"I'm good with the spoon, thanks." And he mixed up his veg curry and rice.

"This gives it a kick," I said as I added raw onion and chilli from the plate in the centre of the table.

"No more, thank you," I said to the grubby man who came back and started piling more rice and veg onto our leaves.

"Free refills. That's amazing." Dolphin finally approved of something.

With full bellies, we went back to the ashram. The same smiling lady checked our papers and gave us purple entry passes, and we entered through the imposing iron gate.

Stepping over the threshold was like entering a completely different world. Flute music filled the air and birds sang in the trees as we walked through a clean, orderly, calm village set in an extensive park with manicured lawns, flowers and drinking-water fountains. "Wow, worth the agro!" I was enjoying it already.

We followed the dust-free, paved path to enter a tasteful, white-domed building and sign up for a meditation class. "Mediation helps to calm your restless mind and bring inner peace," the spaced-out woman behind the counter informed us in a soft voice.

"You sure need that in this country." My baby was not enjoying himself.

"If you're new, I suggest the 'Be Alive' session at three pm." We signed up.

"You made it!" It was Scott, dressed in maroon pants and a long maroon shirt.

"Oh, a purple people-eater," I said, scanning his new attire.

"You get this when you become a disciple. And my name is Yoko now. Come on, let me show you around. You hungry? There's pizza."

"Nah, we just ate off a banana leaf, mate. But there's real pizza?" The Dolphin was finally happy.

"Yes, and it's the bollocks." Scott smiled.

The mediation class involved:

15 minutes: jumping and running to get your energy moving.

15 minutes: sitting to calm the mind.

15 minutes: breathing for relaxation.

15 minutes: dancing.

I loved it. Dolphin did not. So I took him for a pizza before we hooked up with Scott again, to go to the main stage where the guru was going to give a talk.

The grassy area was already occupied by about 300 people, all dressed as purple people-eaters. Some were sitting in meditation; others were embracing. We found a space on the grass and sat down, Scott lying beside us. "I'm doing rebirth tonight, so it's better if I lay down." His straight face warned us not to take the piss.

The place fell silent when a stocky man, with a long grey beard and dressed in black, pulled up in a Rolls Royce. He walked softly onto the stage and sat on a big, red armchair in the centre. He talked in English for 40 minutes about love and universal connection, then got up and walked back to his Rolls Royce and was gone. All the purple people-eaters started hugging and crying. Some were dancing.

"I could feel what he was saying," I said as we got up off the grass.

"What a load of crap! Let's go." Unimpressed, Dolphin headed for the gate. I waved 'bye' to Scot, but I don't think he noticed. He was still lying down with his eyes closed, doing his rebirth.

In the morning, I wanted to go back, but Dolphin wanted to leave.

"Come on. It wasn't that bad. You can have a pizza and enjoy the quiet and clean ambience."

"Well, I suppose it'll be better than anything this town has to offer." So back into the ashram we went. I joined a few meditation classes, while Dolphin ate pizza.

"Let's go now, honey. I'm sure there something in the water that's brainwashing people," Dolphin said after a week. "Look at the people's eyes in here. They're all zombied out, just staring into space. The only time they move is to fuck each other. We're not lost. Come on. Let's go back into the world, even if it is a shit 'ole." My baby was desperate to go.

"OK' I said reluctantly, knowing this was something I wanted to explore more in the future.

~ ~ ~

Our hotel booked us a four am rickshaw to drop us at the bus station for our five am bus to Aurangabad to check out some ancient caves.

"It's four-thirty! Where's the fucking rickshaw? We could have walked it by now!" Dolphin said as we stood outside the hotel in the morning chill.

"It'll come, baby. Don't stress." I tried to reassure him, just as the rusty tin can came rattling through the mist. Ten minutes later, were we in a bustling bus station and the peace of the early morning street was gone.

"Over here!"

"Come here!"

"You! You!"

Clang clang! The conductor hit the side of the bus shouting out its destination. "Aurangabad, Aurangabad," I could hear above the din, and we followed that sound, dodging people and scabby dogs, until we reach a multi-coloured, 30-seater tin drum with 'Horn please!' painted brightly on the back.

"That explains the constant beeping," I said to Dolphin, who was looking at our shit-heap of a bus in shock.

"It looks like it should be in the knackers' yard, not a bus station," he moaned as we squeezed through the narrow door with our backpacks, found an empty, ripped seat and sat down with sighs of relief. It wasn't long before the bus chugged its way out of the bus station and along the bumpy, potholed road, stopping every 10 minutes or so to drop off and pick up more passengers. Soon, the little bus was jam-packed, and people were squeezing onto our seat with us. The heat, the smells, and the noise of the constant honk of the horn and people shouting, gave me a headache. I closed my eyes and waited for the nightmare to be over.

"Aurangabad," the conductor shouted over the din. We were up, squeezing ourselves and our big backpacks through the people and jumping off the bus as if it was on fire. We could see the tops of temples as we walked through a dirty, dusty hillside town to find our pre-booked room, at the top of a rubbish-strewn hill.

"Look, Dolphin, no hands," I said as we passed a woman going in the other direction with a pile of wood on her head.

"Yeah, she needs them free to rob ya," he shouted over his shoulder as he trudged on ahead of me.

Finally reaching the top of the hill, we took a moment to get our breath back while enjoying the panoramic view of the beautiful valley below. From here, it looked amazingly clean, green and lush.

A winding lane took us to our room, which was desperate for a lick of paint and a sweep. It was smaller than the one in Pune and held nothing more than a wooden bed, which Dolphin was quick to lie on with his best friend, the guide book, to rest his back which was aching from the bumpy bus ride.

"*The Ellora caves are one of the largest rock-cut monastery temple cave complexes in the world. They were chiselled into perfection between the fourth and ninth centuries and are the epitome of Indian rock-cut architecture. There are 34 caves: 12 Buddhist; 17 Hindu; and five Jain,*" Dolphin read aloud while I looked for somewhere to hide our valuables (somewhere other than our packs which would surely be the first place a thief would look).

"Fuck!" He jumped up.

"What's wrong?" I was shocked to see him move so fast.

"I don't know. I'm just itching all over." He'd pulled off his T-shirt and started rubbing it over his skin. "We can't sleep here! It's a flea pit!" He was fuming.

"Have a shower. It'll help. Then let's leave our luggage here, go check out the caves and leave."

"Sounds good to me!" And he headed off, grumbling under his breath.

~ ~ ~

Passing through the entrance gate for the Ellora Caves, we stepped onto a paved road through a green-trimmed lawn, surrounding magnificent ruins. I couldn't believe my eyes. "It must have taken forever to build." There was so much detail.

"Amazing they can make this, but not a decent toilet!"

"You make me laugh, Dolphin." And I gave him a big hug.

We walked around for about three hours, trying to interpret the sculptures, imagining what it must have been like in its heyday.

After a quick thali at the shack outside, we headed back to the hotel to get our bags, ran from the fleapit room to the train station and managed to get two tickets for a train to Jaipur, leaving in 30 minutes.

"Perfect timing! Let's have a chai." I was enjoying the adventure.

"That milky shit is not tea."

"But it's tasty and all that's on offer. Come on, Dolphin, lighten up!" I bought two chais, in claypot cups that imparted an earthy taste that mixed well with our earthy, dusty bodies!

"What the fuck is that?" Dolphin shrilled as a big, black, furry—cat? puppy?—ran past.

"Shit! That's a rat!" It was enormous and I was happy when the train rattled into the station, and we could get off the platform.

We scrambled on with crowds of others, all pushing and shoving through the tiny doorway, and tried to find a seat. We squeezed through a cramped aisle, full of sweaty, smelly bodies lying on top of or next to their luggage, to see all the seats already overflowing with people with staring eyes, gaping mouths and crying babies. The stillness of the air, combined with the heat and the smell, was overwhelming, so we squeezed in near the open window in the door to try to get some air to at least breathe.

"It's only nine hours," I said and gave Dolphin's hand a squeeze.

Putting my backpack on the grimy floor, I crossed the obstacle course, climbing over bodies, boxes, and luggage, to look for the toilet, and finally found a door with 'WC' printed on it. I went in. The toilet was a hole in the floor through which you could see the ground passing beneath, and it stunk. I wrapped one arm around the money belt fastened to my waist —there'd be no way to get that back if it fell through that hole—and balanced as best I could. Nonetheless, I pissed everywhere as the train swayed.

"OK, baby. When you go to the toilet, don't breathe, or the smell of piss will kill you." I tried to prepare Dolphin for the experience.

"I'll just piss out the window," he huffed. Well, that's where it will end up anyway, I thought.

"You! You!" It was the guard, waving us to follow him. We picked up our bags and squeezed our way through the sweaty, sticky bodies to the end of the carriage. "Here. For you." He put us in the mail carriage as if he was offering us the bridal suite. "First class, baby." I laughed as we put our backpacks on top of the mail sacks, removed our boots, and snuggled up for a bit of shuteye.

We stepped out of the mail truck the next morning into in a new world, clean and orderly, with pink buildings and palaces with beautiful gardens. We took a cycle rickshaw through this miracle to our hotel, marvelling at the beauty of Jaipur.

Entering our hotel, we were happy to find a shiny, clean foyer with crystal floors and marble walls. A tall, dark Indian, wearing a magnificent, regal-red outfit and a white turban, greeted us with a warm smile and gave us our room key.

Opening the door to our room, we both shrilled in delight at the clean white sheets on the four-poster bed and the sit-down toilet. "This is the place for a princess like me," I grinned as I flopped onto the bed.

"And a king like me," Dolphin rejoindered occupying the toilet like a throne. "There are even museums here." He had already checked the guidebook!

"Let's go tomorrow," I said, pulling him down onto the most comfortable bed we had slept on in weeks.

That evening, we went for a stroll around the town to reach the market for dinner. The market was a hub of noise and merriment, with rainbow-coloured carpets and textiles hanging from pieces of wood or string. Handicrafts, jewellery, gemstones, leather and metal goods were displayed on floors and tables, and smiling-faced Indians beckoned us to buy them. "Every stall sells the same," I noticed.

"Watch out, lady, they'll take your eyes and come back for your eyelashes," some guy shouted to me as he passed. We had hidden our traveller's cheques and passports in the room and were carrying just what we would need for the night, so it would have only been my eyes that they could take anyway!

We sat at a plastic table with plastic chairs, in a little tin shack, and ordered a few vegetable dishes and four roti. "This has to be the spiciest food yet. I can't feel my tongue anymore," I said sticking it out for air.

"Eat more of the bread," he told me as tears fell from his eyes to join the sweat on his face.

Even though, every time we ate, my face felt like I should call the fire brigade, I enjoyed the delicious food—and my baby enjoyed the museums.

But, after a few days of walking around, we decided to move on. The Rajasthani king and his princess were back in first-class on their way to see the Taj Mahal, in Agra. As the train slowly rocked us through urban shit 'oles and poverty, the king slept safely in my arms in our clean carriage.

"The Taj was commissioned by Mughal Shah Jahan in 1632, to house the tomb of his favourite wife, Mumtaz Mahal, and himself when he also died. You see its true beauty at sunrise," Mr Guidebook informed me once we had arrived.

So of course, at sunrise, we sat by the lake in front of The Taj to watch the rays of the sun wash the white marble mausoleum in a glow of golden orange and red, reflected perfectly in the water. "Well worth getting up at dawn for," I whispered to Mr Guidebook.

"Yes, a perfect end to a shitty journey," he laughed.

~ ~ ~

A quick train ride took us to Delhi, and we went straight to the airport for the next leg of our trip: Thailand.

Upon arrival in Bangkok, when I saw people sweeping the roads, I almost cried. "They clean here. I love it already!" I gasped as we walked to the taxi stand outside the airport.

"Khao San Road," Dolphin told the taxi driver, and the taxi took us to paradise. I couldn't believe my eyes as we drove down a long, wide, buzzing road with bars, restaurants and shops on either side and down side streets. The yummy smells coming from the street stalls were mouth-watering.

"Look, Dolphin, they're showing movies tonight, and there's pizza." I was excited as I looked out of the taxi window.

"That one's got live music." He started to dance in his seat.

"Oh my! We're in the middle of it all!" I said as we got out of the taxi and entered the hotel.

The sight of our clean room had us both gasping in shock and we threw ourselves on the bed in fits of laughter.

"Fuck! Where we have been?" Dolphin asked the ceiling.

"Oh my God! A hot shower!" I pulled all my clothes off in a second and let the hot water pour all over me.

"This restaurant sounds good," Dolphin shouted through the shower door, checking his guidebook.

"Put that down. Everything is just outside our door; let's follow our noses."

"OK, baby, let's do that," and he jumped off the bed to join me in the shower.

"Did you notice most people were only wearing vest and miniskirts?" I said, pulling my only beach dress out of my backpack.

"Yes, and that was the men!" he laughed.

~ ~ ~

We took our seats at a table outside a restaurant just as the neon lights of clubs and bars were starting to flicker on, and ordered a few dishes and a bowl of noodles, and two cold beers. "Yes! No rice! No thali! I'll drink to that!" Dolphin said, lifting his cold Chang beer.

"No 'beep, beep' and being stared at! I'll drink to that!" And we clinked glasses.

"I thought the whole trip was gonna be like that, but this is more like it, baby." He was smiling that big Dolphin grin, and I wanted to eat him up right there on the road.

"The entire world is here," I said as I watched the whole of life pass by. We indulged in watching the non-stop live show of street life as we sipped cold beer, complementing the light, spicy, tasty food.

The pretty beach clothes hanging up in the shops were enticing, and I was thinking about what to throw out so I could buy something new. I always wanted to keep my backpack light. "I'm going to buy a beach dress. You want to come?" I asked Dolphin once our bellies were full.

"Yeah, I need a new pair of pants." We paid our bill and walked hand in hand through paradise, checking out stall after stall. There was so much choice.

"You have this in blue?" I asked the petite woman—or was it a man?—in a shop.

"This one look good on you." She picked up a blue, but completely different, dress.

"No, this style?" I showed her the dress I wanted.

"Same-same but different," she insisted.

"Not same-same. Definitely different," I laughed.

"What are these?" Dolphin was holding up a strange-looking pair of lightweight pants, with a wide waistband and ribbons hanging from the side.

"This fisherman pants. You wrap around and tie, then fold. Good for fat people like you." We were not fat, but compared to the diminutive Thais, we looked like giants.

"These will be great for travelling in. One size fits all," I said, trying them on.

Having bought two pairs of pants and my same-same but different dress, we made to leave the shop when I noticed a little, golden house on a dais at the entrance, with food on its terrace. "Ooh, you have a birdhouse." I thought it was cute.

"No. It's for protection spirits. I offer them food," said the shop woman.

"Oh, and who's that man?" I pointed at a framed photo of a handsome Thai man, in a fancy coat, hanging above it—one I had seen hanging in many places.

"That's our king," she said proudly.

Newly informed, we continued on our way, checking out the crazy people on a crazy road.

"Dolphin, look at that beach. It looks too good to be real!" I said, pulling him over to look at a poster on a travel agent's window.

"Of course it's real. This is Thailand, baby."

"Can we go?" I had never seen such a beautiful beach.

"Sure, let's come and book it tomorrow."

"I love you, Dolphin," I said, hugging him, and we continued along the freak show, passing stall after stall, and restaurant after restaurant, full of funkily-dressed travellers having fun.

"You wanna get some dreadlocks and get in the groove?" I teased my love as we walked past a stall that could wrap anything into your hair.

"No. But a massage sounds good!"

"Let's do it." And we went into the first massage shop we saw.

A petite Thai lady took us out the back to a big room that smelt of sweet incense, and was divided into two by a hanging cloth: one side for men; the other for women. Some of the ten clean beds already had people on.

I was given a pair of fisherman pants, and told to keep my top on and lie face down on an empty bed. For an hour, I was almost-painfully compressed, pulled, stretched and rocked—and it felt so good!

"I'm sure I'm a foot longer," Dolphin laughed as we left, heading for a restaurant to watch a movie.

In the morning, we went back to the travel agent to book our tickets to that beach. "We pick you up from the hotel at six pm by bus. Bus to boat. Boat to island. 200 Baht each. Is cheapest," the lady behind the reception desk told us.

"This is going to be easy. Let's do it." I was still looking at that poster in disbelief. We booked it for three days later so we could do the guidebook tour of Bangkok first. We visited all the sights in Bangkok that the guidebook told us to see, and it was terrific travelling by boat along the river looking at temples, shrines and the royal palace.

The smell of delicious food coming from the metal carts was tantalising, and I sampled pleasurable morsels at every corner. "How do the Thais stay so slim," I asked Dolphin as I stuffed barbecued chicken and sticky rice into my mouth.

"They probably don't eat everything they see!" he teased.

Our departure day came, and we stood outside our hotel at six pm. Everything went smoothly and, by ten am, our little boat was chugging away across the ocean.

Watching the island approach, I felt like I was in a dream. Vibrant, green mountains jutted from an ocean lined with golden, yellow sand which was dotted with wooden shacks and fringed with palm trees. "Ooh, I can't believe I'm going there," I shrilled in delight to my Dolphin, who was just as mesmerised.

As soon as the boat stopped, I jumped into the warm, crystal-clear water, grabbed my backpack, held it over my head, and waded to the shore of Kho Phangan. Warm sand was melting under my feet and, unable to contain my excitement, I threw myself onto its soft bed. "This is magical," I laughed as I pulled my Dolphin down to join me, and we lay in each other's arms in disbelief.

"Oh baby, please let's get one of the beach shacks," I pleaded having rolled over to see a line of five bamboo shacks, with a palm tree roof, on wooden stilts, blending naturally with the beauty around them. It was like a fairytale.

"Let's go have a look." He pulled me up, and we walked over to the restaurant.

"I have one left," said the guy wearing makeup and a woman's dress who was sitting in the restaurant painting her nails, and she took us to the one at the end of the row. It was a simple, square shack with a bed, a small table, a suspended bamboo pole holding a few coat hangers, and a squat toilet with tap, bucket, and jug.

"I want it, please Dolphin. We can make love to the sound of the ocean."

"What about mosquitoes? There are gaps in the wall."

"I give you my mosquito net," the receptionist said. I loved her already.

A quick change into my bikini and I was in the ocean having a glorious swim, while Dolphin lay in the hammock on our balcony.

"I'm going to find our mosquito net," I told him as I passed by on my way to the restaurant.

"I only give you. You no tell other farangs, I like you. You my friend," the receptionist said. Really? I just met her. "My name Tam. I kathoey."

"What's that?"

"Ladyboy. You no know ladyboy? A shim?" she said and showed me her penis.

"Well, I knew you had one of them!" and we laughed.

"I knew you my friend. I work bar. Come tonight. We drink." And she pointed to a wooden shack next to the restaurant painted in luminous greens, with a yellow border and splashes of blue and red mushrooms.

"OK." And I walked off with the mosquito net, happy to have a new crazy friend.

After a delicious dinner of seafood pad thai, we went to the luminous bar, sat on the bright yellow bar stalls and ordered two beers. There was a disco ball above a sandy space. Guessing it was the dance floor, I knew I'd be under that swirling ball soon.

"I make you a special bucket." Tam filled a small white bucket with ice, Thai rice whiskey, coke, Red Bull and about five straws. "You suck up through the straw." She showed me like she was sucking on a cock.

"You wanna suck," I joked to Dolphin as I put my mouth around the straw, and his head joined mine over the bucket.

"You like Thai weed?" Tam offered me a spliff.

"Hospitality is excellent here," and I sucked on that too. As the weed filled my lungs to the sweet sound of Bob Marley, my body started to sway all on its own, and I closed my eyes and let go into the rhythm.

"Just arrived?" The voice of a tanned Israeli dressed just in fisherman's pants, brought me back into the bar.

"Yes. It's beautiful here. How long you been here?" I replied.

"About a week. India next," he smiled, nodding his head to the music, his black, curly hair falling over his face.

"We've just come from there. It's same-same but different," I laughed.

"I'm gonna smoke a chillum with the bubbas at the Ganga."

"What that?" Dolphin piped up. And Mossy, our new friend, pulled a horn-shaped, wooden pipe from his pocket and filled it with weed. "This is chillum." He put the pipe in his fist, held it to his mouth and inhaled.

"Try it," he said, passing it to Dolphin, who inhaled then handed it to me.

"Come on, baby." Dolphin had hit the dance floor with his arms flying everywhere, and I joined him.

A few hours later, we rolled into our hut and, as I had hoped, made love to the sound of the ocean.

In the morning, I opened our hut door to the most picturesque sight I had ever seen. I had to catch my breath before running into the calm, blue ocean, singing and laughing all the way. Dolphin was not far behind me, and we frolicked until hunger took us to the restaurant.

"Tonight, full moon party. You come? I get yaba and we dance all night." Tam put bowls of fresh fruit salad in front of us.

"What's yaba?" I spooned in a mix of banana and papaya.

"It's good, and I have makeup and dress you all pretty."

"Yes, brilliant! This sounds fun." I loved dressing up.

We spent the day lazing on the beach, saving our energy for the night's full moon party.

Covered in fluorescent paint, the three of us jumped into a rickshaw, known here as a tuk-tuk, to the beach party.

There were six foot speakers at every bar shack on the beach, and lots of fluorescent everything: paint; bracelets; necklaces; and clothes.

"You gotta run with the wolves tonight," Mossy shouted from the dance floor, still in the same fisherman pants but with a fluorescent-painted chest.

"Yeah, we are," Dolphin shouted back, waving his bucket.

"That tastes strange," I said to Tam, who had just passed me a spliff.

"That's yaba."

"More like rocket fuel!" I was tingling all over and needed to dance, so I passed it to Dolphin and let myself go with the music.

After what seemed like no time at all, the sun started to rise, slowly chasing away the darkness and turning the sky into an orb of orange and purple. Tam rushed off for work while Dolphin and I went for a walk along the beach, watching nature's artwork fill the sky.

As it got brighter, we started to notice that the beach was covered in fluorescent-painted, semi-clad or naked bodies and, there in the middle of it all, lying flat on his back on the sand, covered from head to foot in fluorescent paint, with tissue paper stuffed up his nose for some unknown reason, was Mossy. "He must have been the weakest of the pack," Dolphin said as we tried to wake him up.

"Sleep, sleep," he mumbled. So we left him there and got a tuk-tuk back to our hut for a swim and sleep.

~ ~ ~

"I've had enough of sun, sea, surf, sip and smoke. Wanna cruise?" Dolphin asked one morning after another night of partying, Tam-style.

"Whatever you want, my baby." I could do with getting away from yaba. It was becoming a regular evening event.

"Yeah, we've been here over a week now."

Tam made a phone call to book us door-to-door service, and we were on a boat to another island without thinking or doing anything except buying the tickets.

As our boat took off from the port, we watched Kho Phangan get smaller and smaller, and I smiled at the memories I had made there.

After a few hours of a choppy boat ride, we started to pass massive, jagged, black rock formations staking their claim to the calmer turquoise water that was full of dancing fish. In the distance, many shades of green filled the area before me, rolling down to the yellow ground. "It's like a dream," I whispered into my lover's ear. I could not believe my eyes; it was so beautiful.

"Yes, it's our dream," and he turned his head to kiss me.

We got a beach hut up a hill, surrounded by papaya and banana trees, from where we could see the entire bay from our hammock on the balcony. It was a steep five-minute descent to the beach, where there were a few restaurants and the best snorkelling I had ever done.

I was in my hammock, looking out over the bay, smoking a bong I had made from a papaya stalk in a glass bottle, feeling completely stoned, when the guidebook appeared. "I just thought it's time to move if we want to make Aus for Christmas."

"I'm cool with that." All the climbing was wrecking my knee anyway.

"I've made a route to take us to Bali by land."

"That sounds fantastic. Let's do it."

The next day, we got the boat to the mainland, and a bumpy bus dropped us at a taxi stand, where we picked up a shared taxi to the border with Malaysia.

We walked across the border dealing with the usual passport control procedures, and got a bus to Kuala Lumpur. It was nice to be back in a city after weeks on the beach, especially one that was clean and easy to get around.

With Dolphin's guidebook in his hand, we hit the streets to explore. To get a view of the city, we went up the twin towers to the observation deck and looked over the skyscrapers and river. It was massive.

Although there was plenty to do in Kuala Lumpur, Dolphin had his schedule so the next day we were off on a minibus to Singapore to have a Singapore Sling at Raffles Hotel. "I feel like a tramp in this lush hotel," I whispered as we sat at the bar waiting for our drinks. My pretty, blue beach dress was cute, but it looked worn out and cheap in the luxurious surroundings.

"You look beautiful to me," he said, kissing me on the forehead before he went off to the loo. "I just used a sit-down toilet," he excitedly told me on his return.

"Ooh, I have to check this out." I was off my stool in a second. I almost cried to see a clean, white toilet, a flush, toilet paper, soap and towels. We stayed for another drink just so we could use them again.

Another bus took us to the bustling city of Jakarta, to get a ferry to Bali. Back at a picturesque beach, where volcanic mountains surrounded a vibrant coral reef, rich with colourful tropical fish, I was in my element.

We took a room at the beach's quiet end to get away from the mass of noise from the bars and restaurants, which were full of loud Australian holidaymakers, and watched their antics from a safe distance, getting ourselves into the vibe for our next stop: Australia.

~ ~ ~

"Hey hey!" It was Dolphin's Uncle Bob, who had come to pick us up at Sydney airport. "Welcome to the land down under," he said in a hearty voice, while putting green hats, corks hanging from the brim, on our heads. "And who's your pretty lady?" he said, taking my backpack.

"I'm a ladyboy from Thailand," I told him as I gave him a warm smile.

"Oi, oi! We got a lively one."

Bob had the same beautiful, brown eyes as Dolphin, and he was happy, light-natured and a welcome sight to see. "I got smoked oysters and cold beers in the fridge, I've cleaned the pool and Betty, my beloved wife, has been cleaning your bedroom all day," he told us as he led us to the car.

"That all sounds great, doesn't it, babe?" Dolphin said as he slapped my arse.

"It sounds fantastic, Bob, thank you." I already liked him.

"You've been roughing it a bit for a ladyboy," and he laughed just the same as Dolphin as he pulled the car onto a wide motorway. There was hardly any traffic and I was happy, sitting in the back, looking out the window at my new clean surroundings, while listening to the two Dolphin's laugh and banter.

"This is home," Bob said as he turned into a tree-lined street with huge one-storey houses surrounded by beautiful, well-kept gardens and big driveways.

As we pulled into Bob's driveway, a tall, slim woman opened the door, all smiles and open arms. "I've put you two in here," she said, opening our bedroom door. The room was fresh and clean, with a big window overlooking the pool.

"Paradise!" I threw myself onto the double bed, taking Dolphin with me and giggling.

"Come on you two! Plenty of time for that tonight." Bob was shouting through the door. "I'm filling up the esky." I came out of the room to see Bob putting cold beers into the cool box. Oh, *that's* an esky!

"Grab that tray," he said, and I picked up a tray laden with crackers and oysters, and we moved to the sun loungers at the pool.

I jumped into the pool and, pulling myself onto an airbed that had a handy holder for my beer, kicked back and listened to Uncle Bob's story of his big move to Australia. After the scandal of a divorce, he'd moved to Australia with his new wife, Betty, to start again. They set themselves up well in suburbia, but they were lonely for real friends and regretted the move. They would have liked to move back to the UK but could not afford the transition. Bob's motto was 'speculate to accumulate' and he hoped to win enough money from gambling to return one day.

"We're content but not happy. You'll always be a pom here," Bob said as he put an oyster on his cracker and popped the whole thing into his mouth.

"What's a pom?"

"Prisoner of Mother England. It's what the Aussies call the English."

He introduced us to all the race tracks, and the pokey and lottery shops. Most of these places had smorgasbords, which were the most extensive buffets I had ever seen. "I'm gonna get fat here," I said as I went to refill my plate with yummy barbequed food.

"You could do with some meat on you girl. Eat up," Bob told me, so I did.

~ ~ ~

Not having accumulated any money from 'speculating', Dolphin and I decided to move into the city to find work. "We found a great bedsit in the newspaper. We're gonna have a look at it tomorrow and, if we like it, we can move in straight away," Dolphin told Bob while we were sitting around the pool one afternoon.

"We don't want to leave, but we need to earn money," I added from my airbed in the pool.

"I'll drop you off in the morning, mate." He was hiding his sadness well.

In the morning, Bob drove us through suburbia to the city and, as we passed the Opera House, I felt like I was actually in Aus. I was hiding my excitement and eagerness to get out of the car and play, and I knew I would take the bedsit no matter what.

The room was down a side street of the main high road, which was full of all kinds of shops. It had a comfortable bed, a compact bathroom, a well-equipped kitchenette and a dining table. Through the big window, we could see the bar and pokeys opposite. "Let's take it," I said to Dolphin as I squeezed his hand.

"It'll do the job," he said as he squeezed my hand back.

"Speculate to accumulate," Bob said, and he gave us both a big hug and took off back to his car to go home.

"Once we're settled, we'll come to visit," Dolphin reassured him as he waved out the window and pulled off.

Within a week, Dolphin found a job as a bicycle courier, and I got a job in a mail-order company, selling computer games. I worked in the repairs department, and it was an easy job with easy-going people. A mail came in with a damaged or broken disk, and I sent back a new one.

"Here you go, Sheila. 'Ave that with your smoko." My boss, Hank, handed me a doughnut for our tea/cigarette break. He was a sweetheart and often, on Fridays, I would join him and the work team down the pub for a few drinks. Our weekends were for Uncle Bob, who took us all over Sydney to sights, beaches and gambling halls. Other than that, it was save, save, save.

After six weeks, we had enough money to check out some more of this enormous country so we caught a night train to Melbourne.

The train pulled into Melbourne just as the sun rose, and I noticed it was smaller and cosier than Sydney. I was excited to travel on a tram to the backpackers. We took two beds in a dorm and went to get a newspaper to check out available accommodation, finding a likely-sounding studio and arranging to go that afternoon for a viewing.

"The beach is a 20-minute walk, and there's a market every Wednesday just opposite," the girl was saying as she showed us around a spacious room, with a kitchenette and private bathroom.

"Let's take it, Dolphin." Anything was better than a dorm bed in the backpackers.

"When can we move in?" he asked.

"Now," she smiled.

"Great, we'll come tomorrow." I was so excited I sang all the way to the tram stop. A short ride took us back to the backpackers, and we packed our stuff ready for tomorrow's move.

"This is a great neighbourhood," Dolphin said as we sipped tasty coffee outside a trendy café, watching Melbourne life pass by.

"I love the little lanes and street art. It reminds me of London somehow." We were celebrating that we had both got jobs already. Dolphin's was five minutes' walk from the flat, in a factory, packing boxes, and mine was as a short-order cook in a family pub, two tram rides away. I loved the trams, and I loved the pub life.

~ ~ ~

"Hey, tucker-fucker! Steak and eggs. Surely you can't fuck that up." Oliver, the muscular construction worker, shouted as I washed down my cooker plate on the bar counter.

"One way to find out," I shouted back as I bashed his steak.

The customers were friendly and had a simple diet—usually steak and chips—so cooking was easy, and Mary, the landlady, liked me.

"Here, doll. Stick that in your bag," she said as I was leaving to go home. It was two big steaks. My Dolphin would love them.

We settled into our Melbourne life, and I continued to save money and started to make friends. One day, a girl came into the pub, and we got chatting. "I love it here so much I don't want to go back to Perth next week," she was telling me as I bashed up a steak. "But I have to go to sort out the apartment I rent there." She and her boyfriend had come to see if they fancied moving to Melbourne.

"I'm travelling with my boyfriend, and he only said last week he was ready to move on. Maybe we will buy the tickets off ya?" I told her.

"Really? Do you want to take over our place too? It's a furnished one-bedroom in the centre of town."

"Fuck yeah! That'd be great, and you could take on ours here."

Her smile stretched the whole of her face, and she almost cried.

Dolphin agreed, and we were off to Perth.

~ ~ ~

"We've landed on our feet here, Dolphin," I said as we unpacked our backpacks in a beautiful modern apartment.

"We sure have, baby. Look at the backyard. Shall we 'ave a barbie tonight?"

"Yes! Let's hit the shops." We walked down a vast, tree-lined street, past one-storey houses with beautiful gardens and garages running along each side.

At the end, we found a long stretch of wild beach. "Oh, look at that water; it's almost as beautiful as Thailand." I was itching to get in there.

"Let's get the shopping sorted first, and then we'll get in." He knew me so well.

"Yes, let's hurry." I grabbed his hand and we started to run.

We dumped our bags of shopping on the sand and frolicked in the water like overgrown kids, until hunger took us home for a barbie.

~ ~ ~

As beautiful as life was in Perth, neither of us could find a job, and my money was getting tight. Then, "Look at this, baby!" Dolphin called me into the yard to read an ad in the paper. *"For sale, 400 dollars: Volkswagen in good working order, only four years old, with a back seat that folds down into a comfortable bed. Complete with bedding, tent, and camping equipment. I need a quick sale as I am leaving the country.* This is a bargain. I could buy this, and we could go up north," he said, shoving the paper under my nose.

"That would be fantastic. We can be nomads, camping out and sleeping under the stars."

"Yes, let's go explore this big country."

"Yes, let's," I said, jumping into his lap. I was tired of trying for jobs that had either already gone or were for permanent staff.

He bought the car, 'The Lime Green Dream Machine', and the next day, with our cork hats on our heads, an esky full of food and beer, and the Great Northern Highway spread out before us, we gently pulled away for our adventure. "Our destination is 4,000 km," I told the captain of the ship, checking the map. "First stop: Geraldton. Proximity: four hours away."

"With this view, that's no problem," Dolphin smiled as he pulled onto the coastal road, and a sense of freedom wrapped around us.

~ ~ ~

"Let's pull over for a picnic and a swim before we get to the town, Dolphin." That vast natural beach was calling me.

"Yes, madam. Let's start how we mean to go on," he smiled.

It was beautiful to sit in the sun on the beach, watching windsurfers in the distance, as we munched our cheese and pickle sandwiches. "I'm going in," I said and I ran to the water with Dolphin not far behind.

"These waves are too big even for a Dolphin," he said, running away from them back to the shore.

"You have to dive under them. Come on," I said, going headfirst under the wave. It was exhilarating, and I eventually reached calm water and floated on the fresh, cold, deep ocean.

As I swam back to the shore, a wave got me and dumped me under. I felt like I was in a washing machine and didn't know what to do, so I just went with it until I reached the surface again, stripped of my bikini and with a mouth full of sand.

"Haha!" Dolphin was in hysterical laughter, watching me try to put my bikini back on while avoiding another wave.

"Wow! That was dangerous but so exciting," I laughed as I reached the hysterical man lying on the beach.

"It was bloody funny, that's for sure! Come here." And he wrapped me up in a towel with a big bear hug.

I was still trying to get the sand out of every crevice of my body when we jumped back into the car.

We arrived at a busy port and almost got blown over getting out of the car—so we got back in. "Shit! Battered by the sea; now the wind wants to have a go," I laughed.

"I wonder if it's always this windy," Dolphin pondered.

"I think so. Look at the trees." They were bent over like they were trying to pick something up from the floor.

We didn't see the point of getting windswept, so we drove a short way out of town and slept our first night in our new home.

"Did you sleep OK?" I asked my darling as I was giving him his morning kisses.

"Yes, it was great," and he rolled on top of me.

When we finally emerged from the car, we made banana sandwiches on the windy beach before continuing along the long, scenic coastal road with the scenery slowly changing to rusty red dunes on one side and crystal-clear water on the other.

"This must be Monkey Mia. Only four and a half hours driving, Dolphin. You did well."

"Dolphin wants to swim with the dolphins," and he gave his beautiful Dolphin laugh.

We found a camping ground, had a shower, washed our smalls and went for a walk around the town. Almost every shop sold a dolphin tour and dolphin paraphernalia. "Wow, it's so commercial and expensive. Do you mind if we don't do a dolphin tour? Can we can go swim and see them for ourselves naturally?" I asked my big, handsome man.

"Sounds great. Let's go eat first."

"I hope dolphin's, not on the menu."

"Wah!" my Dolphin laughed.

After a big feed of burger and chips, we went back to the beach and got in the calm, soft water.

"There, there look!" I was thrilled. Just in front of where we were swimming, a dolphin's fin had popped up from the water.

"Let's follow it!" Dolphin swam past me. I followed, doubting my eyes as I swam alongside a myriad of colourful fishes.

The following day, we had a fruit breakfast on the beach while we watched dolphins jumping out of the water, before we took off to the beautiful coastal town of Carnarvon.

"G'day mate," said the guy we encountered as we pulled up, three and a half hours later.

"G'day. 'G'day," we called back.

"You on your hols, are you?"

"Yeah, driving around, mate." Dolphin was trying to be manly.

"Oh, you're pom bastards. Well you'll be pleased to know you can get great fish and chips here. Best in Aus."

"Brill! We're missing our fish and chips," Dolphin joked.

"Go into that bar over there, and you'll get the best feed you've ever had."

"Cheers, mate. We will." And we did.

It was probably *not* the best, but it *was* good.

"Not much to do here. Let's get going in the morning," Dolphin said as we walked around the sleepy little town.

We found a nice, quiet area next to the beach and parked up for the night, then cuddled up on the beach with a beer and spliff for sunset, before bed.

A six am start saw us passing sheer cliffs and rocky red gorges in the perfect sunrise's changing red glow. It was a lovely drive, and we sang along to the radio until we reached the tip of the cape in the port town of Exmouth, where we got out and sat in silence by the lighthouse, taking in the spectacular view below.

"I think my baby wants to get in," Dolphin said and moved towards the car.

"You know I do." I jumped up and got into the car, and my Dolphin drove us down to the beach. I was in my bikini in record time and ran into the turquoise water of the rock pool. "Oh my God! Come look at the colours in here," I called to Dolphin, who was locking up the car. Multi-coloured fish of all sizes, and little turtles, were swimming in and out of the rainbow-coloured coral blooming under me. "It's so beautiful." I was ecstatic as I trod water watching the tropical dance below me.

"Oh, wow, this is amazing," Dolphin said, thrilled, as he swam over to me.

"Let's go to Ninaloo Marine Park tomorrow. There's sharks there," he said, grabbing my leg and pulling me towards him, and we floated face down, fully in tune with our surroundings.

Only hunger got me out of the water, and I set up a big picnic of crackers, bread, cheese, pickles, and salad at the picnic table by the beach. "This is the life, baby." I was so happy.

"Are you ready for the outback?" Dolphin said, slapping cheese on a piece of bread.

"I'm ready for anything and everything when I'm with you," and I ran my fingers through his now shoulder-length blonde hair.

"Let's fill her up with gas, restock the esky with food and beer, and we can be off in the morning."

At six am, we said 'bye-bye' to the beautiful ocean and turned off the highway onto the long and dusty road ahead. There wasn't much to see besides salt bushes, anthills, dust and space—until I saw something bounce. "A kangaroo!" I shouted in excitement. It was our first one and the first thing we had seen in hours.

"Yay, we're in the outback now!" Dolphin shrilled as he slowed down, and we watched it bounce away across the endless barren desert, which stretched out either side, behind, and in front of us.

Then we saw a battered, dusty sign for a roadhouse, and we burst into song. *"Keep your eyes on the road and your hands upon the wheel. We're going to a roadhouse, and we gonna have a real good time"*—The Doors.

Dolphin was still singing about 'the roadhouse' as he pulled up into its dirty, dusty parking bay. A single petrol pump stood in front of a grey, one-storey building. "G'day! Be with ya in a mo'," said the beefy girl behind the counter who was serving a guy who looked like a cowboy. "I'm Charlene. I can do you steak and eggs. The dunny is over there, and we have rooms out back," she said as she wiped down the counter in front of us with a shabby cloth.

"Steak and eggs sound great," Dolphin said as he went off to the dunny.

"What are you poms doing in these parts?" She seemed astounded.

"Checking it out," I said as I bent over to stretch out my legs and back.

"There's nothing but red dust and salt bushes between here and Karijini, but it's worth the long drive. Karijini is a natural wonder. It's beautiful down there. D'ya like swimming?"

"Yes, I love it," I smiled as I sat on a barstool.

"Then you won't wanna leave," she nodded as she whacked two steaks onto a hot plate.

"I see you ain't got any 'roo bars, mate," the cowboy called as we tucked into our lunch.

"What's that?" Dolphin asked, baffled.

"Ya fucking pommie idiots don't know what a 'roo bar is?! You're driving around looking for trouble. They're bars for ya front bumper so, when you hit a 'roo, your car doesn't get smashed up," he told us, assertively.

"What's a 'roo?" I felt stupid asking.

"What's a 'roo?! It's a fucking Kangaroo," he said, laughing his head off as he headed for the door. We managed to stop laughing long enough to finish off our tucker.

"You'll be right. Not many 'roos in these parts, and you only got about another four hours. Just remember, the road is long and you're only as strong as your next move," Charlene said, waving her hands like two pistols as we headed for the door. "Wish I was coming with ya," she called as we got into the car. We waved out the car window and beeped the horn as we pulled back onto the never-ending road.

We would get so excited when we reach the top of an escarpment, wondering what would be the other side. But it just all started again: grey road; dried out saltbushes; anthills and red dust, just like Charlene had told us.

After about two hours, we saw another car coming towards us, and Dolphin beeped his horn in excitement. "Good to see there's life on the other side," he said, tapping the steering wheel in time to the music coming from the sound system.

We nearly wet ourselves with excitement when we reached the top of yet another escarpment to see mountains towering out of the flat valley, and a billboard for Karijini National Park in the distance.

It wasn't long before the two-and-a-half-billion-year-old, erosion-carved landscape was looming over us, and the start of tree-lined watercourses wound their way over the dusty plain. We were so ecstatic Dolphin had to pull over so we could dance, and jump up and down, like two mental cases.

After a short drive, we arrived at a campsite and parked in our allotted parking area, beside a picnic table and barbecue. We eased ourselves out of the car to stretch our stiff bodies, covered in red dust and looking like we had just come from a full moon party.

"It doesn't look real." I was staring at the gigantic rock formations surrounding us.

"Let's get a shower and get out there," Dolphin said, grabbing his soap and towel and striding over to the toilet block. I was right behind him.

Following the marked trail, we stopped in wonder on our approach to the breath-taking, stone formations surrounding an emerald-green pool that was as clear as glass, except where the waterfall made a few gentle ripples.

"I'm in!" I stripped off faster than a whore on a promise, and splash! "Ooh, it's so fresh and no salt. Come on!" I was calling to Dolphin as the waterfall pounded my head, shoulders and back, giving me a welcome massage.

"And no dust," and he splashed in beside me.

"Ooh, what's that?" Something was touching my feet.

"It's fish," Dolphin exclaimed.

"Oh! Oh! They're nibbling me." It was a strange, tickling sensation and I liked it, so I pulled myself up onto a rock and let my feet dangle in the water, giving them a feast and me a natural pedicure.

When we went back to the camp, we set up for an evening feed as the sun set over the rocks and a star-studded, clear night opened up accompanied by a symphony of animal calls.

"Salad ready, wine open, spliff rolled," I told the master chef who was busy barbecuing sausages.

"Let's have another night here before we go to see the crocodiles." Dolphin was spiking the sausages onto a plate.

"I could stay here forever," I replied.

~ ~ ~

A short, dusty, four-hour drive took us to a pit stop in Port Headland, a working town with extensive offshore gas fields, and many bare-chested men in shorts and boots, covered in a sprinkling of red dust. It was great to get back into a calm ocean and wash off the dust, before getting covered in it again along the long, monotonous road.

We were both shocked out of our daydreams when a five-carriage vehicle tore along beside us, nearly blowing us off the side of the road and deafening us with the blast of its horn. "You alright, baby? I asked the Captain, who looked shaken.

"Yeah. I heard about those road trains, but I didn't think they were *that* fucking long!" He pulled over so we could stretch our legs and recover.

"I'll be ready for the next one," he reassured himself as he got back in the driver's seat, and we took off again for the pearling town of Broome.

"Where's Clint Eastwood?" I laughed, as we pulled into what looked like a set for a western movie. The rubble roads held small wooden platforms, which housed a few shops, bars and hotels. "We better learn some barn dancing, Dolphin," I giggled as we got out of the car.

"Yee haw!" He slapped his thigh, and red dust flew off his jeans to meet its red dust friends on the floor.

"Let's go for a swim. This dust is in my every pore," he coughed as we walked around the town. So we got back in the car and took off to the beach to float on the beautiful, calm water. I could feel my skin becoming clean and fresh and, at low tide, we walked along the sand to check out a dinosaur footprint in the sandstone.

"He was a big dude," I said as we both lay down on the warm stone.

"Or maybe just Big Foot? Waaaa waaaa," his famous dolphin laugh filled the space around us.

"Camel ride next," he said, pulling me to my feet, and we walked hand-in-hand back along the beach until we saw a crowd of people gathered around ten camels, and went over for our sunset ride.

A big Aussie man gave me a leg up onto the back of a sitting camel, behind my Captain Guidebook, Suddenly, I was joisted forward, almost head-butting Dolphin, then backwards, almost kissing the sky, as the camel stood up and took off. Her rhythmic pace, and the simplicity of the surrounding dunes and wild beach, relaxed me thoroughly, and I hugged my baby as the sun set into an orange and red glow, projecting black camel-shaped shadows onto the flat sand. "So this is Broome time," I whispered into my baby's ear as I drifted into a blissful and carefree feeling.

~ ~ ~

"Lucky, we had a big dose of Broome time." said the Captain as he checked the map and calculated it was seven hours until the next one-horse town.

"As navigator, I say go straight." And he pulled off onto the long dusty flat road, with anthills and saltbushes on either side.

"I think the car's had enough. It keeps overheating," he said later, as he pulled over to offer her a drink and give her a rest.

As we sat by the roadside, I was sure I could hear a distant noise that sounded like another car. "Something's coming," I squealed in excitement as I saw a truck approaching.

"G'day mate," said the tall, bronzed guy, in boots and shorts, strolling over to our car. "She's playing up, is she?" he drawled.

"Yeah, she's overheating," Dolphin said, stepping into mechanic mode.

"You got a leak, mate," said Boots and Shorts as he checked the oil stick. "You better get her a once over in Hall Creek. It's just up the road." Just up the road? It's three hours away! I thought. "There's not much else between here and Darwin except Abos, and they love to throw a pom on the barbie. They'll have a stick up your arse, and have you over the fire, in no time," he laughed as he went back to his truck.

All too aware of our vulnerability, I was afraid to challenge this casual racism so just thanked him for the tip and watched him speed off, leaving behind flying dust, track marks and silence.

We got back in and started again.

"You'd better cover your arse!" I said ironically as we pulled into the town of Halls Creek. I'd seen my first Aboriginal. He was crossing the road to join a group of about 20 others, sitting under a tree passing around a 'goon', as the locals referred to a box of wine.

"We'll get a hotel room so the car can spend the day at the mechanics and get a full service," Dolphin said, pulling up at the hotel across from the tree.

"Yeah, a real bed and a shower will be fantastic."

"And we can go real local, get a goon and chill at the river."

"Yippee!" I loved the simplicity of our life.

~ ~ ~

With a bit of a hangover, a serviced car and a full esky, we hit the road again, driving through the same deserted scene that made it looked like we weren't moving at all. Only the hands of my watch reassured me we were. Six hours later, when we reached the isolated village of Timber Creek, excitement took us over. We picked up bread and cheese for dinner and parked our overheated car on the outskirts of town so we could all get some rest before attempting the six hours to Darwin, the tip of Australia.

~ ~ ~

Darwin was under reconstruction, having suffered almost a year of cyclones, and looked like an unfinished movie set. We pulled into the backpackers to see if we could arrange to sleep in the car and use their facilities. "You can park in the garden and use the facilities for free, mate," said the tanned surfer guy behind the counter.

"Great, thanks a lot!" We could not believe our luck: a chance for the car to have a rest and us to earn some cash.

I got a job in one of the pubs that were back up and running, and Dolphin got labouring work.

~ ~ ~

"Fancy a game of cards?" Diana, my new English friend, was shouting to me from the backpackers' kitchen window. She had just gotten divorced, sold her house, and was travelling to forget her husband's infidelity.

"Yep, give me a minute." I was hanging out the rest of our fresh, clean laundry. "I got a bar shift tonight," I said as she shuffled the pack.

"I'll come with you to hang out, and then we can walk home together."

"Great. Dolphin's not up too much after a day's labour. It's not his style of work." We played a couple of games of bridge before I had to get ready for work.

I had a shower, put on my short beach dress and a bit of makeup, and enjoyed being a woman again as I went off with Diana to the bar. It was a lively night, and the two-piece reggae band had me dancing along as I pulled the drinks. A few other people from the backpackers were in, and we all walked home together.

"We are gonna chip in for a car and travel around like you," Diana said on the way home.

"It's an amazing journey and such freedom. I reckon you should do it. I can give you all the tips," I encouraged her.

When we got the backpackers, my baby was already lying down in the car, so I climbed into the back and snuggled into him. "Dolphin, you know this car won't make it to Sydney, right?" I whispered into his ear.

"It might." His sleepy voice trickled out of his sexy mouth.

"You know it won't, so why don't we sell it to them and hitch back to Sydney?"

"Will they buy it?" he said, moulding into my body.

"I'm sure I can talk Diana into it tomorrow."

"How soon can we go? I don't want to go back to work." He sounded like a baby.

"As soon as we sell it, I guess." He hugged me tight and fell contentedly asleep.

They bought the car a few days later, with all its mod cons, for 400 dollars, the same as Dolphin paid for it. So I did my last bar shift and took most of the money in the cash register with me as I walked out of the door. Some part of me felt ashamed but I justified it to myself because I was skint.

In the morning, Diana dropped us at the edge of town, and we kissed her and The Lime Green Dream Machine goodbye.

With our thumbs out, our freedom began again.

"You're not from here, are you," said a smiling bald man, as he leaned across to open the door of his ute.

"How did you guess?" I asked as Dolphin threw our backpacks into the back of the ute then squeezed in next to me.

"Cause you were giving the 'Fuck off' sign," he laughed.

"What?" We were horrified.

"Thumbs up in these parts means 'Fuck off'." He was still laughing. "You flag cars like this." He waved his hand up and down. We all laughed so much. "I'm on my way home to Katherine. Any good to you?"

"Yes, great. We're heading to Sydney." It was good to leave the red dust and enter the tropics again.

"I got a spare room, and you can crash tonight. I'll make you a nice Aussie barbie and drop you on the highway in the morning," he told us.

"Brilliant, thanks a lot." I squeezed Dolphin's hand.

Stan invited a few friends over, and we had a brilliant night around the fire eating barbecued meat, drinking fine wine and telling the tales of our dusty road trip in The Lime Green Dream Machine.

"Head to Alice Springs. You won't regret it," Stan said as he dropped us at the roadside in Larrimah.

"What a great guy. I hope they're all like that," Dolphin said as we watched him drive away.

"I told you hitching would be easy and fun," I teased him as a ute pulled up at our side.

"I'm going to Alice. Any good to ya?" came from a beautiful smile with the whitest teeth.

"Good? That's fantastic!" We threw our packs into the back and climbed into the cabin, not believing our luck.

"It's about nine hours away," the driver smiled as we settled into our seat out of the heat of the sun and he pulled out onto the long road. "In about four hours, we'll reach the town camp, get a bit of tucker, have a piss and we'll still get there in time for sunset."

"This sounds great. Thank you. I'm Dolphin, and this is me missus."

"I'm Minijara. It means 'a plum tree'." We sat back, enjoying the long ride listening to Minijara tell us tales of old.

"What's that mean?" There was a big sign that said 'Prescribed Area' at the entrance to the town camp.

"It's a ban on liquor and porn," he laughed, as he passed through the broken, rusty gate and half-naked kids appeared from every direction to run alongside the ute calling out "Min! Min!" He jumped down and started swinging them around one by one.

"The dunny's on the edge of the football field," he told us over the shrills of the screaming kids.

We passed an energetic football game, and a few concrete buildings and scattered tents, to find a plastic tent covering a long hole dug into the ground.

"Over here," Min called on our return. He was sitting under a tree on a big blanket, with a pretty woman in a floral dress. "This is my sister, Kirra." She smiled shyly as we joined them on the blanket. "She's made a pot of veg stew." And he started to spoon brown broth into a bowl. "We've never had gubbahs here before," he said, pointing out the kids spying on us from the safety of the trees.

"What's gubbahs?"

"White folk. They think we eat them." He laughed so much he nearly spilt the broth he was offering me.

"We heard that too," I laughed as I took my bowl and enjoyed a delicious veg stew under the shade of the tree, seeing white eyes peering out from the shadows.

"We better get on the road if we want to reach Alice before dark," Min said as soon as we had finished. So we jumped back into the ute and Min pulled out with the kids running behind us as far as their little legs would take them.

"That was so wonderful, Min. Thank you." I was happy to have met some Aboriginals.

We continued our drive through the red rocky desert mostly in silence, until we reached a dirt track off the road. "Legend says that a caterpillar created this landscape," Min said as he pulled off the road into Alice.

"That's some giant caterpillar! I hope we don't bump into it," Dolphin laughed.

We were soon at the campsite, and we jumped out, got our dusty backpacks, and waved Min goodbye. It started to get dark, so we threw our bags into the tent and headed for the shop to find something to make a picnic dinner before an early night.

We were up early to watch a paint chart of reddish-orange shades bring the imposing MacDonnell mountain range alive while a chorus of birds sang in the new day. Breathing in the fresh morning air, and feeling at one with nature, we went in search of the actual spring after which Alice Springs was named. We were walking through a deep, rugged, red-rocked gorge when suddenly we were greeted by an emerald-green oasis.

"So this is Alice," I said as I stripped off, jumped in and enjoyed the refreshingly cold water that brought my whole body to life. David, from Adelaide, was already in the water and invited us to join him at his campfire for dinner.

"I already put some spuds in the fire, and we can barbie this up," he said, giving me a plate of meat.

"Oh, lucky I know my place," I laughed, taking the plate of meat he wanted cooked.

"Come on, mate. You Sheilas are better at it than us." He was a big guy, with blue eyes and long, curly blonde hair hanging from his crumpled brown hat. He looked more like a boy scout than a man of 30, in his shorts and boots.

"I needed some air after the mines," he told us as we finished off our tucker and sipped beers around the fire.

"What're you mining?" Dolphin asked, more out of politeness than interest.

"Lead, silver, copper, zinc. I've been down them mines 10 hours a day for a year now, but I've nearly got enough to buy me a house, mate."

"Are the mines near here?" I asked.

"Mount Isa, nine hours away. Wanna lift out tomorrow? It's on the way to Cairns."

"Sounds good to me. How about you, Dolphin?" I asked as I lay down to take in the night stars.

"It'll beat trying to get a hitch out of here," he replied, joining me on the ground.

"You can enjoy the sea and The Great Barrier Reef, while he can get busy with the Sheilas in the bars and clubs. I went last month. The sun shines all day and all hotels have swimming pools but, mate, wait 'til you see them Sheilas." I looked at Dolphin and he was smiling. Not at the thought of them Sheilas, I hoped.

David dropped us outside a pub on the highway, just on the outskirts of Mount Isa. We got a simple room, washed a steak dinner down with a few beers, and turned in for an early night.

We were back on the road by six am, to try to get as far as possible before the sun was at its burning peak. With hands flapping, not thumbs up, we waved at our first ute of the day, and it pulled over. Three guys were sitting in the front. "If you don't mind jumping in the back, we can drop you in Richmond," the one sitting at the window told us. We had no idea where Richmond was but there was only one road, so we jumped in.

"It's great, hitching," Dolphin said, lying down next to me in the back of the ute.

"I sometimes like it better than the destination," I admitted.

"We're here," one of the guys called through the glass four hours later. "You can use the dunny in that pub, get some tucker and then keep going straight." And they were gone.

The pub was just opening and provided us with breakfast of eggs and toast. "Shall we keep going?" I asked Dolphin.

"Yeah. Nothing to do here, and all those Sheilas are waiting for me," he teased.

"Do you poms want a lift to Hughenden?" a rugged red face asked as we were leaving the pub.

"If it's on the way to Cairns, then yes please," I answered.

"It's a crossroads about an hour up the road. There'll be more traffic for ya up there. Then Cairns is only about eight hours away. You could make it before dark." We jumped into the back of his ute, enjoying the freedom of the open road.

We had just reached the crossroads when a camper van with two English guys pulled over. "Will Cairns do ya?" Paul said, looking out the passenger seat window.

"Great!" We couldn't believe our luck as we got in the back, out of the hot sun.

"You gonna dive the reef?" John, the driver, said over his shoulder.

"Not sure yet." Neither of us were divers. We had only just learned how to snorkel.

"We've been driving around for months. Didn't realise what a big country it is. Now we just wanna chill in Cairns for a while and check out the chicks."

"Yes, we heard there's plenty there," I said, as I settled down to roll a spliff for the boys.

It was dark when we pulled into Cairns, so we headed straight to the backpackers and got a dorm bed each. I put my sheet under my top bunk mattress, so it hung down to shield Dolphin's bottom bunk, and we snuggled in together in private.

In the morning, we checked out the town, one main road lined with bars, clubs, hotels and backpackers, with a beautiful clear, calm ocean on either side. And indeed, there were plenty of sexy Sheilas everywhere.

"I need to find work. I'm getting desperately low on cash," I said to John as he joined me at the pool, where I was searching through the newspaper for a job.

"Sleep in the van if you want to save on accommodation. We won't be using for a week 'cause we'll be all day on the dive course and all night in the bars drinking, so no driving."

"That would be amazing, John! Thanks a lot." And he gave me the key. Dolphin parked the van up the side road beside the backpackers, which didn't mind us hanging out and using the facilities.

"These reef tours are destroying the reef, Dolphin, I don't want to support it. We see enough beauty snorkelling," I said as we were sitting around the pool checking out the many leaflets scattered around.

"You're right, baby, and they are way too expensive."

"I need to find a job, and there's nothing here. Can we check out this banana-picking place? It's less than two hours away."

"Yeah, the Sheila's are all taken anyway," he grinned.

After a big breakfast, we got a bus to the outskirts of town to hitch to Tully to look for banana-picking work. In great spirits, we were singing, *"Come Mr Tally-man, tally me banana, daylight come and me wan' go home!"* when a petite woman, with short black hair, pulled over and picked us up.

"I never pick up people because I got five kids to look after, but there was something about you I liked," Donna said as we drove down the dusty lane.

"Well, thank you. We're just poms looking for work. Do you know anything or anyone?" I was hopeful.

"I can get you a job humping bananas tomorrow," she threw over her shoulder to Dolphin, who was sitting in the back. "You can stay with me if you don't mind a few dogs, cats, and kids."

"Wow! Thank you."

As we pulled into the driveway of a big, ramshackle house, five kids, four dogs and three cats greeted us, all running around a big, messy garden that had toys all over the grass and a broken swing. "This is home," Donna said as I helped her with the bags of shopping.

The inside of the house was as messy as the garden, and I had no idea where to put the bags of shopping. So I just put them on top of the unwashed dishes on the counter and followed her and Dolphin to our bedroom. Dolphin dumped our bags on the bed and pushed all the clothes and toys on the floor underneath it. "Hard to keep the place tidy with five kids running wild," she said, embarrassed.

"I'm sure it is," I said and hugged her.

We went back to the kitchen, and I made some tea while Donna made a phone call. "Dolphin, there's a job for a week, humping. The truck'll pick you up tomorrow at six am."

Unfortunately for Dolphin, humping didn't mean having sex. It was a full day of hard work. Someone would chop the banana trees at the root, and he had to 'hump' them into the truck. He would come home every night, bent over and exhausted.

I stayed home and helped Donna clean the house and garden, and then we would make a lovely dinner for our humping man. At the end of the week, Dolphin split his wages with Donna, and she dropped us at the highway. "I will miss you two. I'm so happy I picked you up," Donna said as she gave me a tight hug that brought tears to my eyes.

"I love you, Donna," I shouted as she drove away.

The two-hour hitch to Townsville was easy. We just jumped into the back of the first ute that pulled over and the driver, who was entirely toothless, dropped us at the port to get a 20-minute ferry to Magnetic Island.

The ferry let the cars off first so, by the time we were on land, there were no cars to flag down, and we had to walk. The dense jungle dirt track had trees on either side that were as high as the sky. They blocked most of the midday sun but kept in the heat and the track seemed to go on and on. To the sounds of animal calls, we carefully stepped over big tree roots and avoided vast spider webs.

"Look up that tree, Dolphin. There's a koala." We stopped to rest and watch it slowly chew gum leaves.

"It looks stoned," he laughed.

After two hours of hobbling through the jungle, we reached the first rest-house, got a cabin and put our backpacks down. Peeling our sweat-soaked clothes off our aching bodies and putting on our swimmers, we went off for a swim. We were the only ones on the pristine, palm-fringed beach, and we relaxed in its warm water, enjoying the blissful tranquillity.

"Mate, you can't get around without a car and, looking at the state of ya when you arrived, you're no hikers," said the park ranger when we returned to the cabin. "I go to the ferry every day. Let me know when you need a lift back."

We left the next day, on the last ferry, and got a hotel on the highway to make for easy hitching in the morning. The hotel had a smorgasbord, so we filled our boots, as we Brits say, and wobbled up to bed for an early night.

"I can drop you to Bowen," said Dion, who had joined our table for breakfast.

"What's there?" I asked.

"It's got a beautiful coast, friendly people and farm work."

"We need work, and the rest sounds good too." I looked over to Dolphin, who nodded in agreement.

"Well, do you like tomatoes? The season's about to start and they need workers. I can drop you off at the corner where the farmers pick you up, and you can try your luck today."

"Yes, that would be perfect," I said, but Dolphin, who was still in recovery from humping, just ate his food.

By 11 am, we were on the corner and, by 12, a rugged-looking man in Wellington boots came over to us. "Can you drive?" he asked Dolphin.

"Yes, I can drive," he answered, looking relieved.

"Right then, you two can work in the packing shed. And you two can pick," he told the couple from Manchester, standing next to us. "Get in the back." and he walked over to his ute.

He pulled up outside a packing shed with fields of tomatoes stretching out all around it, and walked us to a little one-storey house opposite. "You sleep here." He opened the door to three bedrooms, a bathroom and a kitchen. "At six am, meet me at the shed. There are a few shops and a beach 10 minutes that way," and he was gone.

Paul and Lucy were 23 and travelling round Aus as their honeymoon. Paul had a Beatles look, from haircut to clothes, and Lucy had a long blonde perm, painted nails and full makeup. I was not sure how they would fare picking all day.

At six am, Dolphin and I went into the packing shed where there were a few locals. One taught me how to make a box and fill it with tomatoes, while the farmer taught Dolphin how to drive the forklift, pick up our packed boxes and put them in the truck for the market. It was fast-paced, and by 11 am, I was ready to get out of that shed.

"Fucking hell!" Paul was back from the field, holding his back.

"Look at my nails," Lucy was almost crying.

"Come and have some lunch." I put tomatoes, boiled eggs, cheese and bread on the table.

"It gets easier." Dolphin tried to reassure them by telling them all about his banana-humping days as we munched away.

We were back at it from two pm until five pm. Every day was the same.

After a week, a six-foot woman, stocky with short-cropped hair and brown eyes, walked into the packing shed and joined me at the conveyor belt.

"Hiya, I'm Emma," she told everyone in a strong Liverpool accent.

"Hi," I replied, but I was the only one. Maybe the others thought they would catch 'lesbian' if they looked at her! So I showed her the ropes and we continued to pack.

"I got a car. Do you fancy driving into town after this to get a big food shop," Emma asked me, breaking the silence.

"Brilliant idea! It would be great to get some different food."

Everyone was excited to get off the farm for a few hours so we stuffed ourselves into the car like The Beverly Hillbillies and hit the supermarket, buying up enough food for a week.

Back at the farm, we settled down to working by day and amusing ourselves playing cards and drinking by night. One night Lucy, a beautician, decided to dread Dolphin's hair. It went well with his big brown eyes and suntan, and he now looked like a brother. "Get off me," I laughed as she tried to make a move on my long, golden hair.

"Let's not waste our day off tomorrow. If you all chip in a few bucks, I'll fill up the car and drive to Airlie beach. It's only an hour away," Emma said, pushing Lucy off her hair.

"Yes! Yes! Yes!" We were all in agreement.

I woke up in a house that was buzzing with excitement to go to the beach and, by nine am, with the boot loaded with a few snorkels, towels and sun creams, we were off. Long-legged Dolphin sat in the front, in charge of the tunes and spliff rolling, and I snuggled into the back with Paul, Lucy and a bottle of Jack Daniels. "Boom boom boom," went the reggae and we all danced in our seats as Dolphin's new dreadlocks flew around his bobbing head.

We were pretty smashed by the time we reached the buzzing little town that was alive with shops, bars, restaurants and people walking around in just their swimwear. We fell out of the car, stripped off, locked our stuff in the boot and staggered onto the white sand of the turquoise-watered tropical paradise. "This is our base," Emma said as she put a blanket on the sand, and we all ran into the sea.

"That has to be the best snorkelling ever." Paul shook the water from his hair over Dolphin's and my bodies, stretched out on the blanket.

"It's beautiful, but I still think Thailand beats it," I said, sitting up to pass him the spliff.

"We are planning to go there too, after here." He inhaled the spliff and passed it on to Lucy.

"Let's go eat," Emma interrupted us. Dolphin pulled me up and we staggered off to a Chinese buffet. We filled our plates with a load of dishes and tucked in like farm animals, then got a goon of red, some paper cups, and headed back to the beach.

"Will you be alright to drive?" Dolphin asked Emma.

"I think I'm in a better state than you," she laughed as we piled back into the car.

Emma got us home safe to pick and pack the next day, and the next day, and the next, until one day…

"Argh! I'm fucking fed up of that ostrich biting me. I'm leaving tomorrow, after we get paid." The farm had an ostrich roaming freely around the yard. It was like an aggressive guard dog and bit everything it could. Emma was fuming and checking the latest bruise on her bum.

"Where are you going?" I was exhausted from packing tomatoes and had also had enough of that damn ostrich.

"Mackay. It's a big city, with a great beach full of marine life, and a blue water lagoon."

I looked at Dolphin, and he smiled at me. "Can we hitch a ride?" I was excited at the thought of getting back on the road.

"Sure. Let's get our pay first, and then we just leave before they open the shed. Five am, OK?"

"I'm ready now," I laughed and went to my room to pack.

~ ~ ~

It was beautiful and the lagoon was terrific, but there was no work, and my money was going fast.

"I love it here, Dolphin, but I need work. I'm gonna have to go to Brisbane."

We got a ride all the way to Brisbane with Janice and Bill, who enjoyed the stories of our adventures.

The backpackers' manager was a cool, young dude who gave us a double room for the price of two beds in a dorm. "Check out the park. There's a big fair coming for a few weeks. I'm sure they'll need staff."

I walked the twenty minutes from the backpackers to the park for an interview, and got a job working on the dodgem cars. "It's for three weeks, and you'll get paid on the last day," the boss told me.

"That's fine by me." It would be a great way to be sure I saved it all for moving on.

It was an easy job. I just sat behind a kiosk, selling tickets all day, watching Aussie life pass by, including the strange ways by which they contrived to add tomato sauce to everything they ate. The most popular snack was the 'dagwood dog', a hotdog on a stick, deep fried in batter then dipped into tomato sauce so it was fully covered. A meat pie, with its top a glowing red, came a close second.

After work, a brisk walk would take me home, where my baby would be waiting with a nice healthy dinner.

The three weeks passed fast and, with a few hundred dollars in my pocket, we hitched back to Sydney to spend the weekend with Uncle Bob. "What have you done to your hair?" Uncle Bob said as he opened the door with a loud Dolphin laugh. It was great to see him again and we sat around the pool drinking cold beer, telling him and Betty all about our adventures, as I gently removed the dreadlocks from my Dolphin one by one.

"Speculate to accumulate," Bob said as he kissed us goodbye at the airport.

~ ~ ~

I didn't think you could find anywhere more laid back than Aus, but Auckland managed to top it; everyone was super chilled and relaxed. Mr Guidebook found us a decent backpackers in the centre of town, and we were ready to check out our new home. Walking through a beautiful park, set around an extinct volcano, we found a romantic restaurant on the waterfront and had dinner of New Zealand lamb followed by kiwi fruit dessert.

"It's a pretty skyline, but I'd rather see the stars," I said to Dolphin as we sipped our cold beer.

"We can check for work tomorrow, and if there's nothing, let's hitch out."

"OK." I was ready to hitch out, work or no work.

Hitching through the beautiful mountains was easy, and we got as far as the hot spring town of Rotorua, which stunk of sulphur.

"I'm checking my money Dolphin, and I have two choices," I said as we sat at the sulphur pool.

"Go on. I love your ideas."

"If I stay here and look for work, my money will last for about two weeks, and then what? I'll be in the middle of nowhere with a low-income job. Or we could use the last bit of our 'round the world' ticket before it runs out. We can have a short holiday in Fiji, then onto LA, where I know there'll be work."

"Number two, baby, let's go." And that was that.

We hitched back to Auckland and caught a flight to Suva, the capital of Fiji.

I just about managed to control my excitement when I looked out the plane window and saw the palm-lined beach islands. "There are 333 islands, with coral reefs and clear lagoons. The Mamanuca Islands sound the best," Mr Guidebook informed me.

"Then let's go there." Any one of them would do me.

In the taxi from the airport, I noticed Suva was a dusty, noisy city. It reminded me of India, though without the beggars, and I had no interest in staying. "Let's get straight out of here," I said to Dolphin, who nodded in agreement. We got boat tickets for the next day.

As we arrived by boat at one of the Mamanuca Islands, we could see that it had no roads and was rugged and natural. A woman in a bright-coloured dress was waiting to greet us. She led us into a palm-leaf hut, with a dried cow-dung floor, and invited us to sit around a big wooden bowl where the island's chief, dressed in white, was already sitting for our welcoming kava ceremony. "Bula," the chief said, and we all clapped our hands three times before he offered me an empty coconut husk cup.

"Bula," I clapped once, took the husk, filled it with the muddy liquid in the wooden bowl and downed it in one. The pepper plant's bitter taste slipped down my throat, leaving me numb and chilled. Then we all clapped three times, and I passed the empty bowl to my left.

With the ceremony done, the woman took us to a bamboo hut at the edge of the ocean. Nothing obscured our view of the pristine water where we would sit and watch dolphins jump. Just next door was a tiny kitchen that would serve us spicy food over rice. We had nowhere to go and nothing to do but enjoy a whole week of relaxing, eating and swimming, before going to the big City of Angels.

~ ~ ~

"Look! Marilyn Monroe!" I said as I put my hands on top of her handprints on Hollywood Boulevard. It was a sunny day, and we were enjoying the excitement of a big city, marred only by the challenges of getting anywhere, and the time it took.

"Let's go to Venice beach for the sunset," Dolphin said, checking his bus timetable booklet.

The bus was packed and noisy with loud, twanging voices as it took us through the crowded streets filled with multi-coloured movement. We jumped off into a chilled-out, funky town and walked along the busy promenade which had psychedelic-painted restaurants and bars on one side and an expanse of golden sand on the other. The sand swept into the deep blue ocean which was full of surfers riding the waves. Scantily-dressed women and muscular men worked out in the open gym, and street performers performed all kinds of acts to earn a buck.

"We should move here, baby. I bet I can get a job in one of these restaurants or bars."

"I think we should head out. It's way too busy and crazy." He was right. I think the city itself would have worn me out as much as anything.

We got a driveaway to San Francisco. If you're over twenty-one, with a clean driving license and a one hundred dollar deposit, you can pick up a car with a tank full of gas. When you deliver the vehicle in one piece at the specified time, you get your deposit back.

~ ~ ~

After three days of spectacular coastal road, we finally reached San Francisco.

"Not gonna see it today," Mr Guidebook was saying, looking at the fog that shrouded the Golden Gate Bridge.

"Maybe later. Let's go to the bay."

We jumped on a tram that took us up and down the hills, through tree lined streets with pretty flowers, to reach 'Frisco Bay's spacious marina, which stunk of hot dogs and salt water. Dodging through the tourist hub, we found an empty bench and looked out at Alcatraz in the middle of the ocean. "*No one has ever escaped; not even Capone,*" Dolphin said, reading from his guidebook.

"Bet I can get a job there," I said, looking in the other direction where hot dog vendors were going into a depot under the Bay Bridge. "Wait here. I'll just check." Not what I had in mind, but I was desperate. Dolphin still had loads left from the big money he'd made before we set off, whereas I needed to make money as I went; I didn't want to be dependent on him. But I had been looking unsuccessfully for a job for a week and had been forced to hit him for a loan.

As soon as I walked into the depot, I saw a stumpy man about 40 years old, with greased-back black hair. "Hi. Are you hiring at the moment?" I asked, not sure if I even wanted the job.

"Sure. We hire the pretty girls. Come here tomorrow at nine am for training, and you can start straight away." He smiled at me, giving me a onceover. "I'm Carlos," and he shook my hand.

"See you tomorrow then," I said, wiping my hand down my jeans and walking back to my Dolphin. "I start tomorrow morning. It's shit, but it's money," I told him and plopped myself back on the bench.

"Speculate to accumulate, baby," he laughed.

"Well, it's better than nothing." I had to laugh too.

"Come on. Let's go home, and I'll treat you to a burrito."

Home was a dorm bed in the backpackers in the Mexican part of town, full of bars, restaurants, and cheap cafés serving the best burritos.

"Refried beans please," I said to the man behind the counter. I was salivating as I watched him spread refried beans over a giant flour tortilla, add salad, sour cream and chilli sauce, then roll it up into a big fat sausage and hand it to me. I took my trophy over to the table and dolloped on the extra toppings: salsa; guacamole; onions; and jalapeños. We sat in silence in a world of taste.

I was at the depot and ready for my training the following day. "Good morning, pretty girl. You wear this." Carlos gave me a red baseball cap and a red apron. "This your cart. You keep clean," showing me a cloth and bucket under it. "This card shows you what to put on top of the sausage." He liked that word. "There is seven trays. Sausage here." They were floating in hot, greasy water. "And here tomatoes, onions, sauerkraut, cucumber, gherkins," tapping each one. "Keep the buns dry." He pulled on a plastic bag containing the buns, hanging from the side of the cart. "And here you keep the sauce: tomato; mustard; barbecue; chilli; and mayo," pointing at each one. "You check card, OK, for what put on the sausage." Yep, he liked that word! "You can eat one sausage. You like to eat sausage?" I just smiled. "You work here today. I wanna keep eye on you." He pointed to the marina sidewalk, where I sat with my Dolphin the day before.

I loved it, out in the sun, watching life on the 'Frisco Bay, serving hot dogs.

Dolphin had started a job that day also, packing bottles in a sauce factory. So we were sorted, and started to save money.

But then, one day, I was singing on my way back to the depot, looking forward to a lovely evening with Dolphin, when the earth started to wobble under my feet, and the road in front of me split into two. I froze on the spot, and then I began to run. "Don't go inside, you fool! It's an earthquake!" said the guy that grabbed me and pulled me away from the building I'd been running towards.

"Earthquake!" I had never been in one before, and I knew 'Frisco was expecting 'the big one', so I was terrified. We stood in the middle of a road that was wobbling as if someone was shaking a bedsheet, watching debris fall from buildings. Within five seconds it was over, but it felt a lot longer than that.

I walked back to the depot in a state of shock, carefully stepping over cracks in the ground as big as steps, and looking at the buildings that had separated. I had to stand still to get my breath when I saw the ocean waves reaching almost as high as the high rises. All traffic had stopped, and everywhere was still and silent.

Then suddenly the place was in chaos, and people were running around shouting in confusion and fear. There was no electricity, so no traffic lights, so traffic was going in every direction, beeping, and trams just stood still blocking the way.

I was terrified and still in shock when I reached the depot to put my cart away. "Look up, Pretty," Carlos said, showing me that the top of the Bay Bridge had collapsed onto the deck below. I was horrified. "Go home, Pretty."

Trying to get back to the backpackers was even more chaotic. The roads now looked as battered as an Indian highway, and everyone was in a panic, running around like headless chickens. Everyone was just looking out for themself, trying to manoeuvre the potholes, rocks, and stones everywhere, while burst water pipes created water features all over the place. Cars, buses, trams, and trucks were all full of people who needed to check on their loved ones and homes. Everyone was screaming at everyone else.

"Get off the streets." The police were shouting through megaphones. "The aftershocks will bring the buildings down." Talk about adding chaos to chaos. "Go home and, when you feel the next rumble, stand under the doorframe."

I finally got back to the backpackers, terrified, and rushed to check on Dolphin, who was lying on the sofa in the TV room watching a movie. I jumped onto his lap and held him tight. "I thought I was going to die," I told him through my sobs.

"Here, have a puff on this baby. It'll sort you out." He passed me a spliff.

"No. I'm paranoid enough already." I pushed his hand away.

"All hell has broken loose downtown. People are running riot, partying and looting. Anyone want to go?" A lad had come into the TV room to ask us. I was disgusted and got up and went to the kitchen.

I sat at the table, wrote a letter to my family and friends, put it in my passport and strapped it to my body for identification in case I was to get lost in the rubble.

"You wanna buy my magic number for five dollars?" asked the Aussie twang of Stephan, the surfer, who was watching me.

"What's that?"

"It's a stolen credit card number which you can use to make phone calls. You look like you need it." His deep blue eyes looked at me full of concern. I bought it, went to the call box outside and called everyone whose number I had.

Morning came with no significant aftershocks, but the aftermath was devastating. People had lost loved ones, homes, jobs and cars. Some were temporarily housed in halls and schools, with beds, clothes and food, but others were stuck inside their vehicles in between the decks of the collapsed Bay Bridge. Many volunteers were trying to do their best to help in a shocked and sad city.

"I want to leave, baby. Stephan plans to go to Yosemite National Park in his pickup truck as soon as the roads open. He's offered us a lift," I told Dolphin as we walked around the aftermath.

"Yeah, let's go."

I found a call box and called Carlos. "Hello Carlos. I need to leave. Can you send my wages to the post office in New Orleans?"

"Sure, Pretty. I promise," he assured me.

As the highway leading to Yosemite National Park opened and we began to feel the relief of leaving behind that devastation that we could do nothing about, we broke into a raucous rendition of *Get Your Kicks On Route 66*.

"At least nothing can fall on us here," I said as we pulled into a picnic area at the top of a mountain.

"I'll put the tent up, and you two go look for wood for a fire," Stephan said, tying up his long bleached-blonde hair. We followed the trail into the woods looking for dry wood and kindling.

"I've never seen so much colour and beauty. Look at the size of the trees and the mountains." I felt like they were going to swallow me up.

"Race you to the waterfall." And he was off. A mass of cold water raised my heartbeat again as I jumped into its beauty and let its pounding massage my whole body.

Feeling revitalised, we went back to camp, built a fire and made a pot of veg stew and jacket potatoes. "That was real cowboy food." Stephan put his empty bowl down.

"It was tasty," I said as I gathered up the empty bowls and pot, and put them in the back of the truck to be washed in the river in daylight.

"Is that rock moving or is the firelight playing tricks with my eyes?" I called to the boys who were busy having a spliff by the fire.

"It's a bear! RUN!" Both boys were up and scampering back to the truck. I was quick to jump in behind them and we locked the door. We sat there like excited kids as we watched this great big black bear have a sniff around for food, find nothing then carry on its way. I was nervous sleeping in the tent that night!

Back on the road through Arizona, New Mexico, Texas, Oklahoma, and New Orleans, by day we passed canyon after canyon of a vast and ever-changing landscape and, by night, we would camp out.

New Orleans was full of fun, and alive with all sorts of entertainment and excitement, but there was no money from Carlos at the post office and no work.

"I need work, baby. I'm sure I'll get it in New York. I have connections there, and Grets will let us stay with her until I'm on my feet."

"Ok, let's get a driveaway."

It was an easy highway drive, just pulling off to sleep in the car for one night at a service station, where I dreamt about our destination.

~ ~ ~

"*New York New York, so good they named it twice.*" I couldn't contain my excitement when the ol' familiar sights of Manhattan were before my eyes, and I rang the bell of a familiar door.

"Fucking hell, woman! You stink!" Well, her English had improved.

"It's nice to see you too, Grets." And it was.

"Everything in the washing machine," she ordered as she filled up the bathtub. "Him too," looking over at Dolphin.

"You can't put my baby in the washing machine." The joke was lost in translation.

"You both stink of burnt wood. Now strip," and she threw a T-shirt at each of us. "You can use my spare room," she said, pointing to a door at the back of the apartment. "I sleep here with my wife. No entry," pointing at the room opposite the kitchen.

"Oh, Yana?"

"No, she's gone. Her brother came and took her home, and made her marry a man, and now she has to have sex with all that stuff running down her legs. I'm married to Mary. She'll be back in a few hours, so please be presentable by then." Dolphin was a bit taken back and went to our room to strip off quietly, waiting for me to get out of the bath.

"Tonight, I'll cook, and we all eat together but, after that, you do your own thing. I'm now a professional photographer and I'm busy, with strange hours," she said, giving me a key. She was happy to see me, I could tell.

Mary was a short, chubby girl from Ohio who looked more butch than Grets. "What do you do for a living?" I asked, tucking into pasta and garlic bread.

"I put on exhibitions for artists."

"That sounds nice. Maybe we could come to see one."

"Maybe." Mary was not hiding the fact that she was not happy that there were two strangers in her flat and they were not gay.

Dolphin and I washed up the dishes, and Grets and Mary went into their bedroom. We were soon to get into ours and enjoy being in a proper bed.

"Morning, sexy. It's time for me to show you my city." I woke up excited and ecstatic to be back.

"Morning," and he pulled me on top of him.

The girls were either in bed or out so we grabbed some coffee and toast and hit the streets.

"Let's go up The Empire State building first. My treat," Mr Guidebook said.

"Brilliant idea. You'll get to see the entire city from the window." I took his hand and danced him to the subway. The smell of the electrical circuits shooting up my nose in the airless heat made me feel sick, but it still felt like home.

"Just breathe through your nose, then you don't taste it," I said to Dolphin, who had covered his mouth and started to walk over to the tracks. "Be careful, baby. Sparks fly out when the subway comes in." And I guided him away to check out the graffiti on the walls. We cuddled together waiting for the midtown subway.

Soon a long tube full of people arrived, all wrapped up in their own worlds, and we managed to squeeze through and get a seat together. We sat back to watch a group of people who had turned the whole tube into a theatre of dance while passing around a hat, and I managed to stick a dollar in before we jumped down at Penn Station.

Back on the street, we could see the 443.2 meter high building, with 102 storeys, towering over us as we walked the two blocks to its entrance. Dolphin bought tickets for the viewing platform, and we were whisked up in the lift—or elevator—to reach the viewing deck. It was a clear day, and I could see every building and every brick in the city that I loved. "In the distance, you can see the five states: New York; New Jersey; Connecticut; Pennsylvania; and Massachusetts." The Platform Guide informed us. We were mesmerised and could have stayed there longer but got pushed along so the next batch of people could get to the glass.

"Wow! That was fantastic!" Dolphin said when we were back on the ground.

"I think my stomach is still up there," I laughed as we headed for the bus stop to get a free tour of the city on our way to the Statue of Liberty. I could see Dolphin was in shock with the madness, so I distracted him with food. "I know a great cheap lunch where we get off the bus," and I rubbed his belly.

The bus dropped us just past the monument's entrance, and I went into a supermarket to get a cup of hot noodle soup from the big soup kettle at the front of the store. We sat on a park bench just looking at that green woman, holding her torch to enlighten the world, while we drank our hot soup.

"Can we go check out my old haunts now?"

"Whatever you want, baby." He was happy.

This bus dropped us a few blocks from 14th Street and I was running to the Boom Boom Bar when I was stopped in my tracks by seeing it was now The Sluggers Bar, and there was no one hanging out on the streets.

"Two Buds, please," I told the bartender behind the counter. The bar looked the same, but empty and lifeless. "I used to work here a few years ago. It's changed a lot. Where is everyone?"

"The police did a raid about a year ago, and most peeps got put in the slammer or deported back to where they came from."

"Do you know Starlight, Bingo or Joe?" I asked, hopefully.

"No, none of them kind come here anymore." I was heartbroken as I looked around and the crazy memories flooded my mind. I finished my beer, and we went home.

In the morning, I went to see Cory for a job. "You come back! The crazy friend with you?"

"No, just me, but I need a job, Cory," I pleaded.

"You go look First and First. I have one bar there. You look. Jerry, maybe he give you a job."

"Thank you," and off I went.

It was a dark, dingy, heavy metal bar, with black walls, black floor, and black jukebox. The only other colour was the green of the pool table. "Hi. Are you Jerry?" I asked the skinny, long-haired guy dressed in black, behind the counter. He nodded. "I'm a friend of Cory, and he said you might have a job for me."

"Don't need anyone, dude," he drawled. I could paint your pool table black to match the rest of the decor, I thought.

"Please give me a chance," I begged. I wasn't moving until I had a job, so we just sat there looking at each other.

"You're desperate, right?"

"Yes." It was true.

"OK, come tonight. You can start as a busboy." And he flicked his black hair over his shoulders. "But you have to dress coool, baby." He drawled.

"Thank you!" I was delighted.

A busboy collects empty glasses and returns them to the bar. That would be easy enough; dressing "cool, baby" was gonna be trickier. Molly had given me a phone number for Fishnet, a chick from New York that she was hanging around in London, so I got a magic number and gave her a call. "Hi Fishnet. I'm Molly's friend and I'm in the city. I just got a job and I need to dress cool. Any tips?"

"Hey, anything black and tight. I just left my useless prick of a husband. There should be some stuff in my apartment you can use." She gave me the number of her useless prick of a husband, Noddy. Now in my eyes, *that* was cool!

I quickly called Noddy and arranged to meet at the apartment to pick up some clothes.

Although the neighbourhood was dangerous, opposite a park full of homeless people, I liked it. I knocked on the door, and it was opened by a short English guy with spiky, dyed blonde hair, dressed in ripped black leather pants, with a big, silver-studded belt and an open-neck black satin shirt. "You've come for clothes, right?" he said, walking down the long corridor to the lounge room.

"Yeah. I start a job in an hour, and I need to dress cool."

"Have a look in there." He pointed to one of the two rooms leading off the lounge. "I moved all her shit in there when she left."

It was a small room with a double bed, and a wardrobe with lots of cool clothes. I picked out a pair of leopard skin pants and a pair of black Lycra tights, to go with a skin-tight black vest, plus hair crimpers. "I'll just take these, and I'll bring them back as soon as I can afford to buy some clothes of my own."

"You need a place to stay?"

"Yeah, with my boyfriend."

"You can rent that room off me for ten bucks a night if you want." He pointed to the room with the cool clothes.

"Great! Can we move in tomorrow?"

He nodded and gave me a key. "Let's talk then."

I ran back to Grets' to give Dolphin the excellent news. I could tell he was intimidated there. I think the dykes were jealous of his cock! "Baby, I found us a room for ten bucks a night, and we can move in tomorrow. The guy seems OK," I said as I squeezed in the leopard print pants and black vest.

"That's great. I think I've found a job too—as a bike courier. I finalise everything tomorrow."

"Whoopee!" I was so happy that life was working out.

I finished crimping my long golden hair, Tina Turner-style, and piling on the makeup that, having no spare money, I'd shoplifted earlier. "How do I look?" I asked a wide-eyed Dolphin.

"You look veerry cool baybee," he said, grabbing me in a big hug and I could feel something rising.

"It'll have to wait until I get back. I'm going to be late." And I ran for the door before I changed my mind.

I went down to the basement where Jerry was sound-checking the bands that would play there later. "So, how is this?" I asked him.

"Wow! You look like you're in a band. That's cool!" Jerry's reaction was almost the same as Dolphin's. Pleased I had a foot in the door, I got busy collecting glasses while dancing and buzzing around talking to all the people.

"You look cool and act cool. Can you come again tomorrow?" Jerry asked as we were finishing up.

"Sure can, baby, but I do want to work the bar at some point," I winked. I needed to get at that register and them tips. He gave me my 20 bucks, and I skipped home feeling rich and sure everything was going to work out.

The following day, we kissed Grets goodbye and walked the few blocks to Noddy's apartment.

"Dolphin, we can see the park every time we come out instead of buildings. It's like being in the country."

"Yes, and everything's on the doorstep too. Well done, baby." He slapped my arse as I opened the door with my key, and we were home.

"Noddy, we're here," I called down the corridor.

"I'll put the kettle on." A true Englishman.

We walked through the lounge to the kitchen, dropping our bags into our room on the way. "This is Dolphin."

"Alright, mate," Dolphin said as they shook hands. "I got to go to see about a job, but we can have a chat later," and my baby was gone.

"How was your shift?" Noddy asked.

"It was great. I loved it but I'm hoping to get behind the bar soon."

"I'm in a band, but we're on a break at the moment, same as the wife and me."

"What you doing now?"

"I'm packing boxes in a factory, and I need to go now, so I'll see you later. What's the latest on Fishnet?" he said over his shoulder as he headed out the door with his bicycle.

"I don't know anything about her. A friend put us in touch."

"Good. Let's keep it that way."

"No worries there, Noddy, I'll probably be at work when you get back. Have a nice day."

"Yep." And the door closed behind him.

I fixed our room up cosy for my man and me, popped to the shops for food and made a big dish of pasta for us all, to the sound of gunshots outside my window. Then I dressed up cool and headed back to work. "Hey, Tina Turner!" A shout came from the park. I did a shimmer and ran off laughing. I was so happy to be back in crazy-town.

The bar was rocking again and I had a brilliant time listening to some shitty band that was more like a comedy act, while sucking on a few Buds and pulling on a few spliffs.

Noddy was sitting in the lounge when I got home, watching TV. "What are you watching?" I asked, more out of politeness than interest. I just wanted to get to my man.

"It's a video of my band." It was a punk band, and he was on the drums.

"Nice." I sat down and accepted the line of coke he offered me.

"Do I look cool when I do that Elvis lip?"

"Yeah, Nod, really cool."

"What about that T-shirt? Is that cool?"

"Great T-shirt, Nod. Good music too," I lied. "I'm off to bed now. My feet are killing me." I was hoping for no more intellectual questions. Unfortunately, this was his usual entertainment after a few lines of coke, which happened most nights. Luckily, I worked nights and Noddy worked days, so we did not see each other much.

"Baby, I don't really like New York or my job and, as for Noddy, he's a fucking loser. You don't see him as much as I do. Every night I have to listen to that shit music," Dolphin whispered to me as I snuggled into bed beside him.

"I'm a bartender now. Soon I'll have enough money for a deposit for an apartment of our own, and we can move out. Why don't you look for a different job?" He was not buying it.

~ ~ ~

"I'm going away tomorrow, to stay with friends for a week over Christmas," Noddy said when I got home one night.

"Cool, we'll take care of the place." I was trying to hide my excitement.

"Yeah." He did his Elvis's lip.

I was so excited that Dolphin and I had the flat to ourselves for a romantic Christmas that I went out and bought a turkey with all the trimmings, and some sexy lingerie. "Happy holidays," I told Dolphin in my sexy New York accent, showing him what I had bought.

"Well, I need to tell you something." He put his arms on my shoulders and looked deeply into my eyes, and I stopped breathing.

"I want to go back to England for Christmas, and I'm on a stand-by ticket." I couldn't believe it, but I guess he had 'done' the guidebook of New York.

I went to work on the day before Christmas Eve feeling sure he wouldn't get a flight but, when I got home, he was gone. A simple note on the pillow where his head used to lay said "Merry Christmas" and, under the bed covers, where we use to melt into each other, was a vibrator.

I was heartbroken and missed him so much already. I kept thinking he would jump out any minute with his big Dolphin laugh, but he didn't and I cried myself to sleep.

The city became a ghost town. Most people went back to their home state, and everything was closed. Home alone, in the flat, with my Christmas dinner, I felt lonely and sad and I began to cry. But I couldn't let loneliness destroy my Christmas, so I put the food I'd cooked into a baking tin and went over to the park to share it with the homeless. I didn't know what I was going to do. I just knew I couldn't be alone.

"Hey, what you got there?" said an unwashed guy huddled on a bench in a dirty blanket, as I entered the park.

"Christmas dinner," I said, tearfully.

"Get out of here! Show me that thing!" And he straightened up to look into my tray.

"Oh my sweet Jesus! The Lord, my saviour! Can I eat some?" He jumped up and started dancing from one foot to the other.

"You sure can. It's for everyone." I started to feel better.

"Woo hoo! Happy holidays! Are you for real?" And he grabbed a turkey leg and took a big bite from it. "Don't you cry, missy, I'll make us a nice big fire." He pushed me and the tray onto the bench, still shifting from one foot to the other while taking bite after bite of the turkey leg. "I don't believe it! Lord, you sent me your prettiest angel with dinner. You see the size of that turkey? Mmmm mmmm." He was still chewing while mumbling to himself, as he put bits of wood and rubbish into an empty trash can, lit a box full of matches and threw it in to get the fire started.

"Hey Rasta, you checking this out?" he called to some other people huddled on a bench across the path.

"What the fuck is this, motherfucker?" A big Rasta said, looking at me.

"Christmas dinner." I was still holding the tray on my lap, unsure what to do.

"Rastafari, boombaclart, rass," he said, closing in for a deeper inspection.

"Get out of here," another voice said from behind me.

"You like some herb, sweet ting?" The Rasta asked me, as he took the other turkey leg.

"I got some brandy," someone else offered, coming over with his radio.

We all settled around the fire, eating, drinking, singing, dancing and smoking herb.

"You don't go after that man, you hear me? He must come back to you," the big Rasta told me, passing me a spliff.

He never came back. But walking past the park after that was never frightening again. "Hey, Tina Turner, how's it going? Sure was a great Christmas this year," would sound over the fence.

I loved the neighbourhood but Noddy was getting too much, just sniffing coke and watching himself on the telly most days. He seemed to be getting worse. "Can you stop dressing like that? You remind me of her," he told my tits one night as I left for work.

He looked completely high and crazy, and it made me feel uneasy so I passed by Grets' place to see if she was at home. "I'm not comfortable there on my own. I think Noddy might rape me or something," I told her.

"Dirty fucking men." Any chance she had… "Don't go back there from now on. You sleep here, and I come with you tomorrow to get your stuff." She gave me a key, and I gave her a big kiss and walked one block to work.

"Two Buds," one of the suits at the bar said, passing me five bucks.

"Oh, you're not in a band, I take it," I said, putting the two bottles down on the counter.

"Could be!" the other suit said, and I looked them over. Nah, they looked like mannequin dummies from a high street store.

"So, what brings two suits into a heavy metal bar?" I asked suit number one, the hottest one.

"I heard there was a hot English chick in here." He smiled.

"Oh, you're good," I laughed.

"Wanna go for a beer when you get off?" he smiled with perfect white teeth.

"Sure." He was not my type, with his short black hair and well-trimmed beard, but he looked like fun, and I was lonely.

"I'm Gordie and this is Zak. We live in Long Island and we've come to check out the city tonight."

"Great. I'll be off in an hour and we can go to The Trash Bar. There's a good band on tonight."

After my shift, I grabbed a Bud and joined them at the pool table.

"Let's go." Gordie said, shortly. I knocked back my beer and followed them out of the bar to a red convertible parked outside. Gordie's manicured hands held the door open for me to get in the front while Zak had to jump into the back. I was impressed and even more so when he offered me a spoon of coke to powder my nose.

The Trash Bar was already in full swing when we arrived. Gordie got the beers in and we headed to the front of the stage. The band was playing '60's songs and we sang along and played air guitar.

"I'm a bank manager," he told me in the break. "We're out to celebrate my divorce."

"Well, my boyfriend just left me and went back to London, so we got that in common."

He got some more beers and passed me a spliff and we went back to the stage. When he dropped me home and asked for my number, I gave it to him. I could do with some fun with a generous man.

When I had nights off from the bar, Gordie would come and get me and show me a completely new Manhattan, taking me to top restaurants, bars, and clubs and, when I had a Saturday off, he would send a taxi to pick me up to join him at the races, to watch his horses run. Nothing was a problem or too expensive, and I enjoyed being spoilt and not having to worry about money.

But we still liked to rough it in the naughty bars around Noddy's neighbourhood. One night while we were having a beer just opposite the park, Gordie's red convertible was broken into and his briefcase stolen. "Oh no! I have so many important documents in my briefcase." He leant on his car, stressing out.

"I'll sort it," I told him, rubbing his shoulders and went into the park, with Gordie following behind.

"Hey, Tina Turner, what's up?" came a voice out of the darkness. It was my Rasta friend.

"My boyfriend had his briefcase stolen from the car. Can you help?"

"Sure can, princess. You sit your sweet arse there." and he went off into the darkness while we sat on the park bench. Within 10 minutes, the Rasta appeared with Gordie's briefcase.

"I can't thank you enough," Gordie told the Rasta and gave him ten bucks. "And for you, my little princess, book some time off. I'm going to take you on a cruise around the Bahamas."

A cruise around the Bahamas! I couldn't believe it. "I'll sort it tomorrow and let you know what dates," I said as casually as I could manage, as we walked back to the car.

"Use this to get some gowns for the casino." And he passed me a credit card. Gowns for the casino! I had to contain my excitement as I slipped the card into my purse.

We got a flight to Florida to board the ship for our one-week cruise, first-class with fine dining and wine.

In my new clothes and being treated like a lady, I felt beautiful and finally succumbed to Gordie's advances, finding myself pleasantly surprised by his knowledge and consideration, and secretly thanking his ex-wife for the training.

When I got back to Manhattan, I found a nine-to-five, cash-in-hand job as a saleswoman in a camera shop uptown. It was an easy job in a classy area, but the smelly subway ride to get there was stressful, so I moved into a backpackers two blocks away so that I could walk. It was clean and quiet, with a shared bathroom and kitchen, and I took the top bunk in a four-bed girls' dormitory room.

I was hardly ever there, being out at work all day, in the bars at night, and with Gordie at the weekend. But one night, I stayed home to rest and cook a healthy dinner. "What you cooking, hen?" a gruff Scottish voice came from behind me in the kitchen.

"Food," I answered as I turned around to see a handsome face, framed with long curly blonde hair, with a glint of mischief in its deep blue eyes.

"You want some?" I did not mean food.

"Aye, go on then. I gotta few beers in the fridge that will wash it down nicely," said the sex god with a cheeky smile as he opened one and gave it to me.

As we climbed up the tin ladder to the roof with a pot of pasta, two bowls, some cutlery and a six-pack of beer, I couldn't help noticing that his firm arse fitted beautifully into his jeans, and I had to control myself not to bite it.

"I'm a musician and I thought I'd try my luck out here," Rodders said as he sat on the floor and started to spoon the pasta into the bowls.

"Oh, I love a singalong." He was getting better by the minute.

"Shall I get me guitar?" he asked as he passed me a full bowl.

"Defo, as soon as we've eaten." Ooh, this is dangerous, I thought, and I was right. After a few songs, a few spliffs and a few beers, we made love right up there on the backpackers roof, under a New York sky.

"Rodders, I have a man I see at weekends, but we can hang out during the week." I told him when I was lying in his arms.

"Aye hen, I don't want anything serious. I just got here and want to concentrate on my music." And he pulled me on top of him, and we did it again.

Perfect. I could have the best of both worlds, but weekends were not the same with Gordie. I would miss the excitement with crazy Rodders and his rough touch. "Gordie, I want to spend this weekend with some friends at the backpackers. Is that OK?" I asked him over the phone.

"Yes, whatever you want." And that was it. I wrapped myself around Rodders and forgot all about Gordie and going to work.

"You ready, hen?" Rodders was shouting outside my dormitory door.

"Coming," I said as I climbed off the fire escape through the window, hiding my crack pipe in my jeans and pulling my fringe down to cover my eyes.

My heart swelled as I opened the door and saw his hot, sexy form. "What's the plan tonight, baby?" and I melted into his muscular arms while he ran his fingers through my long curly hair, and brought my face to his soft mouth until it covered mine.

"We're playing in Dan's bar, then onto Night Birds and let's see what happens after that," he said, adjusting his beige fedora, which gave him even more sex appeal.

"Need a party starter?" I offered my spoon to his nose.

"You're a bad girl, but go on then." We had a quick sniff and hit the streets.

Dan's bar was busy, so we started as soon as we walked in with *Help,* by the Beatles, which went down well, and got the requests coming in. Rodders knew all the songs and, if I were unsure of the words, I would make them up and dance alongside him. We were a good team. *American Pie,* by Don McLean, was my cue to get Rodders' hat and dance around the crowd to collect the money. The bartender put us up a beer each, then we headed to Night Birds to do it all again.

"It was a great night tonight, and you're getting more confident," Rodders said as he slapped my arse and split a hundred bucks with me.

Yep. That's the power of cocaine, I thought. "The Statue of Liberty queue is the best earner. We should get there early tomorrow, and then we can do the Staten Island ferry at peak time."

"Whatever you want, my pretty doll," he said, grabbing my hand and leading me into the after-hours bar, where we always ended the night with a few drinks and a lot of blow.

Finally, we saved enough money for a room of our own in a hotel that rented by the month. "Woo hoo!" I grabbed Rodders and threw us both on the wide bed.

"Things are looking up, hen. We'll be able to get an apartment soon."

"Yes, let start to save half of the money we make every night and manage with what's left. I can cook proper food for us now, so that will make the cost of living much cheaper." I was excited.

"Aye, but you need to sort out that coke habit. I think that's your biggest expense." He was right. It had started with a little snort as a confidence booster to get up and sing in front of everyone. But that only ignited my old crack habit and made me crave a more potent boost, then another snort to keep the crack buzz going. I was bang on it.

It became so normal to sniff all day and night that I didn't notice how much I was taking until, one day when I went to visit a friend, I was so paranoid I needed to go back home to bed. "What's going on here, then?" I said as I opened the door to our hotel room.

"It's not what looks like, hen." Rodders said, jumping up naked from the bed as a pile of red hair disappeared under the sheet.

"You can have him," I said as I walked away and back to the backpackers.

Sitting in the backpacker's kitchen where it all started, I could see what a mess I had made of everything and what a state I was in with the coke. I made a call. "Hi Gordie. How are you?"

"I'm fine. What's up?"

"I need to go back to London. Please, can you buy me a ticket?"

A first-class British Airways ticket took me home to clean up and mend my broken heart.

I never saw or heard from Gordie or Rodders again.

3. Wodka Daze: 1992-1995

"Can one of you help me?" I shouted through the dumb waiter to the bar staff downstairs. I'd found work as a cook in a North London bar.

"What do you want?" Jaz, the taller of the two Aussies, was just walking into the kitchen.

"I've got so many orders here, I'm swamped! Can you make the beef sandwich for me?"

"How d'ya do that?" She stared at me, nonplussed.

"Butter two bits of bread and stick some beef in it," I threw over my shoulder from the cooker. I had all sorts on the go, and the orders kept coming.

"You need help up here, mate," Jaz said, scraping the knife back and forth across the butter.

"I know, but that wanker's off shagging the Welsh barmaid again—don't get your hair in it!" Jaz's long, black, curly hair was hanging down all over the food on the table.

"All right! Calm down," she said, her big brown eyes searching for something to tie up her hair.

"Please, just stay and make the sandwiches until it calms down," I begged.

"OK, but I haven't a fucking clue what I'm doing!" She tucked her hair behind her ears.

"You're doing great!" Any help was better than none.

Finally, the orders slowed, and Jaz went back downstairs to work behind the bar. "What a wanker this guv'nor is, leaving me on my own during lunchtime. I should have walked out today." I said to Lee, the other Aussie, whose blonde bouffant hair seemed bigger than any other part of her body.

"Yeah, I'm thinking to quit and head off somewhere. I've had enough of lying to his wife. She's a nice woman." Her big blue eyes were full of compassion as she put a pint of lager in front of me.

"What's your plan, Lee?" Jaz popped her head around the corner from the other bar.

"Don't know. Maybe stick to Aussie tradition and get a camper to go around Europe." she answered fluffing up her hair.

"I'm up for that!" I said.

"Well, I'm not staying here on my own!" Jaz cried and she joined us at the bar, planning.

I had been back in London for nearly a year and hadn't touched any coke or crack in that time. I'd taken a kitchen job as an alternative to the temptations that come with bar work and, to stop me thinking about Rodders, a sweet boyfriend. Plus I was sneaking occasional nights with Dolphin who, until he finally got married, was always waiting for me in London. But none of it made me want to stick around. It took the prospect of the open road with my new girlfriends to bring life back into my blood.

A grand bought us a big ol' van with a fully equipped kitchen, two sofas that converted into three beds, a sink and a toilet. We named her Brucette, and hit the highway.

"It's a bit of a tank." Lee pulled onto the motorway, heading for Calais to get a ferry to France.

"Yeah, but she's *our* tank." My eyes switched excitedly between the road ahead and the map on my lap.

"Just let me know if you need me to take the wheel." Jaz was stretched out on one of the sofas in the back.

"I'm alright for now." Lee's little legs stretched down to reach the pedals.

We parked in the ferry car park, claimed beds for our first night's sleep in Brucette and waited for the morning ferry.

On the other side of The Channel, we called "Bonjour," out the windows as we drove through the countryside to look for fruit-picking work.

Finding a small café, we parked and went for a coffee and croissant.

"Hey girls, we're going to a farm to pick cherries. Want to join us?" A confident French guy was shouting over to our table.

"May as well. We got nothing else to do," I said to the Aussies.

"OK," they agreed, so I called the guys over.

"I'm Fez, and this is my mate, Tommy," the French one said, straddling the chair as if he was going to ride it like a horse or fuck it.

"You get paid by the kilo, so you have to work hard," Tommy said in a broad Scottish accent.

"We can camp on the land, so let's fill up our vans with food and head into the wilderness." Fez seemed like he knew how to go about this.

"Great! Someone who speaks French and knows the score. We're fucking sorted," I said enthusiastically, and the girls smiled.

"Follow us." And with that, Fez pulled off in his luxurious mobile home, with Tommy waving at us to keep up, from the back window.

We parked at the entrance to a field of cherry trees while Fez went to speak with the farmer.

"We can camp here, and we start at five am tomorrow." Fez's tall frame filled our camper door. "I do this every season, so please don't mess things up for me," he added.

"What d'ya mean?" Jaz asked.

"Respect the land, and pick well." He ran his hands through his curly black hair.

"You Aussies know how to climb a tree, dontcha?" Tommy said in his thick brogue. He was pitching his tent next to Fez's van.

"Yeah, and we can make fires by rubbing two sticks together," Jaz shouted back. "Fucking dicks!" she added under her breath.

"True, but they got us work, so let's be nice," I pleaded sweetly.

We chopped up a big salad, and boiled some spuds and green beans, in our van, while Fez cooked steaks in his, and Tommy drank wine. Then we ate outside Fez's van.

"I sleep now." Fez said, after we had cleaned up, and he went into this van and shut the door. Tommy crawled into his tent and we went back to Brucette and lay on our beds.

"Fuck! That Tommy's a bit of a pig. Did ya see the way he ate?" Jaz mimed shovelling into her mouth with her hands, grunting.

"I know, and he looked like he had lipstick on from the wine stains." And we both started laughing.

"You're quiet, Lee. What's up?" Jaz asked when she managed to stop.

"Do any of you fancy Fez?" she asked, fluffing her hair in the mirror.

"No!" Jaz pretended to vomit.

"You can't fancy him: he's an arrogant arsehole!" I was shocked.

"I think he's sexy! And that accent, oof." She swooned right on the spot.

"Ugh! Go have a wank, will ya?" Jaz scoffed, and we laughed again.

"Beauty is in the eye of the beholder." She huffed and got into bed.

"If you twang one-off, keep it quiet," Jaz said, and we laughed as we snuggled down to sleep.

By day, we settled into a routine of climbing trees to pick cherries into the basket. By night, Jaz and I would eat and sleep, Lee would go over to Fez's van and Tommy would drink himself into oblivion outside his tent, chatting and fighting with his imaginary friends.

~ ~ ~

"I'm moving into Fez's van." Lee was throwing her stuff into her backpack after another argument with Jaz. This time it was about the weather!

"Good! More room for us." Jaz didn't like the Barbie doll and was happy to watch her strap on her backpack full of beauty products—as tall as her—and squeeze through the door and into her new life with her French lover.

Jaz moved Brucette further up the field, and we settled down to life without The Beauty Queen.

~ ~ ~

With only a couple of days of picking left, I was wondering what to do next.

"What *you* going do when we finish the cherries?" I asked an almost-sober Tommy one night when he was sitting outside his tent.

"Sell sandwiches and drinks on the beach with my English girlfriend, Sarah. What are you going to do?"

"No idea. Lee's going off with Fez and Jaz is talking about going back to London."

"If you get stuck, you can come to our house. You and my bird would get on great. You'll be able to sell on the beach—but not my beach."

"I'll keep it in mind. Thank you," I said as he passed me their address and phone number.

"What d'ya wanna do, Jaz?" I said, as Fez took off with Lee and Tommy to work at the beach.

"I'm thinking of London because I don't have much money."

"Is it only money that would take you back?"

"Shit yeah! I'd rather be doing walkabout."

"Then have a look at what I've got." From the hollow frame of my backpack, I pulled out £1,000 of traveller's checks. I had stashed £500 up each side.

"Shit, mate! You'd share that with me?"

"Sure! Let's fill up Brucette, head to that beach Tommy's on about and try our luck there." I wasn't worried about my money: I knew I could make more but Jaz had become a true friend and that doesn't come along every day.

So we filled Brucette up and hit the road. She overheated and clunked like a tank through the narrow French lanes, and was barely able to get up to speed on the motorway, but she made it to Marseillan Plage, and we parked her up a side road near the beach.

In high spirits, we walked along the beautiful sandy beach that stretched for miles, while the warm sea tickled our feet.

"Fuck off, then! Don't buy the sandwiches! We've only been making them since sunrise." We heard Tommy before we saw him, shouting at someone on the beach, his skeletal body sticking out of a pair of swimming shorts.

"Empty vessels make the most noise," I said to Jaz.

"Oi oi, come meet the missus." He called when he saw us coming. He took us over to a frail, timid-looking woman, a flowery beach dress hanging from her skinny frame. Her long blonde hair straggled over her shoulders and face, so you could only just see her glazed brown eyes. She looked as drunk as Tommy.

"We've not sold much today," she told us as she opened her cool box of sandwiches. Not surprising given the state of the pair of them. They were mashed.

"I'll take two." They looked tasty.

"40 francs." With a big smile, she passed me two baguettes full of cheese and salad.

"This is great. You make these every morning?" Jaz asked.

"Yeah. We get up at six—and that's when he starts drinking. Then I have one to calm my nerves 'cause I never know what he's going to do next," she looked desperate.

"That's sad." We sat down next to her, eyeing Tommy as he walked up and down the beach, swearing at everyone.

"You gonna stay around?" She asked me.

"Probably. It's great to be here after being in the fields for six weeks, but we need to work."

"You could do this. It's easy, and we always make a profit. You just needed to buy a cool box, fill it up with sandwiches and drinks, and walk the beach."

"We're thinking about it, but where can we park the van?"

"It's illegal to camp here. You'd be asking for trouble. We've got a spare room in our house you can rent. Richard, who plays in the bars, already rents a room from us so it'll be no problem—and we could do with the extra cash."

I looked at Jaz. "The sandwiches seem a bit of a hassle but, if we just did the cold drinks, I'm up for it," she said.

"Let's do it. It could be a laugh."

"We'll be back home by four. Why don't you come over, and I'll make you dinner."

"OK, we'll do that." And we went off for a swim.

After a glorious swim, we went back to Brucette. "Fuck! Another parking ticket! This piece of shit has brought nothing but problems." Jaz kicked the tyre, as though it was the van's fault we'd parked her illegally.

It was true that Brucette was riddled with faults though. "I think we got ripped off when we bought this van" I said climbing in, "but at least we can sleep in her if it's no good here."

"That's all she's good for," Jaz said. She pulled out and we clunked our way to Sarah's.

The house was over three storeys, and we rented the attic room. "'Cause you've got no work visas, you'd be best working the naturist beach. The police never go there," Tommy told Jaz over Sarah's delicious seafood pasta. "Get there for about 10 and just walk up and down shouting out, 'boissons fraîches'. It means 'cold drinks'."

"Shall we start tomorrow, Jaz?" It did sound easy.

"Why not? There's nothing else to do."

A tall slim guy, with neatly cut brown hair and a big smile, walked in. "You got new roommates, Ricky. They're gonna work the naked beach," Sarah told him.

"Nice. I play at the beach bars, and it was busy tonight, so it looks like the season has started, so you should be OK," he said in a soft London accent as he helped himself from the remaining food.

"We'll give it a go tomorrow," Jaz said, and we climbed the stairs to our cosy room and crashed happily out in our new bed.

"How can she disappear?" I was standing, the next morning, where we had parked Brucette.

"Surely no one nicked the piece of shit!" Jaz said in disbelief.

"Well, nothing we can do right now. Let's hitch to the beach and see how this selling goes, and we can deal with this later," I suggested.

"Don't care if I never see her again," Jaz scoffed.

But we did—in the impoundment depot. The parking fine and impoundment fee was a stretch for us, so we sold her for 100 quid.

Hitching to the beach was easy. On arrival, we bought a cool box, stocked it with coke, orange juice, lemonade, beer and water, and covered the lot in ice. Then we walked the long beach full of people, all nude.

"Fuck! They *are* all naked!" Jaz said in shock.

"Haha, it's certainly an eye-opener," I felt overdressed in my bikini. "This looks like a good place to sell." I pulled Jaz, along with the cool box, to a crowd of people by the dunes.

"Boissons fraîches," we called, not realising there was an orgy was going on.

"Eau minérale," a naked man approached us, pointing into the box.

Oh, he wants water, I realised and I bent down to get it. "Dix francs," I passed him the water, averting my eyes. As he was getting his money from a little wallet strapped to his ankle, another naked man approached looking for water.

"Jaz, this is our selling place. We need to buy more water and less fizz." Five minutes later, when we strolled back to the water's edge leaving the sounds of orgasmic pleasure behind us, we had sold out of water completely.

"Yoohoo, girls!" An old queen, with an American accent, wearing just a bright pink scarf around his neck, was calling us over. "Two beers, darlings," he smiled as we put the cool box down next to him. He looked like a sweet man and I felt less intimidated.

"This is our first time selling and being on a naturist beach," I confessed, feeling a bit out of place.

"Let me tell you, sweetie, the beach is in sections. There's a family section—not much action there—a regular section and a gay section, where there's more drinking and open sex, so you'll sell more drinks on this part of the beach." He took a swig of his beer.

"Great, thank you."

"I'm Uncle and this is Marcos." His trophy was hot, with beautiful blue eyes, shoulder-length blond hair and a body that obviously worked out regularly. "I'm in the movie business, darlings, and having a needed break from all the dramas." He was about 50, with a toned body, and hair dyed brown to match his eyes.

"Thanks for the tip Uncle. Let's go, Jaz." We walked along the beach and sold everything within the space of an hour.

"Great tip, Uncle. We sold out," I said as we passed him again.

"Bring more tomorrow, darlings. I can look after your stock," he smiled.

"Well, that was easy and fun, and it was great being on the beach. I look forward to trying again tomorrow," I said as we walked away from all the hanging cocks.

The following day, we bought extra stock and went off to find Uncle. "I'll put them here." I was putting our excess supply of drinks under a towel next to him.

"We've got 30 in the box. That should be enough for now," Jaz said as we walked off down the beach—which was more like an open-air sex show—singing our little ditty:

Coca, orange, citron, beer, doo dah, doo dah.

Coca, orange, citron, beer, doo dah, doo dah day.

Qu' est-ce que vous voulez? Qu' est-ce que vous voulez?

Coca, orange, citron, beer, doo dah, doo dah day.

When we had sold most of our drinks, we went back to Uncle to fill up for round two. It was easy.

~ ~ ~

On a slow day, bored with walking up and down, we sat for a while in the shade. "Let's have a beer," Jaz said with a cheeky smile.

"Good idea." It went down nicely, so we had another—until we'd drunk them all.

"Swap you any soft drinks you want for beers," Jaz said to the passing vendors, until our box was empty and we were totally pissed. We staggered off to the bars to see Ricky, who was none too happy when we fell into the restaurant and danced around the tables.

When a waiter passed with a tray of drinks held at his shoulder, I stood on tiptoe, leant over to rest my tits on his tray and shimmed along beside him. Clocking my behaviour, instead of objecting, the restaurant owner made me an offer. "You can do the dancing for me in my new bar for the opening night, please?"

"Err, sure. How much?" May as well make some bucks.

"I give you all you can eat and drink."

"For the whole day? And Jaz?" I thought I may as well have my mate with me.

"Oui. And you pass the hat and keep the money," he said, nodding.

Bargain, I thought. Free piss up, getting fed and paid, just for flashing my tits. "You're on."

"Merci. I call you The Best British cabaret act," he said, gesticulating with excitement.

The big night came and Jaz and I sat in the front of Ricky's truck on our way to becoming the best British cabaret act. "Don't get too pissed before the show," Ricky said loudly, his face close to mine, as if I was deaf.

"She'll be right," Jaz reassured him. I just kept quiet and turned to look out of the window.

We finally arrived at a hick town that looked like it was out of a western, and parked in the centre outside the bar, its main attraction. Right in the middle of the window was a sign reading, 'Tonight, the best British cabaret act.' I couldn't stop laughing.

"Don't start on the juice yet," Ricky was saying to Jaz, who had just ordered from our free bar.

"Just one," she lied and brought a jug of beer over to our table.

We sat there contentedly sipping and eating until Ricky shouted into my face as if I was deaf, again. "Go and get ready, and don't come out until you hear the intro of *Lazy Sunday Afternoon*."

I went to the bathroom to put on the sexy basque I had borrowed from Sarah. There was no mirror, so Jaz did my makeup. We were taking so long that Ricky came off-stage to see what was happening. "Oh my God!" He took the eyeliner from Jaz and wiped the stuff off my face. "Let me do it." He was not a happy man but, after 10 minutes of being repainted and my hair tousled, I was ready. Jaz went for more refills.

"Right, listen for the intro," he said, again speaking right into my face, before heading back to the stage. Seconds later, Jaz returned with another jug. We were so busy chatting we didn't hear the intro but we certainly saw a very pissed-off Ricky when he came barging in. "I've been playing the intro for five minutes. Now get it together, for fuck's sake! It's packed out there." And he stormed off.

Looking like I should be in an Amsterdam window, I staggered out of the loo with blown-up condoms sticking out of my cleavage, and swung my hips as I walked onto the stage. I danced slowly, grinding the condoms, then gave each one a blow job and threw them into the crowd. One at a time, I removed my hat, my belly chain and the basque, so I was topless. I finished with a moony. Dancing around with my hat, I got 700 francs. Meanwhile, Jaz made friends with a man at the bar, telling him our woes with Brucette, which, to our surprised delight, resulted in him giving us a tent.

"I wish I'd seen it." Uncle was crying with laughter as Jaz told him about the best British cabaret act. "Come party with us tonight. It's my last night. You can sleep in my room. There's lots of space."

"OK, we'll go home to shower and dress—or undress," I laughed.

We arrived to find a classy resort, decorated in natural, soft colours with sprinkles of neon, alive with naked people. We walked the wooden paths checking out the fancy shops, restaurants, bars, and nightclubs until we spotted Uncle on the terrace of a bar, waving like he was having some kind of fit. I could see his wrinkly cock swinging through his transparent dress, and Marcus' tight red rubber pants left nothing to the imagination. I felt overdressed in my shorts and T-shirt, so I removed my top and bra to blend in. Jaz stayed dressed: she was a shy girl.

"I got us a bottle of the best French wine," he said as he poured us a glass each. We sat watching people pass in bits of string, belts, nipple covers, piercings, dog chains or just body paint. The waiter, wearing only a frilly pink apron to hold his notepad, came to take our order. Uncle ordered a few dishes for us to share, and another bottle of wine.

"Let's go to that straight nightclub. Same sex couples are not allowed in," Uncle said after dinner. So off we went dancing to relieve our stuffed bellies.

The only light in the club came from a big screen showing porn, above sofas that were covered in people shagging. The music was good so we all had a dance on the rotating mirrored dance floor. "That cannot be pleasant," I said to Jaz as I looked at a woman with cocks in her mouth, arse, hands and fanny.

"It's shocking." Jaz was not amused.

"Let's go get ice cream." Uncle could see Jaz was uncomfortable and we took off to the ice cream parlour before bed.

~ ~ ~

"Good morning, girls." Uncle woke us with croissants and coffee. "I have to leave now, but I hope to see you next year." And he was gone.

Without him, the beach was boring so, with a few quid in our pockets, we hit the road.

"I didn't realise hitching was such fun and so easy," Jaz said as we crossed the border into Italy.

"The best way to travel, mate. No schedule, no timetable, no tickets. Just freedom to flow with the wind," I said as I stood on the edge of the road, holding out our sign for the sleepy little mountain village of Lana, where we planned to find farm work.

"Yep, and the people that pick us up are so cool," she said just as a fit-looking guy pulled over. He took us home, fed and watered us and put us back on the motorway in the morning.

Our next lift dropped us in Lana. The main square consisted of barely more than a water fountain, a supermarket, and a pub. We followed one of the many lanes, with adorable houses and churches, to reach the river and make camp. "This tent is brilliant," I said as we pitched it on the grassy bank next to the river, along with loads of others.

"Yep. Good score, mate."

"You girls, OK?" Milko, the Polish guy whose tent we were pitching next to, called.

"Yes, we're nearly finished."

"So, tomorrow at six am, you stand there." He pointed to the road above us. "The farmer will come and take you to work. Tonight, I make fire. You can cook on it. Or you go to the churches and they give you a bowl of cooked food. It's usually pasta—and tasty." Having thanked him, we headed off to check out the village and buy food and wine.

We both got work the next day, picking apples. Luckily Milko was on our farm too and explained everything to us. "You hang this sack around your neck, then tie those straps at the bottom around your waist. Put the apples in gently: they bruise easy. Then when it's full, empty it into the big crate—gently."

"Alright, I get it! Gently it is."

We climbed the trees and—gently—started putting the ripe apples into our capacious bibs. It was a comfortable, carefree life, and we settled into it fast. Pick, eat, get pissed, fuck someone and sleep.

Until one day the rain came—and never stopped. The farmers stopped coming, the tent flooded, my knee was swollen from the rain and tree climbing. I was ready to move on.

"Will you wait for me?" Jaz had a job with accommodation for two weeks.

"Sure. I'll go see if I can stay with the nuns."

I knocked at the church door where they gave out free food, and was greeted by a beautiful nun with a peaceful, loving smile. "Please Sister, can I rest here for a few days?" I asked hopefully, showing her my swollen knee.

"Yes, my child." It was that easy.

Sister Agatha gave me a room, with a cosy bed, at the top of the nunnery, ran me a hot bath, gave me a pair of pyjamas and took all my clothes for washing. Every day she would bring three hot meals to my room. I enjoyed the simple lifestyle, kindness and purity of the nuns, and I hoped one day I would be able to live that purely and simply. But the party animal inside me was alive and kicking and I had no control.

After a week, my knee was less swollen, so I offered service to repay their kindness. In the mornings, I helped with kitchen chores and, in the afternoons, we would take disabled people to church.

Eventually, my partner-in-crime's job came to an end and she fetched me. It was great to be out again and we hitched around Italy, taking in the Colosseum, the canals of Venice, Pompeii, the leaning tower of Pisa, Florence and the Vatican.

We stayed in cheap hotel rooms and mostly scavenged food that restaurants and supermarkets threw out, unsold, at the end of the day into big bins at the back of their buildings. But because we couldn't speak Italian, there were no jobs to be had, so we hitched around Europe searching for work, getting picked up mainly by truck drivers. We slept at truck stops and sometimes hotels as we passed through Monaco, Switzerland, Germany and Czechoslovakia, taking in the sights. Finally, we reached the port in Greece to get the first boat to Israel where we knew we could easily get work.

"Two deck class tickets please," I asked the man behind the ticket counter.

"The ship leaves tonight at nine. Boarding starts at seven." He handed me our tickets.

We just had time to go to the nearest supermarket and shoplift supplies for our three-day trip, before boarding the giant vessel. We climbed the wooden steps to the deck and set up camp under a tin roof, next to a bench, away from the toilets.

We were chilling on the bench, watching the deck fill up with travellers that had just finished working the summer season in Greece, when a tanned guy, with long curly black hair and the bluest eyes, came and joined us. "Moshav or kibbutz?" he asked in an Irish accent.

"What's the difference?" Jaz replied.

"Well now, a moshav is a community of farms in the middle of nowhere. The farmers are cunts and the workers are called volunteers.

There's a volunteer leader in charge of you. The work is hard but you get paid and a house. While a kibbutz is a farm where you do community work in exchange for food and shelter."

"We need to earn money, so I guess we're going to work for the cunts."

"Haha, I like you. I can tell you like a laugh. I'm Ben. I'm on my way back to the moshav I worked last season. Do you girls fancy a shindig?"

"Fuck, yeah!" Jaz, as always, was up for it.

He left and we continued to watch groups gather to play backgammon, scrabble, or cards. "Did you see that? Three stars just shot across the sky." I pointed upwards.

"It's so clear because there's no light at sea. You'll see plenty more." Ben had returned with a guitar and a bottle of whiskey. "Do you know *Wish you were here,* by Pink Floyd?"

"Yes." I loved to sing.

"It's one of my favourite songs." He played, I sang, other deck class passengers joined us sharing whatever supplies they had, and the party was on until the halfway stop in Cyprus.

~ ~ ~

"Nice to be on land." Jaz said before eating her kebab almost in one bite.

"Maybe we should stop here on our way back. It looks nice."

"Yeah, maybe but, for now, let's find some booze for tonight." The kebab was gone.

"Good idea. Celebrate our last night on the boat. Tomorrow, Israel awaits!"

~ ~ ~

With mighty hangovers, we gingerly got off the boat and adjusted our eyes to the bright sunlight and busy port of Haifa. "Get a bus from over there to Main Street where an agency will set you up with a moshav," Ben told us as he jumped into a car.

"We better behave here," I said, looking at the soldiers walking around with machine guns.

"It's fucking tense all right," Jaz said as we dodged people to get to the bus stop.

A short bus ride took us to Main Street where we entered a small agency office, with a lone woman sitting behind a desk. Within minutes of us walking in, she'd given us a job on Moshav Infar, handed us some kind of employment slip and directed us to a bus stop from where the bus pulled onto the dusty, barren desert highway towards the distant mountains. Only a few trees dotted around gave the landscape definition.

Everyone on the bus seemed tense and looked at us suspiciously from the corner of their eyes, even though an armed solider stood at the doorway. "Shit, they're paranoid little fucks," Jaz whispered, watching people getting on and off the bus.

"It should be better on the farm," I reassured her, though I felt uncertain myself.

"Infar," the driver announced, and we jumped off into the dust. As the bus pulled away, we found ourselves alone in the barren desert. Only a metal fence topped with barbed wire reassured us something was going on, and we walked through double metal gates under the sign saying 'Infar'.

"It's like a prison camp," Jaz looked around her new surroundings.

"I wonder if the barbed wire is to keep us in," I laughed.

"Well, we got this far. May as well check it out, hey?" Her big brown eyes were looking at me uncertainly.

"Yeah. If Ben can do it, so can we." With that thought, we relaxed as we walked down a dirt track, with fields on either side of us filled with row upon row of peppers. Finally, we saw a few large houses and a shed with a sign that said 'Volunteers' office'.

"Hi. We've come for work," I said, handing the spotty-faced woman in the office the paper we'd been given in Haifa.

"Welcome to Infar," she said from behind her long black hair. "I'm Pip, your Volunteer Leader," and we shook hands. "We're a peaceful farming community. You'll be working on Farm 25. I'll take you there in a minute. One thing to be aware of though: each farmer employs two or more Thais on two-to-five year contracts. Most of them are from rural areas and have never seen white people so they'll be curious about you. But there are big cultural differences: it's best you stay away from them. If they give you any problems, you come to me."

Not knowing what to make of this advice—I *liked* meeting foreigners and exploring our cultural differences—we followed her out to a jeep.

She knocked on the door to a big house, and a scruffy man, with a long beard, came out. "Come, I'll show you the house you'll share with the other workers. They're in the field and will be back soon." We followed him to the back of his house and entered a large packing shed with a conveyor belt.

At the end was a long building: our house. Actually a bedsit with a kitchen, plus a toilet which we shared, via adjoining doors, with the room next door, which was occupied by a South African couple.

"You start tomorrow at five am. First, load up the trailer with these crates, then jump on the back and the Thai will drive you to the field that we're picking. You pick until eleven, then have lunch that you cook yourself. At two pm, you pack until it's all packed. Saturday is your day off for Shabbat, the Jewish holy day. You understand?"

"Yes." I wasn't sure if I should salute!

"What do you think?" Jaz said once Hitler had left.

"I think Ben was right about the cunts." We pissed ourselves laughing.

~ ~ ~

We were in the shed at five am. The trailer was already stacked with crates and the two South Africans, so we just jumped on. "Hi. I'm Wendy and that's my boyfriend, Leon," said one as the Thai driver pulled out onto the dusty road. Leon was half-asleep and just waved.

We lay down and silently watched the sun rise in the distance, and other tractors filled with workers on their way to the fields.

Soon we reached our destination and jumped off the trailer.

"First, we line all the rows with the crates and then, with a pair of shears, we cut a ripe pepper off the bush and put it in the crate," Wendy told us, picking up a stack of crates and putting a pair of shears in her jacket pocket. We copied.

Five hours later, I could hardly straighten up as we packed the full crates onto the trailer and headed for home.

"I'll show you the shop but don't get too excited. There's not much in it," Wendy said as our tractor dropped us off outside.

"I can't move." All my muscles were aching as I tried to jump down from the trailer.

"You'll get used to it after a few days. Come on." Wendy offered me her hand.

"Be careful of the Thais. They try to touch you up and are always looking in your window," she said as we entered the shop. The Thais *were* staring at us but wasn't that simple curiosity? I was keen to get to know them.

"We can eat our veg but don't get caught taking from another farm. It's stealing and you get a fine. It's better to swap with the other volunteers." Wendy continued her briefing.

"Fucking hell! Prison rules," Jaz said.

"It's a village, with a village mentality," Wendy told us, then went off to get her shopping from a shop that consisted of two aisles of dried goods and a few boxes of fruit and veg.

After lunch and a lie-down, I dragged my aching body to the shed for two pm and leant on the conveyor belt, where a Thai was emptying the crates of peppers. Another Thai was making boxes from flat pieces of cardboard, and putting them above the conveyor belt to be filled with peppers. "You have three boxes: ripe; medium ripe; not so ripe. You put the full boxes on the trailer." The farmer told us.

"When your eyes need a rest from looking at peppers hour after hour, you can make boxes and give 'em a rest," Wendy told me as I approached the conveyor belt.

"You like singsong?" Our Thai colleague finally talked. "You go bar Friday. Many singsong." Then he went back to throwing the peppers onto the conveyor belt.

The bar was a barn on the edge of the moshav that sold beer, played dance music, and was full of dancing seasonal workers. "Now this is more like it," I said, and we hit the dance floor.

"What the fuck?!" A group of Thais was dancing behind Jaz and one had grabbed her arse.

"Shit!" Another had grabbed my tits.

We could not work out which ones it had been, so we shoved them all away and went to sit outside on one of the few benches.

"Want a shot," Paul, a black guy from London, offered me a glass of clear fluid.

"What's this?" I said as I took the glass.

"Wodka. Israeli firewater. It's cheap and cheerful."

"Not to be mistaken for the Russian brew vodka. This is a chemical-and-water cheapo version." Tommy, the Aussie, said. I knocked it back and passed the glass back as I felt the enamel come off my teeth.

"Where do you get that?" Jaz liked it.

"The shop. They only sell it to the select few, on the sly. They keep it under the counter, so you have to ask for it." Paul winked.

We finished the bottle, washing it down with beer. Then Jaz went home with Tommy, and I thought I would try a Thai so went back into the bar. I found one with beautiful big brown eyes, the blackest hair and a silken body that was all muscle and hairless. I stroked him all night.

"Tonight, party my house. You come, OK?" he told me in the morning.

"Yes. I'll bring my friend."

That night, Jaz and I walked around in the dark for about half an hour, lost, until we found a house with a few lights on. "Let's just try this one," Jaz said, and she knocked and opened the door. The five Thais inside jumped up as soon as we entered. A few started cooking and the others set up a sheet on the floor for a table.

"Sit, sit," they shouted excitedly, handed us glasses of wodka and lit fags.

"Thank you." I was horrified to realise that I wasn't sure which one was my friend from last night so just sat down next to the one I thought it was. The others put plates of food and a saucepan of rice in front of us.

"This is so delicious." I was stuffing in the different tastes of Thai cuisine.

"Let's dancing," and they were up, moving to the music with graceful rhythm.

"I have Fung Mok," my host told me as he pulled me up to dance.

"Whatever." I had no idea what he was on about and was more interested in his dance moves but, once we reached his bedroom, I found out exactly what Fung Mok was—and that he was *not* the same guy as last night. Fung Mok is a bead, usually a pearl, or two—or five—inserted under the foreskin of the penis. Because there were no pearls on our farm, the Thais used glass beads. They smoothed a piece of glass into a ball the size of a ball bearing, made a small cut under their foreskin, pushed it in, and then worked it down to midway, pushing it little by little each day. They had to move it around often to prevent infection, which was also an excuse for them to play with their deformed, lumpy dicks.

"Are you going to fuck the whole Thai community? They have AIDS, you know." Wendy said as I waved to the Thais we were passing in the fields.

"They're so sexy, I just can't resist, especially after a few wodkas." As well as finding them sexy, I felt sorry for them: I didn't like the way they were treated as second-class citizens and separated from the westerners. I did my best to treat them equally and fight for their rights with Pip, the Volunteer Leader. I became good friends with most of the Thais.

"I heard they stick their cocks into the calves' mouths for a blow job," she mocked.

"Well, I'm giving the calves a break then, ain't I?" That shut her up.

"Give her a break, will ya? She's just got the one now," Jaz said, backing me up.

"Well, there were two in there last night!" Wendy scoffed.

"What?" I was shocked.

"I saw them in our bathroom, and our two Thai workers were watching the whole thing through the window."

"I don't think so. I came home alone from the bar when Jaz went off with Tommy."

"I know what I saw!" Wendy snapped irritably.

To be honest, I didn't really care what she thought she'd seen. It had just dawned on me that my missing Tampax must be inside me. I knew I hadn't removed it.

Coming back from the field, I noticed a chair outside our window and started to realise that Wendy might have been right. "Shit, that must be where the Thais looked in Jaz. I don't remember a thing." I just stood there distraught.

"You better get to the doctors to check about that Tampax," Jaz said and went into the house.

There was no one else waiting to see the doctor, so she examined me immediately. She did indeed find the Tampax and removed it with forceps.

Returning to our packing shed, embarrassed and confused, I sheepishly stood next to Jaz at the conveyor belt. "It *was* up there and I sure as hell didn't push it up like that. Wendy must be telling the truth," I whispered as I started to pack the peppers.

As soon as we had finished, I went to our room and broke down. "I thought the Thais were my friends. I am always acting as a mediator for them and I'm the only one that invites them to the parties so they can make friends with us," I said between sobs.

"I'm sorry it happened, but you can't blame all of them. Let's go get ice cream," Jaz said, hugging me.

At the shop, a group of Thais were looking at me, whispering and giggling. "Sexy!" said one. "Sex free!" sniggered another, and I wanted to punch him.

"You should not mix with them, drink that wodka or go to the bar." Wendy still had to stick in the knife, like it was my fault.

"A bottle of wodka, please," I asked the shopkeeper, and he gave me a bottle wrapped in a black plastic bag.

"I thought we were getting ice cream." Jaz laughed.

"I need to forget. Will you join me?"

"Sure." And we went home and got pissed.

~ ~ ~

"I always follow in your footsteps," Jaz said a week later. She had just come from the doctors with the same Tampax problem.

"It's got to stop. If we don't do something, the Thais will think that it's OK to do this. I'm wondering, are they spiking our drinks because it's strange how we don't know or remember anything."

"I think they must be. The problem is we don't even know who it is, or if it's different ones or the same one."

"Something has to be done to stop it. The cunt farmers don't care." I was fuming and went to see the bored Israeli soldier who protected our main gate all day.

"Shalom, Ami."

"How are you?" He smiled.

"Good. Why don't you come over to mine when you finish your shift on Friday? Jaz is going out so we can have the place to ourselves?"

"Sounds cool." He was bored shitless.

"I got a bottle of wodka and we can make a private party."

"I'll be over at eight pm." He smiled again.

True to his word, on Friday at eight pm, he knocked the door, put the safety catch on his M16 and put it under the bed. I poured a large wodka and coke for him and a small one for me. "Drink up, Ami." I smiled as I gave him a full glass.

"You don't have to get me drunk to seduce me," he said, pulling me onto his lap.

"Let's have one more first." And I fixed him an even stronger one.

After sex, he was out cold, and I slowly and quietly slipped the gun from under the bed and went sneaking through the darkness to the bar. From the bushes outside, I could see it was full of Thais so I put the gun into place and pushed through the door of the bar. "Get against the wall, you Thai fuckers. Move! Now!" I shouted.

People were scattering as I pointed the gun at the Thais, and they hurried against the wall. "You want some?" I shouted at the barman who came towards me to try to disarm me, and he backed off.

"Who's fucking raping the girls? Who?!" I was pointing the barrel of the gun at them. "Is it you?"

"No! No!" They were huddling in a corner.

"You?" I went closer, pointing the gun at them.

Duf, the barman, finally seized his chance, rugby-tackled me to the ground and got the gun. "Get out of my bar," he shouted at me.

"I take home," Thiang, my Thai boyfriend, said as he picked me up from the floor.

Ami was still fast asleep when I entered the room, so I woke him up. "Your gun is in the bar," I told him.

"What? Shit! I can go to prison if I lose my gun!" And he jumped up and ran out, just as my farmer appeared.

"What were you thinking?" He was fuming.

"They're raping us, and no one here is going to do anything about it. What was I meant to do?"

"We told you to stay away from the Thais. Stay in your room until we decide what to do with you. This is a serious case. If a soldier is without his gun, he can get a $500 fine or even go to prison." And he stormed off.

"You did well," Thiang said as I fell asleep in his arms.

A loud banging at my door woke me with a jolt, and I hurried to open it. "We decided to protect the soldier and will keep this quiet, but you must leave the moshav today." The farmer shouted, still fuming.

"Come my house," Thiang said.

"I'm coming with ya," Jaz said, and we packed our stuff and walked over with Thiang to his house.

"You fucking hero!" Tommy said as he came into Thiang's house with a bottle of wodka. It was Shabbat so no one was working, and soon the place was full of people all assuring me I did the right thing.

"Well, we're out of booze. Thiang, go see if you can find some," I ordered.

"Let's go see what we can find," Jaz said to Tommy.

I knew they weren't going to look for booze, so I went to the bar to see if I could find a drink there, but it was closed. I noticed that the window was half-open so I forced it and climbed in. I grabbed as many beers as I could carry and climbed back through the window.

"What are you doing there?" Some farmer spotted me climbing back out.

"Nothing!" I jumped down, clutching the beers, and ran back to Thiang's house.

"You're the girl that took the gun, and now you've robbed the bar." Thiang's farmer stopped me in my tracks and looked like he was about to hit me. "Get off this land now, you alcoholic," he shouted.

Still clutching the beers, I sneaked over to Tommy's to find Jaz. As expected, they were in bed. "I just got caught robbing the bar," I said to the two of them as I handed out the beers.

"Fuck mate, you're getting worse," Jaz said as she cracked one open.

"I know. It's best I get out of here. I'm gonna hitch to Eilat."

"Get your head down here tonight and I'll drop you on the road at first light," Tommy said as he clinked his can against mine.

"I'm coming with ya," my faithful friend said.

~ ~ ~

"I'm sorry I fucked up, but it's great to see the ocean." We were sitting on the beach, with stinking hangovers, watching young Israelis walk around in swimming trunks and M16s.

"Let's go to Egypt. It's a dry country, so we can dry out," Jaz proposed.

"Sounds good." The way I felt, I didn't want to touch another drop.

We went back to our shitty hostel and packed, ready for an early morning hitch.

We were on the one dusty road by eight am and the first car that picked us up dropped us at the border. From there, it was just a short bus trip through the desert to Dahab, a Bedouin village by the Red Sea.

"This is so beautiful and laid-back," I said as we lay down on a soft mattress at the beach, drinking fruit juice.

"You can see the fish from here. The water is so clear."

"It's amazing," and I got up and went for a swim. Floating in the soft, warm water, I reflected with horror on the person I had become. I was out of control.

"I shouldn't drink, Jaz. I lose it every time." She had joined me in the water.

"I think it was everything combined. Don't beat yourself up. It was fucking funny though, mate. First you hold up the Thais and then you had the audacity to go back and rob the bar. You're fucking class." We both started laughing. But my laughter became hysterical as my frustration, shame and anger came flooding out.

"Look. Why don't we chill here for a few days and then go see the pyramids?" Jaz said, when I'd calmed down.

"Defo." I was feeling better already.

Drying out was challenging. My body craved a drink, but there was none to be had so I had no choice but to get sober.

After a week of chilling, we were ready for some action and the big city, so we got a bus to Cairo.

"Fuck! This is worse than India," I said as we got down from the bus into a sea of people and tried to cross a road that was a mess of jumbled-up traffic.

"Mate, you think we should get a cab across?" Jaz jumped back onto the curb.

"Nah, let's just do it." I grabbed her arm and we walked out in front of the beeping traffic, reaching the other side with faster heartbeats but unharmed, and checked into a room near The Great Sphinx.

"It looks amazing. Let do the camel ride tomorrow." Jaz was excited, looking at the pyramids from the safety of our window. As usual, we hid our valuables around the room and then we showered and went out to book our camel trip.

"This place is mental! The streets are a jungle and everybody wants something," Jaz yelled, covering her ears against the noise.

"Yeah, let's do the pyramids and go." I was feeling rattled already and relieved at the few minutes of respite afforded by entering a shop to book our tour for nine am the next day.

We grabbed a plate of rice and beans from the shop next door and went back to the room to watch the light show over the Sphinx in peace.

"Wow, this is worth all the bullshit," Jaz said as she took off on her camel across the Giza desert, with me and the guide following.

"These are tombs for pharaohs and their consorts, and one of the wonders of the ancient world," the guide informed us. "Menkaure, Khafre,

Khufu," he pointed them out, "can be seen from outer space. They are 4,000 years old and took 20 years to build using strength, sledges, and ropes."

We parked our camels and walked around the pyramids and the Sphinx, speechless.

A few hours later, we were back on the rhythmic beasts and heading back to town. With very sore arses, we jumped off our camels and pushed our way through the crowded streets back to our room.

Later that evening, from a rooftop restaurant's sanctuary, we watched the light show over the pyramids while eating a hearty bowl of spicy chickpeas and rice.

A short road trip took us to Luxor to see the Valley of the Kings and Karnak temple, and take a riverboat down the Nile to chill out at Alexandria's waterfront. After refusing yet another offer of the best and cheapest papyrus and perfume, we'd had enough of the hassle so we got a bus back to Cairo.

We were preparing to return to Israel when our guesthouse manager offered me a deal on four ounces of hash at a reasonable price. "I'm gonna take it and sell it back in Infar. I can treble my money," I told Jaz. So with the hash stashed in the hem of my jeans, we hitched back to Infar.

"I miss you every day. You stay here with me," Thiang insisted. Well, that was our accommodation sorted. Now to get rid of the hash. I put the word out and sold half of it on the first day. People just kept coming.

The following day, the barman was at Thiang's door. "The farmers know you are up to something, and I know what it is. The police are coming for you tomorrow."

"Don't know what you're on about." I shrugged.

"I've just come to warn you. Do what you want with it." And he walked away.

"Greece?" I said, looking at Jaz.

"That sounds lovely," she smiled.

We packed up and left for the port early in the morning, and managed to get a boat to Athens for that evening.

"I was a little nervous," I said as we passed through Greek customs with the hash stuffed down our pants.

"Me too, but we did it."

After a few days checking out Athens, we got a boat and watched islands passing from the deck. None had much appeal until we approached Paros. "This is where we get off," I said.

"Paradise," Jaz said as we disembarked just as the sun was about to set. It was like a postcard. Little alleys led you through a labyrinth of shops, restaurants, bars, and churches, painted white with bright blue roofs and set against a natural rocky landscape. Fruit and olive trees gently danced in the breeze, and the beach was pristine, with the whitest sand and clear blue sea.

"Let's save on a night's accommodation and sleep on the beach tonight. Then we've got all day tomorrow to walk around and find a nice room to tide us over until we find something more long-term," I suggested.

"Good idea."

We walked to the far end of the beach, found a big tree, and huddled up in our sleeping bags. My body moulded into the sand as the ocean gently sung a lullaby under a sky that was full of twinkling stars. "This is a good start Jaz," I mumbled as I gently closed my eyes and drifted off to dreamland.

We woke to a glorious sunrise, packed away our stuff then walked the charming lanes to find a room.

"We'll take it," we said in unison as we looked around an elegant room with a window overlooking the garden, a bed, a table and a bathroom. After a good scrub up, we were off to hunt for a job and an apartment.

We walked the winding road, with closed restaurants and bars on one side and the beautiful beach on the other, clueless but hopeful. "Not much open," Jaz observed.

"Um, but it's good we got here early. We'll have the pick of the jobs and apartments," I was sure.

"Yassou," I said to a man opening the door to a café.

"Yassou," he smiled back.

"Can you speak English?" That was my Greek done!

"Yes."

"We're looking for work and an apartment. Can you tell us anything, please?"

"You can clean?"

"Yes, we can do anything," I smiled.

"OK. I have a big new bar complex at the end of this road. We are preparing for opening and it needs cleaning. You go there and say Yannis sent you." We couldn't believe our luck and skipped excitedly to the complex. Five bars needed cleaning and it gave us three day's work and an invitation to the opening night.

"You can clean? I need a cleaner." George, who was standing next to me at the bar, said. He was in his early thirties, tall, muscular, with sandy hair, blue eyes and a red sports car.

"Yes, I can clean."

"I have six apartments. You meet me at the port tomorrow morning and I take you there." I was happy.

"You can work restaurant?" the just as handsome man with him was asking Jaz.

"Yes. I do many times," she lied.

"OK. You come tomorrow and help me clean for the big opening next week. Then you can work restaurant." He gave her a business card.

Jaz and I looked at each other in shock. "All we need now is an apartment," I was delighted.

"All we need now is another drink," Jaz said and ordered some more ouzo. Our new friends were happy to teach us some Greek dancing as the ouzo flowed.

"I'll see you in the morning," Jaz whispered as she left with George. I staggered home alone.

George's apartments, just a few blocks back from the beach, were posh. "OK. You clean ready for guests, remove all the spiders' houses, put clean sheets and wash everything. The toilet paper goes in the bins: you always empty. If you need me, I'm at the port." And he was gone.

After I finished the cleaning, I went to find Jaz at her restaurant. "My job is easy, Jaz and, after your antics last night, I'll always have one up on him, especially when his girlfriend's around."

"He was more interested in the mirror than me. I won't be going there again," Jaz told me as she washed down the counter in a beautiful taverna. "I've been told about an apartment. D'ya wanna go check it as soon as I've finished?"

"Yeah, great." I helped her finish the cleaning and we went to check the apartment.

"Yay! A bed each and a kitchen." I liked it.

"Hot shower! And look at this balcony!" Jaz opened the sliding door. It overlooked the road but it was somewhere to sit outside.

"I like that it's off the main drag. Let's take it." I was hoping it would keep me away from temptation.

"I don't think we'll find better."

We put down a deposit, moved in the next day and we were set for the season.

In the mornings, I would walk to work along the beachfront, passing crashed-out bodies all over the beach, collecting a few empty beer bottles to return them to the shop on the corner for the deposit. This bit of cash would buy me a few sunset beers, my starter for the night. Then onto the side road to pick flowers to put on the pillows in the apartments. I usually only worked a few hours, cleaning the checked-out rooms, tidying the other ones, before heading to the beach.

"How was work?" Cindy, who I had met in a bar one night, asked as I sat down next to her on the sand. She was a pretty 23-year-old, from England, who had come to work the summer season.

"No checkouts today so it was easy. Just swept the courtyard a bit, cleaned up the loo's and emptied the shit bins."

"Oh, I couldn't do that." Her job was dancing in a bar to make it look lively.

"Yeah, that's the only crap bit, but the tips and leftover stuff I get is brilliant and I can do it on little or no sleep, still drunk from the night before or hungover."

"I love my job too. I get paid to drink and dance." Her beautiful smile lit up her pretty face.

"A couple of lads checked in today. I'll bring them tonight."

"Great."

"Do you know what that blue truck does?" I said, pointing to the road.

"No." Her flowing blonde hair fell over her shoulder as she turned to look.

"It's the shit truck. A thick tube gets inserted into the tanks in the basements and sucks out the contents. Then it's emptied into the sea on the other side of the island."

"You're joking, right?!"

"Nope. Coming for a swim?" And I ran laughing into the sea.

George always hung around the port until the last boat came and left, accosting people as they came off the ships to get them to stay at his apartments or rooms. It was illegal to do this and, one night, he was arrested and gaoled for two days. When he got out, with a warning not to do it again, he came right back to Paros.

"Malaka," he asked affectionately, "Will you go to Mykonos for me and work the boat for people to stay in my rooms?"

"How much will you pay me?"

"I'll pay the boat fare and give you enough for a drink." He winked.

I was on the next boat. I had nothing else to do anyway and a free drink, especially from George, was a bonus. When the ferry reached Mykonos and the passengers disembarked, I remained on board, having a beer. When we took off again, I chatted to the passengers, telling them about the great apartments in Paros. By the time we docked in Paros, I had seven tourists follow me straight into the hands of George. He worked his magic and filled his rooms, and I went off to see Cindy.

We partied all night and, as the sun rose, I persuaded Cindy to come to the apartments to help me clean. I wanted to finish quickly and continue to drink at the Sunday session everyone was going to.

"I feel sick," she said as soon as we entered the first apartment, and flopped onto the bed.

"Yeah, I need to eat something."

I'd just made myself a coffee and a sandwich, using stuff out of the guest's fridge, and sat down to pull myself together for some work, when in walked George. "Malaka!" he shouted at me, using the term less affectionately this time! But then he just walked away, shaking his head. I was surprised that was all he had to say but, not caring, I finished the sandwich and coffee and did my best to clean.

"Wake up. I've finished." I was poking Cindy.

"Where am I?" she tried to open her eyes.

"Come on, we're going to the Sunday session. But we can't go past the port. George was just here and not impressed. He can't see me sneaking off."

"OK, red car alert it is," she slurred as she pulled herself up, and we sneaked off to the party. I was often sneaking off once the work was done and had to keep an eye out for George passing me in his red car. He would not be happy paying me a full day's wage to sit at the beach or a bar.

The next day, in my ouzo bubble as I dodged the bodies and did my collection of bottles on my way to work, I noticed a girl cleaning the apartments. "Hello. What are you doing here?" I asked, thinking that maybe George had got me a helper.

"George hired me yesterday. He said you'd finished up or something." This was news to me!

"No. I *haven't* finished up. Can you go down the port and tell George that his cleaner is here? I know there's a job going for a cleaner at The Paradise. It's at the top of this road. You should try there."

"Alright. I don't want any trouble." And she was gone.

About half an hour later, George drove up in his sports car and just looked at me.

"Yassou, George." I waved.

"Malaka," he laughed and drove off.

~ ~ ~

"Things are slowing down now: the restaurant is empty most nights. And I miss hanging out with you," Jaz said one morning, as I was about to leave the apartment.

"Yeah. I feel like I've not seen you all season what with me working days and you working nights."

"Shall we do a bit of island-hopping before the season's over?" Her eyes willed me to agree.

"What a wonderful idea!" Within a few days, we were off.

~ ~ ~

"None of these islands are as beautiful as Paros," Jaz said as we sat at the port in Eros, with killer hangovers. I had no recollection of the night before apart from the police taking us to our room and asking us to leave in the morning or go to gaol.

~ ~ ~

When we were done with our island-hopping, we hitched around mainland Greece, gradually making our way to the port where we boarded a boat back to Israel. I lay on the boat's deck unable shift my hangover no matter what I tried. I slept throughout the three-day boat journey.

I still felt rough when we arrived. Was it the movement of the bus that was making me shaky or was it alcohol withdrawal? I still felt like shit when we got off the bus at Infar.

"I don't think we'll get a job but I want to leave a message for Thiang," I said as we walked through the gates.

"You're fucking brazen, mate!" She laughed as we walked to the volunteers' office through surroundings so familiar they felt like home.

"I can't believe you have the nerve to come back here!" The Volunteer Leader said when she saw me.

"I've stopped drinking now." I reassured her. "We really need work. Please help us."

"Oh, alright. Let me try at Ran for you. It's just down the road." And she picked up the phone.

"Ran will take you. I'll drop you there but there must be no fun and games like before." Jaz and I were trying not to laugh as we got into her truck.

Our farmer was happy to have experienced workers, who knew the work conditions and how to pick, and showed us to the part of the packing shed that formed our house. "This is your room," he said as we entered. It had two bedrooms, a kitchen and a bathroom—and needed a paint job. "You share with Dennis. He'll be back from the field soon. And that house is the Thai house." He pointed through the kitchen window to the one opposite. "You stay away! I don't want trouble here." His brown eyes stared into mine. "You can start this afternoon, with packing." And he left us to settle into our new home.

It wasn't long before a tall, skinny man with dark eyes entered and introduced himself, with a Dutch accent, as Dennis. "I had a message from God to come here." He smiled, showing us disgusting, misshaped yellow teeth.

"Oh, what did he say?" I asked.

"It's personal." And he touched his heart and stared into space.

"More like bullshit," Jaz whispered. We went to our room and left him to his lunch.

At two pm, the three of us went to pack and meet our Thais workers, who were distant and seemed shy. "Nah, they're not shy: they're scared. Everyone knows you're the crazy lady with the gun," Dennis said as we packed peppers into boxes.

"That was then and this is now." I did not like my title and continued to pack in silence.

In the morning, we all jumped onto the crate-packed trailer to be taken to the fields. "What's that?" I asked Dennis as we passed a big cross on the top of the mountain we could see from house.

"That's where I go to talk to God on Saturdays."

"We live with Moses," I giggled to Jaz.

~ ~ ~

"Friday night is dinner night," Moses said, rubbing his stomach. This was the highlight of the week. Our farmer would invite all the workers for a get-together over a big dinner. Jaz and I would stuff it down fast so we could get to the bar to join in with the antics.

"You girls are late," the beautiful Cindy said as I joined her on the dance floor.

"Yeah. We had to have our family dinner. He thinks it'll put us to sleep." I laughed and took a cold beer from Jaz.

"I'm having a party at mine after but I've only got one bottle of wodka," Debbie said. She was dressed like a fashion model and looked incongruous on a farm in the middle of the desert.

"The night is young. We'll find some more." I had good hunting skills.

"Look." Jaz poked me. Thiang had walked into the bar.

"Now the party's started," I said as I pulled him onto the dance floor and took a big swig from his bottle of wodka.

Debbie's party was wild. Everyone from the bar had come to join in, bringing whatever booze they had, and people were dancing all over the place. Some Thai boys started cooking, while others ran around like naughty monkeys let out of a cage, taking sneaky gropes at the dancing girls.

"I'm taking my man home, Jaz. You alright to sleep here?"

"Yeah, go. I'm gonna hook up tonight," she smiled.

Thiang and I spent the day in bed until Jaz came home all excited, and he left to hitch back to Infar.

"Wow! Now I get it. Thank you for opening that door." Jaz had just experienced her first Thai lover, Pepe.

"Haha! Hate to say I told you so."

"He was everything, mate. I was treated like a queen and fucked like a whore. I can't wait to see him again." It wasn't long before she was spending almost every night at Pepe's house, and I was home alone with Moses. I used this opportunity to try to stop drinking and get in touch with God which didn't last long. There was too much madness around me that I wanted to enjoy.

~ ~ ~

"We brought you a present." It was Pepe and his mate, Donkey, at the door, with a sack. Inside was a dead turkey they had robbed from the turkey farm. Because the Thais sent most of their money home to their loved ones, they had to live cheaply. Most of them walked around with a catapult in their back pocket, waiting for an innocent bird to fly by for their evening meal. When that didn't work, they stole a turkey. "Oh shit! Don't let Holy Moses see stolen goods in the house! Get in the bathroom." And I pushed the drunken pair, with their sack, into the bathroom. Within twenty minutes, they had plucked it and gutted it and got busy cooking up delicious dishes to wash down with wodka.

"What are you doing for your 21st birthday, Cindy?" I asked as we gathered outside the shop at lunchtime.

"Well, it falls on the Jewish holiday, and we got two days off, so John and I are going to Jerusalem to celebrate." She went into the shop.

"Let's go and surprise her," I said to Jaz.

"You always have brilliant ideas." She was excited already.

"Can I come?" asked Debbie, who was listening.

"Of course. The more, the merrier." Now I was getting excited too.

The big adventure day came and Pepe picked us up on his tractor and took us to get Debbie. "Jump on," I said as we parked outside her house.

"Just finishing packing," she shouted through the window.

"We're only going for one night. What do you need? Just grab some cash and your toothbrush," I shouted back.

"Posing till closing that one," Jaz said.

"Yeah, I know, but she's good fun."

After five minutes, she came running towards us in a bright-coloured minidress and with a small backpack that I knew would be full of cosmetics.

"First, we go see a friend," Pepe said as we took off across the dusty dirt track.

"Party," his friend said as soon as we pulled up outside his house. He threw a blanket on the floor to be our table and placed on it a bottle of wodka and delicious Thai food from the fridge—an offer we couldn't refuse.

We were pissed and singing our heads off, on the back of the tractor, as Pepe did his best to drive us to the main road. He kept swerving off the dirt track into the dusty desert and only just managed to get through the moshav gate without crashing into it. Still singing, we rolled off the trailer and stood on the side of the road, watching Pepe's tractor sway back through the gate.

"We don't split up," I said to the girls as I knotted my white vest into a crop top and adjusted the hem on my cut-off jeans to make them even shorter. "This is as sexy as I get." Jaz rolled her tracksuit pants up into shorts and tied a knot in her T-shirt to give it some style. Debbie didn't need to do anything.

I put my thumb out and it wasn't long before a car pulled over, and the three sex goddesses were on their way to Jerusalem. I got into the front and readjusted my clothes while the other two got into the back. "You are so beautiful. Come into the desert with me," the unsightly driver suggested.

"Have a look in the mirror, love," was my reply. He looked like a camel and smelt like he'd shit himself. He kept putting his hand on my leg and smiling at me, wiggling his eyebrows up and down. I kept pushing his hand off.

Once he realised he was getting nowhere with me, he started on the others in the back. "Any one of you will do," he said, licking his tongue over his brown teeth.

"Stop the car. It's enough," Jaz said, pushing the back of his head.

"I have a strong, beautiful dick," he informed us as we were getting out.

"Then go stick it up one of your mates," I told him as he pulled off.

He did a U-turn and pulled over to us, shouting out the window, "I have a strong, beautiful dick. You girls are crazy. I will please you all." That put us in fits of laughter, with Jaz kicking the car as he drove away. We each had a quick piss behind a tree, and a fag, and then waved down the next car, which took us, with no dramas, to Jerusalem's old city.

Jerusalem is a vibrant, energetic compact city behind a big wall, divided into four quarters—Jewish, Christian, Muslim, Armenian—each with a gated entrance. Through each gate, you enter a different world, full of labyrinths of tiny lanes and steps, in which it's easy to get lost, but we managed to find the hotel where Cindy was staying.

"Surprise!" we shouted in unison as Cindy opened the door of her room.

"Hurray! Hurray!" she squealed, jumping up and down. "I wondered why you wanted to know where I was staying!" she said, giving me a big hug.

"Where's John?" Jaz said.

"We had a row and he left. I was just sitting here feeling sad."

"Feel sad no more!" And I handed her a bottle of vodka.

"A birthday present from us girls."

"Fuck! Real alcohol! Let's start," and she unscrewed the top.

"For sure, but let me sort us out a room first," and I popped down to reception and haggled us a dormitory from the young Israeli guy behind the counter.

"We've got a massive dormitory room just for us. Let's party there," I told the girls. So with our precious bottle of vodka, we did just that before our hangovers could kick in.

"Let's go to this bar first," Cindy was making a plan for the evening, looking through fliers she had collected from the front desk. "You get a pint glass on entering, which you can refill as many times as you want in twenty minutes." She laughed.

"Hey-hey! Sounds good. And look at this one: a live band and buy-one-get-one-free," I said, passing a flier to Jaz.

"Let's party, party!" Jaz said, and we did another shot.

Staggering through the labyrinth of lanes, we managed to find the gate out and reach the first bar in time for the 20 minutes of free beer.

"Three pints in 20 minutes! We Ran girls don't mess about," Debbie said as we were leaving the bar, still managing to look sober.

"I feel like I've swallowed a football," I laughed, unbuttoning my jean cut-offs.

"Right, buy-one-get-one-free. Let's go." Cindy was leading the pack.

The band was funky and we hit the floor as soon as we entered. "Have you seen Jaz?" I asked Debbie, who was busy doing her usual 'come fuck me' dance. She shook her head, no.

"She's on stage, touching up the drummer," Cindy laughed, pointing her out.

"Haha! Look at his face; pain and pleasure." And I went over to get her.

"Jaz, come down. We're over here." I pulled her onto the dance floor to the drummer's relief.

The last thing I remember about that night is Debbie and Cindy kissing on the dance floor, surrounded by applauding men.

"Can you please check out!" The hotel guy was at our door in the morning.

"Yeah, we're leaving today," I told him, trying to raise my head from the pillow.

"Last night was bad. There were maybe 20 people in here. It was so noisy and out of control I was going to call the police, but I didn't want trouble." He shook his head at us and walked away.

"What?" I was shocked and looked around our room to see that Debbie and Cindy had brought their sexy dance to the bed, and it looked like two guys had joined them. Jaz lay naked on the floor, and I was also naked—in a bed that was wet with piss.

"And I thought we came home and went to bed." I laughed.

"You gonna hitch back with us, Cindy?" Debbie asked as she untwined herself from her.

"Fuck, yeah! I'm not leaving you girls ever." And she went for a shower.

With hangovers kicking in, we hitched back to Ran. The Thais were happy to see us return unharmed and threw us a party, with delicious Thai food and, of course, turkey, but there was a wodka shortage.

"Do you fancy hitching to Eilat after work tomorrow, Jaz?"

"What you up to now?"

"I'm thinking to go get wodka. We can fill up both backpacks with 15 bottles, keep five for ourselves, sell the other 25 and triple our money."

"Fucking great idea! This place is too dry. But we'll have to stash it at Pepe's because of Moses." I agreed.

The business was a success, and we went to Eilat to restock three times a week. But Pepe kept drinking our stash so we had to shift it to our house, which was not a good idea for us two pissheads.

"You're partying again?" Moses said as we four girls were sitting at the kitchen table doing shots.

"Nothing else to do," Jaz replied getting up to opened the door in response to a knock. Pepe and Donkey came in with a bag of food and started cooking.

"You get fed. What's your problem?" I asked him.

"I love the food, but singing and dancing all night disturbs my sleep. Then bodies all over the floor in the morning. It's no way to live."

"Then move out." Jaz did not like him at the best of times. And he stormed out over to the farmer's house.

"No other place for me to sleep," he said on his return and went into his room, slamming the door.

In the morning, the Holy Born Again tried to punch Jaz in the face as we were leaving for work, but she managed to get into the bathroom and lock the door. I complained to the farmer who decided to keep us separate during the working day. Moses picked with the Thais a few rows away from us, and packed at the end of the conveyor belt. He took to staying in his room at home, so he didn't notice the comings and goings of the wodka business.

"That must be his third bottle," I said to Jaz as a drunken Thai man was leaving our house.

"There's a party somewhere. Shall we go find it?" she wondered.

"Nah, we got all we need here." I was too pissed to walk.

In the morning, I went to work with the usual banging in my head, still drunk from the night before. I found this state better for picking because it made the time go faster. By the time I sobered up, it was time to go to the shop to catch up on the gossip, find out where the party was that night, buy lunch, and pop into the Volunteer Leader's office to see if there was any mail.

"Come by the house tonight after work." The Volunteer Leader said, one afternoon.

"What have I done now?" I could tell from her face there was something.

"Let's talk later." Then, that night, "Are you selling wodka?" she asked as soon as I walked through the door.

"Not really." What could I say?

"Well, we heard you *are*, from the Thais you sold it to last night. You know they were running around the moshav like savages, trying to kill the livestock for a barbecue, fighting each other and smashing up the house."

"What?"

"This morning, when the farmer went to see why his Thai workers hadn't turned up for work, he found the door off its hinges and Thai bodies lying all over the floor, surrounded by empty wodka bottles. They were too sick to work today."

"Ooh, I'm so sorry. But why do you think it's me?"

"The farmer threatened them with deportation if they didn't tell him where the wodka came from, so they had to tell." If a Thai had been deported, he would have been in disgrace, and his family would have been without the money he was sending home, so I did not mind them telling on me. "You can continue to sell it. Just please, not to the Thais."

"It's alright. I'll stop selling it. Hitching to Eilat is boring anyway." And I walked out.

The season was coming to an end, and I started to feel like I would always be pissed and out of control. Sober, my body ached like an old lady's and I'd taken to mixing coffee, milk, sugar and wodka in an empty plastic water bottle, and putting it in the fridge overnight for my morning frappé.

"Don't know about you, Jaz, but I'm feeling fucking rough. D'ya fancy a dry out?"

"Yeah, it's getting too hot anyway. Where do you fancy going?" she asked, taking a swig from my frappé bottle.

"Turkey?" I shrugged.

"Well, we've been eating it for months, may as well see it." And we both laughed.

~ ~ ~

We flew into Istanbul, excited to be back in a colourful, buzzing city after being in the desert for four months. Pretty painted mosques were everywhere, looking like something from a fairy tale, and the calling of the muezzins was enchanting.

"Let's go shopping and eating," Jaz said in response to the smell of spices calling to our stomachs. We went into the first restaurant we passed and ordered kebabs. The taste kept us hungry even after we had eaten—it was so different from Thai food—and we managed to munch our way through various flavours throughout the day as we went into almost every clothes shop and got a much needed new wardrobe each.

"A Turkish massage?" I said as we passed a big stone house.

"Yeah, my muscles are fucking tight from all that picking."

I was not sure about being naked when a muscular woman laid me down in a hot room on a marble slab, threw hot water all over me and lathered me up with a rough cloth. But, once I relaxed into her pummelling and pounding, it was bliss.

"I'll do that again," Jaz said as we left.

"Me too. D'ya know we've spent £1,000 already today?"

"Was worth it, mate." And we went home for our first sober sleep in months.

Hitching was easy but most of the drivers were predatory, and I had to beat or bite a few of them. However, we got to see some sights, including Ephesus, an ancient city of mighty monuments, built by the Romans, and the stunning white terraces at Pamukkale, formed from calcium deposited by hot springs. We finished with a beach chill at Ölüdeniz's beautiful lagoon. We hadn't had a drop of alcohol for nearly two weeks and I was feeling good.

"Cash is dwindling, Jaz. I think it's time to settle for a while and save."

"London?"

"Yeah. My mumma will be delighted!"

We hitched through Europe, back to France, and got a ferry to England and that British pound. My mumma was happy to see us and tuck us into her nest while we looked for work and we soon found a live-in job in a lovely pub on the River Thames.

The customers were either from the rowing club, old gents, or tourists and were a pleasure to serve. With my focus on saving and getting back on the road, I worked every possible shift and didn't hit the booze, except on naughty nights out with Dolphin.

But London life just didn't cut it for me anymore. My family made me want to stay but, once I'd saved enough of those beautiful pounds that would stretch so far in other countries, my feet would start to itch and I just needed to go.

"I need to get out of London now, Jaz, and Thailand's chilled out happy people and pristine beaches are calling. Do you want to come?"

"Fuck, yeah!"

And we were off.

4. LIFT LIFE: 1996

Arriving back in Thailand brought tears to my eyes and, now I could speak some Thai, it was even better. I couldn't wait to party, eat and get at them Thai men. "Home sweet home," I said to Jaz as we sat outside a bar on Khao San Road, with a few spicy snacks and a bucket, watching the street life.

"Let's go to a night club." The first bucket had started to kick in and I needed to dance.

"Yeah, let's go everywhere." Jaz answered raising her glass. Ooh, one of those nights was on the brew.

We got a taxi to the famous red-light district of Bangkok and entered a multi-coloured neon world packed with people, taxis and tuk-tuks moving in every direction on either side of the length of Patpong Road. The bars, restaurants and free-entry nightclubs had prostitutes and ladyboys, dressed in glittery bikinis and glittery makeup, beckoning everyone who passed by to come inside with the call of "Hello! I love you long time. I suck your cock. Come here, handsome." The only thing enticing *me* was the smell of the street food.

"They're fucking kids, not women," Jaz said as we passed a bar in the middle of the street where scantily-clad children were pole dancing on the bar.

"I know. These kids have no other choice, Jaz. Most of them are from poor farming families and their parents send them here. They can make more money in one night than the farmers can make in a year."

"Look at that pig. It's grossing me out." Jaz was looking at an overweight foreigner sitting at the bar, with a girl on one knee and a boy on the other.

"I know. It's disgusting. The bars hire them out, by the hour, day, week or month and, once they're used up or HIV positive, they're sent back home. Some go to Khao San Road or the islands and work there." We continued to walk through the freak shows to reach the nightclub at the end of the road. "When I was here last time, I chatted with a few and they told me they try to keep the customers drunk so they don't have to have sex with them and can cream off a bit of their money from their wallets while they're out cold."

"What a life," she said as we entered the nightclub, full of old men and scantily-dressed kids. And before long she was freaking out. "Can we leave?"

"You wanna go back to Khao San?"

She nodded yes, and we got a taxi back and set ourselves up with a bucket outside a bar. It wasn't long before we pulled two Thai men and were off dancing in a decent neon nightclub. They were cute and we spent a few days hanging around with them in Khao San and going to shows and Thai boxing matches. But really it was the same ol' song, and I was starting to get bored with the party life and the hangovers. There must be more to life than this.

"I wanna go home to Aus. Do ya wanna come?" Jaz said one night at the bar.

But more and more, I was feeling a pull to explore Buddhism. I had a sense it might help me to live a different way, without the drinking and

'Bang cock', which was starting to make me feel like my life had no meaning and was pointless. "I need to stay in Buddhist countries, Jaz. I'll come to visit later." I felt sad she would leave but this felt right. "I've been thinking to travel overland to Hong Kong and look for work there. I saw there's a night bus to Laos."

"Sounds great, mate," she said encouragingly.

The next day I sorted out my bus ticket, Jaz bought her flight to Aus, and we had our final party.

Jaz waved me off on the night bus to Laos and I watched her frame get smaller and smaller until she was gone. A pang of sadness took me over and I wanted to stop the bus and jump off but I just sat there with an ache in my heart. We had travelled together for four years. It was as if she had become me, and I had become her. We were one person.

But I also started to feel a thrill of excitement as the bus moved through the darkness into the unknown of my new life; a life of exploring myself and finding my real interests, but mainly of stopping drinking and behaving like an arsehole.

I needed my wits about me now. I was alone, under no one else's influence and with no party invitations. I started to feel lonely but, I've been lonely before, in company, I reflected.

The vast open jungle and long roads through Laos, Vietnam and China, by bus and jeep, were perfect for letting go of the past and reflecting on my life so I could try to make the changes I needed to make. Slowly, I was becoming the person I was struggling to be, and leaving behind the person I was expected to be. Change can be a slow process but I knew I was at the start of mine, as I began going to temples instead of bars, and meditating instead of doing drugs and booze. Old habits die hard and sometimes I'd slip back to my old ways when I met up with someone for a drink, but at least I was *trying* to control the drugs and drink instead of them being in control of me.

It was at this time that, in a café in China, I came across *The Tibetan Book of Living and Dying*, by Sogyal Rinpoche. It was enlightening, giving me a new perspective on many of the questions I increasingly found myself pondering.

Why are we here?

What is the purpose of life?

What happens after we die?

Are there other dimensions, ghosts, spirits, demons?

My life wasn't just about me and my gratifications. Its purpose was for me to purify myself of the impact of my past misdeeds, and to prepare for my death moment so that I could control my consciousness once it left my body. After all, death is the only certainty we have. This book was just what I needed to be reading during this transformation. I was hungry to learn more but unsure where to go, though I had faith I would be guided.

Jamie, a stocky girl from Liverpool with an angelic face and a fantastic sense of humour, was also sitting in the café. It was great to have good company to laugh with again. "There's plenty of Buddhist temples—and work—in Hong Kong," she told me as we sipped our coffee. "I was working in a bar and saved some money, but you do go out drinking a lot. The big money is in hostessing."

"I'm trying to turn my life around and clean up my act. It's best if I stay away from the booze. It only takes one beer, and I become a different person. And I never know what she will do next. I'm tired of her." I felt like I was in a swamp, and trying to pull myself out, but the world around me kept sucking me back in.

"Not sure what else there is, but you'll get a cheap room in Chunking Mansion."

"A mansion? That sounds nice." I was hopeful.

"It's a fucking madhouse. Every nationality all living together in one tower block, which is a city in itself. The ground floor is like a big shopping centre where you can buy anything you need from every country. Then, on each floor, there are restaurants, hotels, hostels, temples, brothels and long-term apartments."

"Have the toilets got proper walls?" The toilet walls in China were only a foot high. They just about gave you some privacy in the lower region but you could see everyone's head and shoulders as they went to the loo.

"Haha! Yes, the walls reach the ceiling."

"Well, that's something positive," I laughed.

I said goodbye to Jamie, who was off to Tibet, a country I had just heard of and had no interest in visiting, and caught a train to Hong Kong.

~ ~ ~

As the train pulled into the station, I was shocked to notice the richness and cleanliness of Hong Kong and instantly felt like a tramp in my travelling clothes.

Slipping into a gap in the crowd, I was swept along a flow of busy, busy, busy bustle as people rushed in every direction in smart, trendy clothes, with cool hairstyles, on mobile phones and pagers. Little kids had shoes that lit up and squeaked when they walked: where I had just come from, they had no shoes at all. Feeling overwhelmed, I jumped on a bus that took me to Nathan Road and Chunking Mansion, which was just as Jamie described.

I joined a long queue of people waiting for the lift and stood mesmerised for at least 20 minutes as it slowly advanced. Every nationality and every style of dress was coming and going in the foyer. Finally, it was my turn to push myself through the jumble of people and squash into the tin compressor.

When we reached the 16th floor, I unstuck myself from my comrades and squeezed out to find the guest house Jamie had told me about and knock on the door.

"You lucky. Today we had check out," the diminutive Chinese lady told me as I walked through the entrance into the sitting room. The room I was in had three doors leading to bedrooms and, at the back, a little kitchen area. This area, which was next to the combined toilet and shower room, contained a sink and a shelf holding a barrel of cold drinking water, but no cooking facilities.

"Can I see it?"

"This only single bed and only window. You take?" On each side of the room were two sets of bunk beds, and the single bed was at the back under the window. Nine beds in the one grubby room. "Other rooms all full, all men. You only woman, so I give you the single bed."

"I'm tired. I'll take it." And I lay on the bed to rest my back for a few minutes, until I heard the buzz of a TV from the sitting room.

"What you watching?" I asked the guy in front of the TV.

"A load of shit." He continued to look at the screen.

"Why does the screen keep jumping?" I asked.

"Because it's an old TV but, once you focus, you don't notice it anymore." He stayed fixed on the screen.

"So you're watching a load of shit on a shit TV?" I mocked and went back to my room to unpack.

I set up a space to hang my clothes, built a small Buddha shrine over my bed, and made a deal with myself that, if I ever started to watch that TV, that would be my sign to leave!

"What's that you're making?" A voice interrupted my thoughts.

"A shrine to the Buddha," I said to the guy emerging from under the sheets of the bottom bunk, near the pillow end of my bed.

"Oh, that's new around here." He slowly got out of the bed in just his pants, adjusted his balls and offered me his hand. "I'm Gordon." He was a big, muscular guy from Newcastle, all sweaty and spotty, and looked like he needed a wash.

"Hi," I replied, ignoring his hand, and continued to make my shrine. "It's to remind me that I don't drink or party anymore, so I need a job other than in a club or bar."

"Good luck there, lass. There's not much other work about, like, except in bars or at the airport. You'll soon be drinking. It's the only thing that gets you through, like. Me and the lads have been here a year and havnae saved a penny. Cannae even get a flight home." On which note, he left the room to go to the toilet.

I took a walk along busy Nathan Road, saw a sign for staff in a restaurant window, and went in. "You start now and you stand there," the greasy man behind the counter said, handing me a bunch of fliers and pushing me outside the restaurant.

For eight hours, I stood outside Chunking Mansions in a mass of moving people, trying to pass them fliers that they didn't want.

"Copy watch." A small Chinese guy in a black suit called to the people passing by, from behind a wall.

"What's that?" I asked.

"It's Lolex at cheap price." He showed me a gold-coloured Rolex watch in a box.

"Why are you hiding?" I asked.

"That undercover police." He pointed to a tramp standing at a bin. "I careful. He behind that wall is selling drugs. She a hooker." I watched the street open up to hold characters rather than just faces in the shadows.

"My feet are aching," a Scottish voice said.

"Yeah, mine too, but it's great for getting the street lowdown. I'm only doing it for a week to get enough cash for a month's rent, and then I'll have time to look for a different job." I was trying to stay enthusiastic.

"I do extras work but there was nothing today, so I came to do this. I'm Alice."

"What extra work?"

"No, *extras* work. In the movies. Every day at eight am, a guy comes to the garden hostel and picks out people to be extras in the movie they're making. Come tomorrow. If you don't get picked, you're still in time to start here at ten. It's a great earner—better than this—and you get fed and watered."

"Sounds great. I'll be there."

But the Chinese man didn't choose me as an extra because I was wearing sandals and he only wanted people wearing shoes.

"Go and see this English guy, called John The Book. He sells secondhand stuff. You'll find him in The Travellers Hostel on the top floor of Chunking Mansions," Alice told me as she went off for her day's shoot.

The lift to the top floor of Chunking provided the usual stuffy, stinky ride, and I was relieved to get out at The Travellers, find John The Book's room and knock on the door. A man of about fifty years, with snow-white skin and hair, opened the door. His body was so arched over he looked like he was trying to tie his shoelaces.

"Come in, luvvie," he said as he shuffled his feet to move around his cramped and stuffy, windowless, 10-foot-by-10-foot room. Junk left behind by travellers was piled against the walls, covering most of the floor and half the bed. "I started just selling books, but now I have a whole shop."

"It's a bit cramped in here, John," I said, as I carefully tiptoed between the gaps on the floor, looking for somewhere to sit.

"There's loads of space, luvvie," he replied, sitting on the only corner of the bed that was clutter-free and gesturing me to sit there also. "These are all I have in size seven." And he handed me a pair of purple and pink shoes. Not what I had in mind but, if they got me a job, they would do.

The next day, in my new shoes, I got picked out and taken off to the studio for makeup and costume. It was an airport hijacking scene. An armed man took me hostage, by grabbing me around the neck at gunpoint, and pulled me into the departure lounge. I had to scream.

"It's not fair you get a speaking part on your first day," an old guy said to me on our break.

"Sorry that you didn't get the part. I think it was because they needed a girl," I tried to reassure him.

"It should have been me. I've been working here for months." Pete was upset. This was his full-time job and he was waiting to be discovered, like most of the extras.

"I just want to pay my rent," I told him and moved away from the glares of the regular extra crew, whose speaking part I had stolen.

Juggling the two jobs, I managed to pay a month's rent and spend my days looking for something else, finding a little set-up that delivered lunch to the offices. "You'll be working the four tower blocks in Wai Chai. Try and sell it all but keep a sandwich for your lunch," the English woman said as she handed me my basket of sandwiches, salads and cakes, and my cool box of cold drinks. "Put this on." She handed me a navy 'Having lunch' T-shirt.

From 10 to two, Mondays to Fridays, I was whooshed up in a lift, leaving my stomach on the ground, to sell some of my heavy load, then whooshed back down to pick up my stomach on the way out.

One day, feeling shaky from all the whooshing, sitting by the sea, I noticed a sign for a fair coming to town and went to see if they needed workers. "Roll up, roll up," I said jokingly as I entered the room for my interview.

"You got the job," the Irish lady told me. "You start at four pm, finish at 10 pm and the weekends are all day, from 10 am to 10 pm. You'll be working in the cash box, selling tokens for the rides." And she gave me a flier with a map to the fairground site.

"This is great. Thank you." And I walked out very happy, with two jobs in alcohol-free environments.

At the end of the sandwich round, I would take the leftover sandwiches to the fairground and sell them half price to the other staff, then sit behind the counter to rest my leg while selling tokens. And the best thing was: there was no time to play out.

"I took these from work," Gordon said when I got home, handing me a bag full of tokens. "Can you resell them and we'll split the money?"

"I sure can." I smiled, stuffing them into my bag.

Gordon got me tokens every day and our fiddle became an excellent extra income.

With research, I found a small Buddhist centre inside one of the high rises and started going there between jobs. Little did I know then that I was going to a temple whose Kagyu lineage would become my breath, my blood, my life.

"What are you doing?" the red-robed monk asked me as I sat in front of the Buddha statue in his temple.

"Meditating, I think," I answered shyly.

"Just watch your breath coming in and going out," and he sat next to me.

We sat for a while, and I started to relax. "I have to go to work now but I will come again tomorrow," and off I went to the fairground, happy to have a Buddhist friend. Every day I would leave home at nine am to do the sandwiches, go to the temple, go to the fair, then return home by 11 pm. Weekends were all day and night at the fair. I was busy, happy, saving money and sober.

When the fair finished, so was I. I'd had enough of running around the busy high-rise city, and sleeping in a room with eight smelly men, so I booked a flight to The Philippines and the beach.

On my last night in Honkers, I decided to have a night out to see what I had been missing, so I tagged along with a few guys from home who were going to a nightclub with no entrance fee.

There was a 7-Eleven outside where you could buy beer and drink it on the street with everyone else, before popping into the club for a dance. It was my first drink in a while and I was up for a crazy one, glugging down the beers outside then shaking it away on the dance floor in my alcohol bubble, until I noticed one of the boys from home having a row with a Chinese guy next to me.

"Leave it. Let's go get a beer," I said, trying to be diplomatic.

"You! Outside!" My arm was up my back and the bouncer was pushing me through the crowd.

"You're fucking hurting me!" I shouted as he pushed me face-first through the door.

"OUT! And don't come back!" The bully walked back into the bar in triumph, obviously too much of a coward to fight the men.

My nose was bleeding, my arm felt detached from my body and I was in agony, so I went to the hospital. My face was only bruised but my shoulder was dislocated. So this was what I was missing with the Honkers nightlife! Ha, bloody ha!

I couldn't carry my backpack but I was determined to get on that flight so struggled with it over one shoulder to get a taxi to the airport.

I was still in pain when I landed in Manila so I got a taxi to the backpackers and took in my new environment from the car window. It was a step back in time after Honkers as we drove through a run-down Spanish colonial city on a dirty bay, the beautiful old buildings surrounded by modern skyscrapers reaching up to the dull, polluted sky. The signs on the doors of banks commanding you to leave your guns outside were a bit of a worry but, otherwise, I liked the vibe.

The backpackers was in the centre of town and I stayed one night, to rest and leave my backpack in their storage.

The following day, with a bag of toiletries, a bikini and a change of clothes, I headed to the beautiful island of Boracay to relax and heal my shoulder.

The ship was huge. I walked through the lower deck, which had a few shops, restaurants, bars and a big lounge area with comfortable chairs and big screens playing music videos, to reach the top deck which was full of bunk beds. I found mine and lay down until we docked.

My heart skipped a beat as we approached the sun-kissed tropical beach and I almost ran off the ship. Kicking off my sandals, I walked along the warm, soft, white sand and let the clear and refreshing water roll over my feet.

I saw a beautiful wooden shack restaurant with a few cabins, and managed to get a cabin with an attached toilet and a sea view. Throwing my bag on the bed, I went to eat. "I'll have veg on rice with a fried egg on the top," I told the ladyboy waiter.

"Nasi goreng," he clarified and wiggled his arse into the kitchen.

"That was tasty," I told the shim as he removed my empty plate.

"What problem, your arm?" he asked when he returned to my table.

"Accident." I didn't want to recount the events of that night.

"Tonight there is a party. You come with me? No need arm, only legs."

"OK." I could do with some dancing.

We went to a disco bar and I danced under the disco ball all night with my new friend, Johnny, who was 'same-same but different' from the Thai ladyboys. His nationality might have been different but the sex, drugs and rock 'n' roll was much the same.

After three weeks of rest and gentle exercise in the ocean, my shoulder was much better, so I travelled around a few other islands. But they soon started to look all the same. Boredom was creeping in, along with the drinking.

Sitting in a bar where scantily-clad women danced seductively around poles, I met Brad. He looked like a bald beached whale, seated on a bar stall, smoking weed from an empty Coke tin he had made into a pipe. "You want a hit on this," he asked, passing me his can.

"You're alright." I was trying to stay clean. The booze did enough damage.

"I need adventure. I can't sit here day after day getting stoned," he said as a cloud of blue smoke left his lips.

"Do you want to travel north and see some mountains?" I was also ready to move on.

"Sound's super-duper. Let's do it." And he sucked his can again.

The next day we went to a travel agent to get ship tickets back to Manila. "One ticket for you and one for your dad," the travel agent said to me.

"Don't let *him* hear you say that!" He was not much older than me.

~ ~ ~

The boat dropped us in Manila and we stayed one night in the backpackers to reunite with my backpack, which I'd stored there while I was away healing my wounds, before catching the early morning bus to Spelunking.

I enjoyed the view as we rolled past lush, green mountains and rice fields, while my dad puffed on his can at every stop.

"Separate rooms, please," I said at the reception of the guest house. I didn't want any confusion.

The room was nice and clean and, after a hot shower and a spicy nasi goreng, we went to check out the town. "The people are more genuine and kind up here," Brad noticed as we walked around.

"Yeah. Fewer holidaymakers, I guess. The only attraction is the tour of the limestone caves. But it does look amazing, we should do it." I wasn't sure if my dad would be able to, considering he was never off his can, but we booked it for the next day.

We met our happy, English-speaking guide at the mouth of the cave. "These are the coffins of our ancestors," he informed us as we passed them hanging at the opening, and entered the darkness. "You must stay close to me because slippery and I have light," he said and switched on his head torch. The whole space in front of us lit up—yellow limestone formations were covered in rainbow stripes. There was a narrow gap in the middle and that was our path. "Protection," he said and tied a long rope around our waists, connecting us.

He was a natural as he guided us through the space between the rocks, and manoeuvred us from one fantastic rock formation to another, over a slippery floor covered in bat shit. "Put your leg here, your arm here and slide over my body to that rock." He was acting as a bridge. "Now you can swim." We were at the edge of a little freshwater rock pool and I stripped to my bra and knickers and jumped in.

"It's freezing!" My echo bounced off the walls.

"Not for me," my dad said, sitting on the edge making another can.

I jumped out and ran on the spot to warm up, feeling invigorated.

Having dressed and slipped over the rocks—and our guide—again, we reached the cave entrance and sunlight, then went for lunch.

"What is that?" I asked the guide, looking at the large boiled egg he was cracking open for lunch.

"Balut. It's a 17-day-old, fertilised duck embryo. You want to try?" he offered, passing me a cooked baby duck.

"Happy with my rice, thanks." I felt sick at the sight of it.

"Where to next?" My dad slurred.

"We can get a bus from here to Banaue to go see rice terraces," I told him excitedly, and he nodded his wobbly head. I left him staring into space with his bloodshot eyes and went to get the bus tickets for the following day.

The bus took us through rural villages, built with straw, with a few livestock grazing on the grassy hillsides, to a beautiful green mountain range, cut into big flat steps where the local tribespeople grew their rice. We decided to do the two-hour hike across the rice terraces to stay in the little guest house in the middle.

It was a challenging hike, along a thin ledge with the rice fields full of water on one side and a long drop on the other. My dad struggled with his cumbersome, stoned body, and my knee was screaming, but we pushed on, taking short breaks whenever we reached a plateau and enjoying the breathtaking mountain views.

Finally, in the distance, we saw smoke coming out of the chimney of the sweetest wooden, straw-roofed guest house. We hobbled the last stretch to be greeted by a middle-aged couple, happy to see us. With big smiles, they showed us three empty guest rooms so we could make our choice. "Not surprised they're all empty, the effort it takes to get here," my dad said, picking the first one and getting his Coke can out.

"Worth it though, Brad. I think we should stay a couple of nights," I said, going into the room next door rubbing my hot and swollen knee.

"Yes. At least three. Not sure if I can handle that walk again so soon."

"Brilliant." I was happy with that and settled into a step back in time.

There was no electricity and we had to get water from the well outside, and warm up metal buckets on the fire for a shower. They served us a lot of rice with various tasty sauces. During the day, I enjoyed watching the wildlife and, at night, the dancing light of the stars around the moon. And my dad enjoyed his can.

After three peaceful days, we said our goodbyes to the smiling couple who'd never once spoken to us, and carefully stepped our way along the edges of the rice fields back to the main town.

After a few bumpy bus rides, we finally arrived back in Manila. I gave my Coke-can dada a kiss goodbye and flew to Indonesia to pick up a few buses to Bali and a flight to Australia. I wanted to see my old mate, Jaz, in Perth for Christmas, and earn a bit of cash. I had already used my work visa when I was there with Dolphin so I could only get a holiday visa, but I knew I would get a job off the cards.

You can always get a job if you don't mind what you do.

5. Down Under: 1997

I could hardly contain my excitement when I landed in Perth, knowing I would see my old mate, Jaz. My luggage couldn't come quickly enough and I was itching to reach Arrivals where she'd said she'd be waiting.

"Hey hey!" She shouted, sounding even more Aussie than before, as I came through the door. My heart jumped, I ran into her arms and we hugged and hugged until I could hardly breathe.

"Wow! Look at your hair." Jaz fondled my long, golden, sun-bleached locks. "This is my mum, Ann." A tall, slim woman, with cropped red hair was smiling at me.

"Hello Ann." I smiled back and she also squeezed the life out of me with a bear hug.

"Thank you for looking after my little girl when she was overseas," Ann said once she let me go, and Jaz and I laughed.

"It was the blind leading the blind, Ann," I told her as we jumped into the car and she pulled onto a spacious highway to reach their suburban house outside Perth.

"This is home," Ann said pulling into the big driveway of a one-storey house in a tree-lined street.

"Wow! This garden goes on forever!" I said as I walked across the manicured lawn, with its pretty flowers.

"Wait 'til you see out the back," Jaz said taking my hand and leading me through the house to my bedroom. I dropped my backpack on the floor of my bedroom as we passed and continued to the back door, which led to another perfectly-manicured lawn, with a boat on a dolly platform and a big barbie, where a bare-chested, bald man, with a beer belly, was happily turning over pieces of meat and fish.

"G'day. I'm Jimbo." Jaz's dad greeted me with a cold beer. "I hope you're hungry." He patted me on the back.

"Starving," I nodded and sat at a table laid with bread, cheese and salad.

"Tuck in." Jimbo nudged me as he put a plate of mouth-watering barbecued meat on the table.

"We'll go crabbing tomorrow," Jaz said, nodding over to the boat.

"Do you like water skiing?" Ann asked.

"I can't do that kind of sport because I have a knee injury, but I can sit in the boat and watch you lot."

"Terrific. We'll show you the great Aussie outdoor life," she said, raising her glass.

"What a welcome. Thank you all so much." I felt delightfully at home.

Jaz had a driving job, delivering cooked pies to various outlets, and I would sit up front in the van with her, while she gave me a tour of the town and introduced me to all the people. In the evenings, we would hit all the bars and drink with all her friends. It was a whirlwind of fun and hangovers.

~ ~ ~

"I could stay longer but I need to look for work," I told Jaz as we were sitting in her favourite bar, getting pissed.

"Let get ripped, rest off the hangover, then I'll drop you to Donnybrook. It's only a couple of hours down the highway, and you'll find picking work there easy without a work visa."

"I'll drink to that." And we downed a B52—and then another.

Donnybrook was a highway town. The one road had two bars/hotels and a backpackers, which was also a job centre for fruit picking in the area. You put your name on the job list at reception and, when a farmer needed workers, he would call Sheila, the owner of the backpackers, a tall, attractive woman with a happy smile. Each day, Sheila would work down the list, giving out jobs. When your job was over, you went back to the bottom of the list. If you were short on money, she would let you stay on credit, keeping your passport for payment security. It was a good system, especially if you were skint.

"You can have a bed in dorm number three, and I'll put you on the bottom of the list. The season's taking off, so you'll have work in a few days," Sheila informed me when I checked in.

"Thank you. Anything to do around here while I wait?"

"You can swim in the river but be careful of the leeches. I'll show you to your room." We walked down a dim corridor, with three doors on either side, to reach the last door on the left. She pointed to the bottom bunk in a mixed eight-bed dorm. A shared bathroom was down the hall.

"Hi," I said to the girl lying on the bed above mine.

"Hey. I'm Cazza," she answered, in a jolly Kiwi voice.

"What to do in this place, besides lie on your bed?" I asked as I pushed my backpack under the bed.

"Nothing mate, except the pub. You wanna get a beer?" And she sat up and buffed her long, curly, blonde hair.

"Not really, but I guess it's a way to meet the locals. Let's go."

She jumped off her bunk and led the way down the one road to The Donnybrook Hotel, which was nothing like a hotel. It was a big room with a bar full of men, in checked shirts and cowboy hats, swigging back beer. "Two middies, Bruce," Cazza said, straddling the bar stool with her long legs.

"Who's your mate?" said the short, tubby man as he put two small glasses of cold beer on the counter.

"Just another drifter, looking for work," I answered.

"Ooh, a pommie! We love a pommie in these parts, especially on the barbie." His pot belly shook as he laughed.

"Let me know if you ever need a barmaid." I liked him.

"You wanna work at the weekend? It'll be busy. We have a live band and a skimpy."

"Sure. What's a skimpy?"

"What's a skimpy? You *are* a fucking pom." And he walked off laughing.

"A skimpy is a barmaid who wears nothing but sexy underwear hiding her tattoo and, if you give her a cash tip, she'll flash you her tattoo and sometimes her tits," Cazza told me, her big blue eyes full of mischief.

"You want me to do that? I've got a few tattoos!" I called to Bruce, who was pulling more drinks.

"Nah, you just pull the drinks, mate."

"Great, I'd love it."

The night was a laugh and I enjoyed serving the rednecks as their cowboy hats bounced along with the band. The skimpy was fun, dressed in just a camisole, G-string and high heels, parading up and down the bar. Every time she got a tip, she lifted her up camisole to show off the multi-coloured swallow tattoo on her left tit. I filed it as a work possibility for if I ever got stuck.

"Come look at this," Bruce said, taking me upstairs after the shift. "Do you like it?" It was a single bed in a floral-decorated room.

"Yes, it's cute."

"You can move in tomorrow if you want. Just give me what you pay at Sheila's."

"Great, but you ain't gonna get me from my bed to throw me on the barbie, are you?" And we laughed.

I loved my little room, with its bedside lamp—the dorm had been too noisy and had no privacy—but I was now off Sheila's list, so I had to look for a picking job myself. I hitched to the nearest farm and knocked on the door. "You picked tomatoes before?" Bert, the stout farmer, asked.

"Yes, in Bowen and Israel."

"Right, I'll pick you up at The Donny Hotel at six o'clock tomorrow morning and drop you home again when we've finished work."

Fuck, that was easy!

He was a nice, easy-going guy of about forty-seven, who was having an affair with a vacuous twenty-year-old woman who found everything funny. They moved away from their village because of the gossip and bought this farm to live in peace.

We soon became like a family and would pick until lunch and pack until the last tomato was in its box. But the tomatoes were ripening quicker than we could pick them, and some nights I would not get home until 11 pm.

"We got a full shed that needs packing. Can you please stay on?" Bert asked one day.

"I'm tired, mate," I told him, although I could see the work.

"Go on, mate. I'll make you a special bit of tucker for your tea," he begged.

"Alright, Bert, but let's speed it up." I couldn't leave him to do it all and I fancied trying out this special bit of tucker. I only ate ten-cent noodle packs on my budget, so something good to eat was a bonus.

"I need a break, Bert. All the red is blending into one and, when I close my eyes, all I can see is tomatoes," I told him as I held my back, aching from standing on the same spot for hours.

"Alright, I'll sort you out your tucker. You just hang on in there." He went into the kitchen and I continued packing until he called me.

Guts a-rumbling, I sat down ready to scoff and could not believe it when he served me stewed tomatoes on toast. I thought it was a joke, but the look of triumph on his face told me different. "Go on. Tuck in. You deserve it," Bert said as he watched me eat.

"This is great. Excellent tomatoes." What else could I say?

"Tomorrow, my brother, John, and a few backpackers from the hostel are coming in. It'll give you a bit of a break, doll," Bert said as he ate the rest of the stewed tomatoes from the saucepan.

"Brilliant." I could do with some help and other company.

"And I got a machine." He smiled, proudly. "I'll show you," and he led me to a shed at the back of the house. The metal contraption was in three sections, each of which had two seats, and could go down three rows of tomatoes at a time, enabling you to pick tomatoes from both sides of the bushes. It had a shaded roof, and a rusty lever in the middle manoeuvred it forward or backwards. We would put the empty boxes on the front, load them until they were full, then put empty boxes on top of them and fill them. At the end of a row, we would remove all the full boxes, replace them with empty ones and fill them hour after hour.

"It's so hot under here," I said to Marcel, the Dutch guy that sat next to me on the machine. The sweat was pouring off me and I was starting to feel faint.

"Take your top off." He had already removed his.

"Yeah, fuck it!" I was wearing a sports bra that looked like a crop top.

"Put your top back on," Brother John shouted through the bushes of tomatoes.

"Leave it out, John. I'm roasting," I shouted back, wondering how he could see through the bushes.

"I said, 'Put your top on', or there'll be trouble."

"I'm not putting it on, John, so let's just get on with the work." He stormed off the machine into the packing shed to his brother, like a baby.

"Sorry mate, can you put your shirt on? It's upsetting John but, if it were me, I'd get you to take the lot off." He was laughing. I just wanted to get the work done, so I put the shirt back on and we started picking again. But John didn't come to work again, and I picked in my bra and shorts after that.

"Hey, she's home early," Brucey Baby said as he put a middy on the counter for me. "We've missed you around here lately." He winked.

"We got extra staff now so things should be easier. Thanks for the drink." I said and knocked it down in one.

"Thirsty little pom," and he put me up another one.

"Ooh, this is dangerous, Brucey Baby!" It was going down like nectar.

"Can you organise a party in the yard for all those backpackers this weekend?"

"It would have to be Sunday. It's my only day off. Discount drinks for them and free for me."

"Yep, I can do that. If they buy tickets to cover the cost of a barrel, I'll throw in the barbie."

"I think that'll work."

I sold thirty tickets. Sunday came and, excited that we were having a party, I went down to help Bruce. "Get the salad from the fridge and put it there with the sauces," he said as he threw the sausages on the barbie. "Then fill up the paddling pool." He nodded over to an inflated pool.

"Oh, this is gonna be fun. Good idea," I laughed.

As the sun belted down over the one-horse town, the pub rocked with people who'd turned up with guitars, puff, and lots of happiness.

"The barrel's all done," I shouted through to the bar to Brucey Baby.

"Then half-price pitchers for everyone, you greedy fuckers." He was pissed and happy.

"We're not greedy. We just like a lot," I giggled and announced the good news to the crowd. The pitchers kept coming and I sat next to the man with the guitar and sung every song he knew.

"The pub's never been so busy. Let's do it again next week!" Brucey Baby called after me as I staggered up to bed with the guitar man.

"Sure! I loved it."

"Phone call." Brucey Baby was knocking at my door the next morning.

"Who is it? I've got an awful hangover and need to go to sleep. Can they call tomorrow?" Every time I tried to get up, I felt dizzy and sick.

"It's Shelia. Just take it, mate."

I forced myself up and went downstairs to the phone.

"What you playing at? The whole place came home drunk last night, creating so much noise, and hardly anyone's gone to work today." She was spitting down the phone.

"Well, that's not my fault. I didn't force them to come over."

"I don't want you coming here anymore."

"What?"

"Stay away!" She slammed the phone down and I went back to bed.

~ ~ ~

Let's go to the beach after work, Saturday. We can camp the night and come back Sunday evening," Marcel was saying as we picked, picked and picked some more.

"Yes. Can I bring Cazza?"

"Sure. We have a big campervan."

Saturday afternoon came and I was as good as kidnapped by a group of ten travellers in the back of a psychedelic campervan. "Get in," Cazza shouted from the back door as I stepped over boxes of beer, took the bottle of bourbon and a spliff, and kicked back for the two-hour drive to the beach.

"The last one in makes the fire," I said as I ran into the water, throwing my clothes off on the way.

"Hey! Skinny dipping!" Cazza was right behind me, throwing her red dress onto the sand.

"The boys are out surfing. It looks like we're left to make the fire," I observed as we waded out the water, and I pulled my jean cut-offs and white vest back on. We gathered wood from the forest behind the beach, got a blazing fire going, and wrapped potatoes and squash in tin foil and threw them on the coals.

"Right, that's dinner on the go. Let's have a spliff." Cazza was an efficient rolling factory.

"Do you want coke or lemonade in your bourbon?" I asked as she sparked up.

"Coke, darling."

We sat on the sand, getting off our faces while watching the boys surf. One by one, they came back and sat around the fire to enjoy the barbie washed down with bourbon.

"Can you play Pink Floyd?" I asked the guitar man, who came to sit next to me.

"I'll play it. You sing it." The pleasure was mine.

In the morning, I untwisted my naked body from the guitarist, climbed over the sprawled-out bodies to get in the sea to freshen up, and noticed that Cazza had also pulled.

Slowly heads were stirring and it started all over again. By the time we got back to Donny, we were pissed, stoned, skint and knackered. I fell into bed and slept through the morning alarm clock, so I had to hitch to the farm and I arrived three hours late.

"Glad you could make it, Sheila," Bert said as I was climbing onto the machine.

"No bother, boss." I smiled back at him.

He was a sweetheart but, the next day when I slept through the alarm again, I knew I was done with the tomatoes and it was time to move on. "Bert, I've done it again. I think I must be exhausted and in need of a holiday, so I've sacked myself."

"Alright, mate, if that's what you want."

"Yeah, that's what I want." It had been four months of pick, pack and eat tomatoes.

Cazza and I hitched to Manjimup. It was a lovely town and we rented a caravan next to a natural swimming pool, and got a job picking apples. "I love this caravan. It's like our own little house," Cazza said as she made a sitting area outside.

"Let's hitch into town, get supplies and cook." We walked past the apple field we would start picking tomorrow, and onto the road.

"Jump in the back," a guy in a ute said before we even reached the road and, fifteen minutes later, we were in a supermarket shoplifting everything we needed. We made a big feast and had an early night ready to start the next day's picking.

"How do I put this bag on?" Cazza was fiddling about with the apple-picking sack.

"Let me show you." Drawing on my experience in Lana, I explained to her how to do the job properly and we climbed the trees and gently picked apples. We were paid by the kilo so we worked the hours we wanted, which was all morning, leaving ourselves time to chill at the pool in the afternoons. There wasn't much to do in that little town so we just picked, swam in the pool, shoplifted luxury food and saved our money.

As soon as we'd picked the whole field and got our cash, we hitched to Margaret River to pick grapes. "Ooh ooh, check out the surfers! I'm gonna like it here." Cazza big blue eyes were bulging as she looked out of our caravan window at the blonde, bronzed, fit bodies waxing their boards and smoking weed.

"Yes, nice to look at, but they've only got one brain between 'em." They were not for me.

"I'm not looking at their brains, mate!" Fuck, she made me laugh.

At six pm, we were standing in the kitchen with the rest of the flock, waiting for the campground owner to hand out the picking jobs. "Dwayne's got a truck so he can take you girls with him tomorrow," he told us. "You got this field for a week, alright?"

"Alright," I replied.

"I'll come by your drum at six am. Be ready," a skinny, dopey-looking guy said to us and took off. Happy we had work sorted, we went home to have a spliff and chill out.

At six am, we were waiting outside the caravan just as Dopey was pulling up. "Great, you brought the radio. We can have music while we pick," I said as I settled into the passenger seat.

"No, mate, it's to check the surf. Surf's up, grapes down!" he smiled, flicking his long sun-bleached hair, and pulled out of the campsite and onto the road.

We arrived at a big winery and the farmer gave us each a bucket and clippers.

"Fuck! I've cut my hand again. These fucking clippers!" I was on my arse, clipping grapes off a bush.

"It's because you're sitting on the floor. You need to clip from the top," the farmer told me.

"But I can't bend my knee. I have to sit," I said, showing him my deformed, scarred leg.

"You should put some wheels on Dwayne's surfboard and roll along," Cazza laughed.

"No one touches my board, dude," he said sternly.

"Tense or what! You should try waxing something else. Why don't you and your friends come over to ours tonight?" Cazza offered.

"Session on, mate." He winked.

We got a complementary bottle of wine at the end of each day, so it was 'session on, mate' every night.

~ ~ ~

"My six month visa's nearly up, and I need to see my mate, Jaz, before I go. Do you fancy coming to Perth?" I asked Cazza as we sat in our garden, sipping the last of our wine.

"Sounds like a hoot, since we've picked all the grapes, drank all the wine and fucked all the surfers."

That was true.

Jaz had organised a big send-off party for me that included an acid trip, which I was still up on when they dropped me off on the highway to hitch a ride to the airport. The car that picked me up was full of surfers on the piss, who passed me a bottle of bourbon on entry. "Mull up, dude," the voice next to me said, passing me a bag of weed.

"No worries there, brother." My rolling factory began.

I got out of that car, clueless as to where I was or where I was going. I wobbled through the airport rigmarole on automatic pilot and, before I knew it, I was landing back in Honkers. I checked into a shoebox room with six beds and no window, put my bag down and went to check out my old place.

"Gordon, my man!" He was watching the flickering TV as I entered.

"Yeah, still here, lass. You back for work?"

"No, I'm on my way to Thailand in the morning. I've been working in Aus."

"You put on a few pounds. All them barbecues, I bet. I got some good coke if you wanna line, lass."

"Why not? I may as well finish the party here. I'm going to detox on a beach when I get to Thailand. I went off the rails a bit in Aus." He chopped up a couple of lines and we went out to dance until sunrise.

Another hazy flight got me into Bangkok, where I caught a bus to the port and a boat to Kho Chang. I was longing for my bed so I took the first beachfront hut I found.

"Please help me to stop this debauchery," I was saying to the Buddha shrine that I had just made, when there was a knock at my door.

"Hi sweetie, how's it going? I'm David, your neighbour. Come and visit me once you've settled in." I watched his pert arse, in tight cut-off jeans, wiggle away as he went back to his bungalow, delighted to have a friend already and happy he looked like an interesting one. Feeling it could become a messy night, I dug a hole under my bungalow, buried my valuables and went over to see him.

"So, what you up to?" I asked as I approached his bungalow.

"I'm glad you're here, baby. I bought these beauties in Germany and have been waiting for someone to take them with." He brandished a plastic bag full of pink pills.

"What are they?"

"Ecstasy" and he put one in my hand and one in his mouth.

"Oh fuck. I was planning to dry out before going to London to look for work."

"No sweetie, not tonight. I'm an air steward and I've got a two-week holiday. Please play with me."

And so it began.

After two days of partying, I needed to sleep, went to my hut and crashed out. I woke up feeling like I'd had a lobotomy, and went for a swim to try and bring some life back into my body. It didn't work so I thought I'd try some food.

"How are you?" David asked as he sat at my table. I could only grunt. "That was some storm last night," he said as he drank his coffee. *That* was what was different about the beach! It was half washed away and covered in debris from trees.

"I need to go back to bed," was all I could manage to say, and I went back to my bungalow. Only then did I notice the coconut on the floor next to my bed and the massive hole in the roof. Fuck! If that had landed on me, I would have been severely injured or dead. Someone must be protecting me, I thought, as I fell back to sleep.

When I woke up, still feeling shaky, I was delighted to find my valuables still safely buried, but shocked to realise my flight to London was in two days. "I have to leave," I told David, who was deep in concentration building an enormous, detailed sandcastle, although he did manage to stop for a second to give me a big hug and kiss. I jumped onto a boat, looked back at the island I'd just spent a week on—and realised I didn't remember any of it.

6. Institutionalised Concrete Jungle: 1998

Looking from my window as the plane flew over London, I saw the River Thames with all its bridges, and lush green parks, and started to get excited. *Maybe it's because I'm a Londoner* started rattling away in my hungover head.

As soon as the plane landed, my emotions exploded and I realised how much I'd missed my family and friends, but mostly my mumma. "I'm here," I said into the plastic mouthpiece of the phone in the Arrivals lounge.

"Hurry up," her excited voice sang in my ear. I put the phone down and rushed to get a black taxi cab. As the cab drove through the clean, organised, busy streets, I started to feel warm and content. I was home.

My mumma had decorated the outside of her house with balloons and a big banner saying 'Welcome home.' She ran to the taxi as soon as it stopped and we kissed, hugged and cried right there in the street.

The house looked the same and we immediately opened the bottle of duty-free whisky I'd brought, and sang and danced to her favourite tunes by Chas & Dave. People came over to visit me and it wasn't long before we took the party out on a pub crawl.

Waking up with a throbbing hangover, I went to see if I could get on unemployment benefit to help me out while I looked for work but, instead,

I got put on a free seven-month NVQ Level 2 course in Healthcare. That wasn't my original plan but I'd never studied before and didn't have any qualifications, so I thought I'd give it a go. After all, I was 36 and maybe it was time to settle down and get a normal life, especially if I wanted to have a baby: my body clock was ticking.

My placement was in a nursing home for the elderly in Acton, four days a week, and I spent one day a week in a classroom in Kilburn. "This is the first time I've ever studied for anything, so I want to do well," I told my teacher, Glen, who was a kind, helpful man.

"Really? Most people just come because their benefit money'll get stopped if they don't."

"Not me, I've been on the road most of my life, and now I'm yearning to do something other than party. I want to become a healthy, sensible, responsible person. Maybe this qualification is the start." I was serious.

"OK. I'll support you all the way." And he did.

I spent time at the library, researching for my course work, and was always the first in class and the last to leave, squeezing all the knowledge out of Glen like he was a ripe piece of fruit.

On weekends, I would hang out with my old mates and join in with the piss-ups at the pubs, clubs, or people's houses. On one of these drunken nights, I met Michael, a handsome blue-eyed, blonde rascal from Scotland. When he invited me, with that irresistible accent, to join him in a game of strip pool, I was at the pool table in a flash. Every time one of us missed a ball, we had to remove a piece of clothing. It wasn't long before he was bollock-naked at the table, with his own balls on display, and an angry landlord was telling us to get dressed or get out.

We had many crazy nights like that, and I would always end up sleeping at his flat so, eventually, I moved in.

"How was your day, hen?" he asked as I walked in, enjoying the smell of the lovely stew he was cooking.

"Physically and emotionally draining." It was a relief to be home and I fell into his arms for a big bear hug.

"You'll get used to it," he reassured me, pulling my long golden hair out from its ponytail. But I wasn't sure I would or even whether I wanted to. I had never been to a nursing home before and now I was working in one.

Standing alone, surrounded by a well-kept garden, the home looked like a beautifully-maintained hotel but, once you entered, the smell, and the reality of death, hit you in the face. Boom! Old, sick, confused people walked the corridors, on frames or sticks, while others just lay in bed or stared blankly at the TV. My job was to wash, dress and feed them, and take them to the toilet.

No one wanted to be there, not even the lazy staff. It was a horrifying, depressing place, but it opened my eyes to old age, sickness and death, something I had never thought about before.

"Help me, help me." A distressed, male voice came from behind a closed door.

"Just ignore him. He shouts for nothing," the fat arse in a nurse's uniform said, and walked off.

But I couldn't. "What do you need?" I asked the old man, who was lying in his bed crying. Due to gangrene, one of his legs had been amputated and doctors were trying to save the other one that was also full of it.

"I'm in so much pain. Can you move me?" He grabbed at my arms in desperation.

"I'll try," and I rolled him onto his side and propped him up with pillows.

"That's better," he sighed.

I returned to the corridor to the sound of "Fucking cunts! Arseholes!" coming out the mouth of one lady, calling into the space around her.

"Mrs Brown has gone wandering. We had to call the police. Can you take over the breakfast?" Fat Arse said, attempting to move fast.

I went into the dining room, sat down a few stragglers and busied myself getting out the cereals from the cupboard. When I turned around, to my horror, I saw that a woman had lifted her skirt, taken down her undergarments, climbed on her chair and shat in her bowl! "I take it you don't like the food!" I said, wryly. There were bits of shit all over her, the table and the floor, and it stunk. I quickly cleaned around her, helped her up and led her to the bathroom for a wash, still hearing "Fucking cunts! Arseholes!" bouncing off the walls in the distance.

"No, Alice. That's not your room. Go put that back and get your breakfast." She was leaving someone else's room with their hairbrush. With my free hand, I guided her in the right direction and continued to the bathroom. I put Shitty Pants into the shower and soaped up her sagging skin, while she pulled gently on my hair. With a soft rub of a towel, some talcum powder in the creases and clean clothes, she was ready to go back into the dining room, which was getting cleaned up and set for lunch.

"Get your break while we're quiet," Fat Arse said as I was preparing bread and butter for Shitty Pants.

I washed my hands a few times but they still felt like they had shit on, so I ate my sandwich with a knife and folk. "I don't think I'm cut out for this job," I said to the nurse stretched out in the armchair in the staff room.

"You should try the hospital. That looks more like your style," she lazily drawled.

"I don't think any of it's my style." I was overwhelmed by it all and wasn't sure I could manage the seven months, let alone a full-time job.

"Mine neither, but I have to pays me rent." And she sucked her teeth.

"Your time's up. I need help." A head was leaning around the staffroom door. "You need to clean up Alice."

I reluctantly got up and went back to work while the nurse stayed slumped in the chair. Alice had shit and pissed all over herself and the floor, and was trying to eat it. It was hard to keep my sandwich down but I did what was necessary, while the police brought Mrs Brown back home.

And that's how it rolled four days a week for seven months.

When I finished my nursing home training, they offered me a full-time job but I joyfully declined it. Instead, Glen convinced, and helped me to fill out an application form for a hospital job as a Dialysis Technician. I was completely astonished when I got invited for an interview, completely shitting myself when I went for it and completely flabbergasted when I got it. I had never had a proper job with a contract, annual leave and a respected uniform. People were calling me 'Nurse' overnight. It was a total transformation and, with Michael by my side, I was willing to give this 'normal' life a shot.

The haemodialysis dialysis unit was in three sections, with six beds in each. Outpatients came in three times a week to get their blood washed by the machine, which acted as an artificial kidney. The treatment usually took four hours.

"If I just think that the red stuff in the tubes is Ribena and not blood, I think I'll be OK," said Lyn, from Jamaica, who was also on her first day.

"As long as there's no piss and shit to clean, I'm happy."

"It's not enough pay for me to do that." Her face screwed up in disgust. We were standing at the entrance of the ward, not sure what to do.

"You two!" The little Chinese nurse called us to join her at one of the machines. "Today, I'm going to teach you the procedure. We disinfect and clean the machine after every use. These lines are used to wash the patients' blood. The red line brings blood out to the artificial kidney. The blue line puts it back into the patient via their fistula. A surgical procedure joins an artery and vein to create a special big vein for good blood flow; that's the fistula. We use these special needles to attach the lines." She showed us a packet with two big needles in it. "Lara will be your mentor. You'll follow her today."

Lara was a petite, Caribbean woman with a warm, soft smile that made me relax a bit. "Take all the used lines off the machine, wash it with disinfectant, then put a new set of lines on top. Put the sheet in the laundry trolley, wash the bed down with disinfectant, dry it and put a clean sheet on it. Then get Mr Johnson from the waiting area," she told me in a no-nonsense manner.

It was an excellent job but it was hard on my damaged knee which became swollen and painful. I was back on painkillers and my doctor told me I needed a knee replacement.

"Oh no, I'm too young for that! Please, can we do something else?"

"I could give you an arthroscopic knee wash-out. It'll improve things for a few more years, but you're going to need a knee replacement in the end."

"I'll try anything," I pleaded.

"The procedure involves introducing irrigation fluid into the joint using an arthroscopic port, which allows the fluid to collect before it's flushed away."

"Sounds easy, let's do it." Because I was staff and it was only a 20-minute procedure, he squeezed me in that week. I recovered quickly and was back on my feet running around after a few weeks.

I worked and studied hard, and it wasn't long before the manager chose me to do my NVQ Level 3 as a Dialysis Technician. It was a great course. I learned the machines inside out and backwards and was soon confident enough to put the big needle into a patient's fistula and put them on the machine. I cut my hair into a short, neat bob for a more professional look, and would meditate before each shift and go to work with love in my heart—and a smile on my face to spread it to everyone, especially the patients. I enjoyed making them laugh, telling them stories of my travels and brightening their day by doing something stupid or singing and dancing to them. I got to know them well, and they got to know me. As I put them on the machine, I would often feel a gentle shuffling in my pocket: it was usually sweets or chocolate. One guy used to bring me a £10 phone card to top up my mobile every week, another would bring me a packet of twenty cigarettes three times a week, and I would often get home-cooked meals and fruit. My boss dubbed me The Dancing Disco Nurse.

But this created a lot of jealousy with the other staff, and they made my life hell. I would be sent on unnecessary errands around the hospital, given dirty jobs and ignored in the staff room. Worst of all, they had to be constantly chased up to sign off my course assessments.

I kept on smiling and dancing but, when I got home, I would often cry, and have a drink or two and a little spliff to even myself out.

I was lucky I had Lara. She helped me get through the bullshit and finish my course. The Dialysis Technician course was new. I was the first to complete it in the UK, though that was less to do with my efforts and diligence and more to do with everyone else's laziness. The other students had no interest in learning new skills to, as they saw it, do more work for the same pay. And the nurses didn't want to do the extra work involved in signing off our assessments. As a result, the others on the course progressed slowly, if at all. But I was keen to learn and found the course interesting.

Michael was an electrician and earned a fair wage but, even with his support and my nursing salary, I still didn't have any spare money to save, probably because we went to the pub a lot. I couldn't face doing more shifts at the hospital: I already spent enough time there. So I got a fun second job as a barmaid in the local football club on match days; three or four times a month for football and two or three times a month for rugby.

My bar was on the football stadium's top floor, in a first-class luxury lounge, with first-class customers who needed a VIP invitation to enter. This gave me confidence that no one from the hospital would be coming in for a drink or walking past, and I could keep it a secret.

It was an easy job, and I worked with a young party animal, called Mel, who was in charge of the tea and coffee station. The bar opened an hour before the game, and closed an hour afterwards. The flow of customers was relaxed apart from the madhouse that took over during the thirty minutes of half-time, when everyone would come in at once, and I would be doing a juggling act with bottles and glasses to get them all served.

Next door was a fancy restaurant that served a free gourmet lunch to the chairman and his elite guests. As soon as the second half of the game kicked off, Mel and I would be in there, filling up our plates with mouth-watering delights.

It was more like a day out than a job and, after work, Mel and I used to go out to party with the other staff, and sometimes the players, and I would have a wild boyfriend-free time. Due to my crazy antics, I often got invited to the after-game parties, and people would usually buy me drinks. They liked me pissed because I was good fun and free entertainment. There wasn't much I wouldn't do for a laugh.

"I love coming here to work," I told Mel as we were setting up the tea and coffee station on a Saturday morning.

"Don't you like nursing, then?"

"Yes. I love helping the patients, but some of the nurses are hell to work with. They go from school, to college, to nurse training and then to work. It's like being back at school. Instead of solving problems with other staff, they run to the boss. They've not had much life outside of an organisation and are institutionalised. Instead of using their brains, they do everything by the book, even if the book is out of date."

"Ooh, robots."

"Yes. Lazy, boring ones. I think every nurse should be a patient before they're allowed onto a ward. Then maybe they'd have a bit more compassion for the patients. Some of them have no idea what it's like to be disabled and stuck in bed unable to do anything for yourself." I was having a big moan.

"You sound sick of it already."

"Yeah, I am. But I love the patients and need to finish this course." To drive the hospital's torment and frustration out of my mind, I went out onto the platform to watch the football game. I soon felt better as I soaked up the chanting and shouting while watching fit muscular men run around in shorts.

What a job!

It was fascinating how the supporters knew all the words to the songs and would sing together even to stuff that had only been in the papers that day.

"We've got an invite to the Player of the Year party!" An ecstatic Mel came to join me.

Now this was an honour of an invitation, and I could not believe it. It was a sit-down meal in a posh hotel, while the football players were given awards for their performances that season.

The big night came. After work, Mel and I went to my flat and dressed in our finest clothes while drinking a bottle of wine. We were half pissed before we even got there.

The doorman opened the door and showed us to the function room, where another man led us to our table. Trying my best to look like I belonged, I sat down and poured myself a glass of red from the complimentary bottle on the table. "Let's have a spliff, Mel." I needed to subdue my naughty drunken demon, who wanted to come out to play already.

"No! Not here at the table." She was horrified. Other staff, our boss, the chairperson, the players and people from the press surrounded us.

"It's all right, Mel. No one will notice" And off I went skinning up under the tablecloth.

'No one will notice'! The hash smelt so strong *everybody* noticed and was looking to see where it was coming from. But I was too pissed to notice them noticing, then too stoned to care and needed to dance.

"What's up with these people?" I asked Mel, when I was put back into my seat by security.

"They're still giving out the awards, and dinner's about to be served." She was pissing herself laughing.

Soon the table became a slow-moving conveyor belt of delicious food that I was too pissed to eat, so I just looked at it and drank more wine instead.

Finally, it was time to dance, and I lost myself in the music until it stopped.

I staggered over to a group of people sitting in the lounge, where one of the players was playing the piano, and leaned against the wall. "You play the piano like you play football," I told him as he was banging away at the keyboard.

"Thank you," he said, pleased.

"Yeah, crap," I laughed as we walked off to get a cab home.

Sitting in the back of the cab, I started to feel melancholy. "I haven't seen a happy, contented nurse yet, Mel. I'm starting to think 'If that's my future, then I don't want it.'"

"You're just drunk." She put her arm around me like I was a child.

"But if I'm going to end up like the people in the nursing home, do I want to spend my life doing this? I'm not happy."

"But the patients love you," she tried to reassure me.

"I know, but do I want to wake up next to the same man the rest of my life? Do I want a baby?" I rambled.

"Sleep on it, mate." And she gently kissed the top of my head.

In the morning, looking at the head next to mine on the pillow, I knew it was over. I didn't want to spend the rest of my life with Michael or have his baby. I got out of bed, walked around our home and realised I didn't need these possessions.

I was deep in thought on the bus ride to work and, as I entered the hospital, I felt a heavy depression fill my body at the idea of another shift with these ignorant bullies. I knew I couldn't do it anymore, and this was not the life for me. I was living a life that other people were telling me I should be living, but it was not the one I wanted to live. I was not happy. Something was still missing, and I was filling the gap with alcohol and drugs again.

As soon as I finished my NVQ, I gave my notice at the hospital. Since I had annual leave left, I took that and walked out right away. I went home, finished with Michael, and was out of there on a flight to Africa a week later.

'Normal' life had been tried and tested and was most definitely not for me.

7. Mzungu: 1999

Jamie, who I'd met in China, was now working in Botswana teaching people how to use computers. She had a four-week break from work and I flew out to travel around neighbouring Namibia with her.

I felt nervous being back on the road again, embracing its unpredictability after months of knowing exactly what tomorrow would bring, especially as I gazed at the city of Gaborone, surrounded by a barren desert, from the window of the plane. After all, this was Africa and I had heard that it was dangerous and primitive.

The plane landed—and I just sat there in shock. Why hadn't I continued with my mundane but secure life? What was I going to do here? Here I was again, drifting. An air steward tapped me on the shoulder, interrupting my thoughts, and I got up and stepped out of the aircraft into the unknown.

Then I saw Jamie in the tiny arrivals lounge and, when her big white smile and sparkling brown eyes met me, excitement took over. All my doubts melted away. My life might have been secure but it wasn't happy.

"I thought you weren't on the plane," she cried, in her Liverpool accent.

"I was adjusting to the transition," I laughed, and gave her a big hug.

A short taxi ride took us to the hotel she had booked, in the heart of the city, and I was impressed that it was modern and not run down. "Oh my! This place is a lot better than I was expecting. And it's clean!" I said as we entered the lobby to check in.

"And there's a swimming pool," she smiled.

"Really? Let's go swim." I still couldn't believe I had escaped a life I didn't want and was back out in the world.

"Tonight, we're going to a bar," Jamie said as we sat by the pool.

"What, a real bar, with booze?"

"Yes, and food." She laughed.

"Music?"

"Haha, yes. What do you think? Everyone is running around with bones through their noses?"

"I don't know what I think. I'm still in shock."

The bar was full of foreigners, and heavy metal music was playing from a large screen. If it hadn't been for the heat and the dust, I would have thought I was still in London. "Looks like a meat dinner then," I said, looking at the menu.

"It's mostly meat because of the game parks. The beef stew is good." Jamie sat down on a comfortable sofa and I went off to order two of those and two beers.

An hour later, "Have they gone hunting for the beef?" I said to Jamie.

"It's Africa time: slow; very slow; stop; tomorrow! But it'll be worth the wait."

"Maybe we should order breakfast now, then." I laughed.

The next day, we chilled at the pool so I could acclimatise and get ready for the road trip we were starting in the morning, and so that Jamie could teach me about this new way to communicate, called email. What a discovery! It was so easy and so life-changing. I could send an email in seconds. Until then, I'd relied on a post office address, telling people weeks in advance where to send letters.

"I'm just going to pick the truck up from the garage. She's getting a full service. I'll be back in thirty minutes." Jamie left in a cab and I jumped into the pool.

She returned in a gleaming white pickup truck. "She's brilliant! We're doing this in style," I said as I checked the truck out.

"Indeed. I've got a tent, mattress, music tapes and even a couple of deck chairs."

My excitement grew and I couldn't wait to get on the desert road. I was up early the next day and, after a big breakfast, I was ready for action. "Let's go," Jamie said, sitting at the wheel.

"Yep. Windhoek here we come!"

Jamie pulled onto the highway and it wasn't long before we were on a dusty road flanked by just a few dried-up trees. That continued for a few hours, before the landscape changed to a vast, open, undeveloped desert that stretched for miles all around us. "Lucky we got the truck. I've not seen a bus stop yet." I said as we passed through the unchanging empty desert.

"It's definitely not on the top of the tourist list. I've never seen such a deserted road," Jamie agreed.

"It says in this guide book, you have to camp in authorised campsites. It's illegal to camp anywhere else—and you don't want to be gobbled up by a lion in your sleep."

"Yes, there's some kinda spa coming up in about an hour. I heard they rip you off but they do provide somewhere to put the tent, a shower, toilet and an overpriced restaurant."

We could see the open-air spa resort, shimmering like a mirage in the sunlight over the deserted plains, thirty minutes before we reached it. "Shall we get a room for tonight?" Jamie said as we stepped out of the truck.

"Cool with me." I was stretching my aching back and longing for a shower.

"A room?" said the chilled-out guy sitting at the reception desk, looking at us with big eyes as if we'd asked for something strange. After a long pause, he reluctantly got up, walked to the computer and started tapping away at the keyboard. Tutting, he tapped away some more. "OK, one person, number 27."

"No! Two people," Jamie pointed at me.

"Two people." He looked at Jamie and then at me, shaking his head, then tapped away again for another few minutes.

"OK, two people, number 27," and he passed her a key.

"For fuck's sake!" Jamie was unimpressed.

"This seems the norm. It's better if we slow down and adapt or we we're only gonna get stressed out and ruin our trip," I said as we walked an immaculately-paved path to room 27.

"This is luxury!" I was gobsmacked. The large room held a massive, clean bed and fancy furniture, and had a big window overlooking a well-manicured garden decorated with water features.

"Very cosy and clean. Let's go check out the spa." Jamie was smiling.

We dropped our bags and walked a dust-free paved road, lined with flower-filled pots, to a white building. Inside, white marble floors surrounded two giant hot tubs and a swimming pool. Everything gleamed. "I can't believe this is Africa," I said as I took a hot shower before getting into the tub. I was so impressed. "I thought it was going to be all mud huts and poverty!"

"What are you like?!" Jamie laughed. "I think we should stay an extra day," she added as she floated in the pool.

"I think you're right!" And I lowered my body into a steaming hot tub.

After two days of luxury, we continued our drive along flat roads, passing a few sun-shrivelled trees, the landscape slowly transitioning to rusty red dunes, then back to a flat, dusty road. The continuous flow of ever-changing landscapes and colours provided an excellent backdrop for reflection or, as I thought of it, 'doing my laundry' regarding what I wanted from life. I'd come to realise it wasn't a career, husband, babies or mortgage. That felt like going through the motions and boring. I was happy on the road. But could I stay on the road forever? Maybe a bit more of that Buddhist stuff would help me work it out.

"Wow! What a dress code," I remarked as we pulled into the modern city of Windhoek. The women were wearing Victorian-style dresses, tight at the bodice, with about ten petticoats underneath sweeping up the dust as they walked.

"They look great, but in this hot sun..." Jamie was sweating from just looking at them.

We managed to get a room at a hostel whose other guests were all on safari. "Let's go up to the hilltop and check out the Independence Memorial Museum," Jamie said. "I bet the sunset will be great from up there too. I do love a sunset."

Happy to be out of the truck and in civilisation, we walked the elegant, orderly streets to the top of the hill. The museum was interesting, with tanks, statues and lots of paintings and we were out just in time to watch the sun become a glowing ball of fire and disappear into the distant desert, turning everything pink and red.

A stroll back down brought us to a lively bar, with German beer and safari tourists talking excitedly about Etosha National Park. "I can't wait to get there, Jamie. It sounds fantastic!" I'd always dreamed of going on safari.

"Let's have another day here and then we'll go. I heard there's a pizza restaurant." Her stomach was important to her.

"Sounds like a plan." So was mine.

The next day, we walked the broad open street, found a neon sign advertising pizza, entered, and sat down with rumbling stomachs.

"I'm sure we've been sitting here for more than 10 minutes," I said and got up to see what was going on. "Can we order, please?" I asked the guy I found sitting down, staring into space.

"No cheese. No cheese," he told me. A pizza restaurant with no cheese!

We were in search of an alternative when I noticed the tourist information centre. "Ooh, Jamie, let me see if there's a Buddhist place in this city."

"Alright. Can you ask about a gay bar too?" she said shyly. Aha! I wasn't the only one doing my laundry on the long drives.

The woman behind the counter looked at me nonplussed, not sure how to answer my questions. "We do a city tour. Would you like to do that instead?" she offered.

"No, thank you." I left.

The next morning, I was so excited I could hardly sit still. "That guy we met last night said it's only a four to six hour drive to the park," I gushed as I sat down for breakfast of bread and eggs.

"If we hit the road after brekkie, we should be there in time for lunch." Jamie was as excited as me.

"*Nellie the elephant packed her trunk and said goodbye to the circus,*" I sang on our way to the truck.

"*Off she went with a trumpety trump. Trump, trump, trump.*" Jamie joined in and we laughed as we strapped ourselves into our seats, ready for another long drive on a desolate, winding desert road.

We were each smiling ear-to-ear when Jamie drove through the gate, its wooden sign reading, 'Welcome to Etosha National Park'. "Look! Look!" I nearly wet myself with excitement when I saw through the window a herd of grazing springbok.

"Look ahead," Jamie squealed, pointing out a herd of elephants crossing the road.

"Oh, this is unbelievable!" I couldn't contain my excitement and called, "Nellie! Nellie!" from the window as they stomped past us.

When Jamie pulled up at reception, I jumped from the truck, took a deep breath and looked up to the sky in gratitude. With enormous smiles, we entered a clean, air-conditioned room, one wall taken up by a map of the park. A man in a safari uniform sat behind a counter. "Camping for three nights," I told him, wondering if I was in a dream.

"Lot number six." And he pointed in the direction we should take. "The toilets and showers are next to the restaurant behind here. Don't leave any litter and no fires, please." He smiled.

"Thank you." I smiled back and we went to park up and get some lunch.

"Well, we've seen all the animals," Jamie said, looking at all the meat laid out on the buffet. "I was hoping to see them alive, not sure if I can eat them!" It made me sad but Jamie was less sentimental, saying, "Well, it's that or nothing!" and piling various types of meat on her plate.

After putting up our tent, we drove the dusty grey pan to a watering hole to see if there was any action and sat behind the protection fence in silence, listening to distant grunting and birdsong while watching antelopes drinking. A purple-black sky was kissing goodbye to a red ball of fire slipping behind the rugged rock backdrop.

"The elephants are coming!" Jamie whispered, and we watched them slowly stomping along the dry ground, dust flying behind them. When they reached the water, they gently nudged each other out the way to flop in their trunks, while their babies copied as best they could.

"It's surreal!" I said. The stars were starting to twinkle like distant diamonds. It was breathtaking and only the need to sleep drew us away and back to our tent.

"You'd never know you were sleeping in a tent. That mattress is brilliant," I said as we woke to the orchestra of a million birds in full song and prepared to watch the sunrise.

"After this, we can drive around the whole park," Jamie smiled.

My whole body fizzed with excitement as we took off along the track through vast open plains populated with wandering springboks and pink flamingos. "Zebras ahead!" Jamie said as they crossed the track in front of us.

"Look out my window. There's giraffes!" I was ecstatic as I watched their long necks reaching up to the few trees that grew on the deserted plains. I sat back to take it all in.

"Shit! We've got a blowout," Jamie said as she pulled the swerving truck to a halt.

"What're we gonna do?" We had just seen a lion running through the bushes and it was still out there somewhere.

"We'll have to get out and change the tyre."

"But the lion will eat us." I was shitting it.

"No choice, baby. You keep watch." And she handed me a monkey wrench and started jacking up the truck. Twenty minutes later, we were back in the truck unscathed to continue our drive through this untouched, natural animal kingdom.

"I feel alive again! I'm so happy!" I said as we drove back to the campsite.

"You gave up getting married, having a baby and a career for this." She laughed.

"I know! What a fool!" And I started laughing too.

"Look at that monkey," I whispered, as we sat in deck chairs outside our tent, having a cup of tea. He had unzipped a tent opposite us and crawled inside, coming out with a jar of peanut butter and running up a tree to eat it.

"Guess that's what you call a 'cheeky monkey'," Jamie laughed.

"Let's go back to the watering hole." I wanted to make the most of our last night. We did just that and sat in silence watching the antics of the wild animals until Jamie's stomach demanded food.

~ ~ ~

"Get the chairs." We were loading the truck to leave for an 11-hour drive to the salt and clay plan of Sossusvlei, and its high sand dunes. Once we'd packed up, we took off through what seemed like an endless sea of rust-red dunes and bleached-white plains dotted with ancient gnarled trees.

Then the truck came off the road and would have turned over if something hadn't stopped it: it felt as if someone caught it and put it back on its wheels. Our hearts racing, we clambered out. "Are you OK?" I asked an ashen-faced Jamie.

"Yeah. I think I took the corner too fast," she said, looking back at our skid marks.

"Did you feel as if something stopped the truck from toppling over?" I was sure of it.

"It did feel like that. Someone's looking after us, baby girl. That's for sure." She got back in the driver's seat and we hit the long, dusty road again.

"Here in one piece," Jamie said as she jumped out of the truck outside our lodge.

"Well done." I ran around the jeep to hug her.

We checked in, washed a big dinner down with a few beers and crashed out early to be up at four am to watch the sun rise over one of the world's highest sand dunes.

"Wake up, Jamie. The jeep'll be here in 20 minutes." I was gently rocking her.

"It better be worth it," she moaned as she dragged her sleepy body to the bathroom.

"Good morning," I said to the other eight people as I climbed into the jeep. They all looked like they had just had an anaesthetic and barely responded. The four-wheel-drive bounced and swerved along a dark, dusty road to our destination.

"Climb up to the top to see the best sunrise in the world," the guide told us, just as the sunlight was starting to lift the darkness.

Other jeeps surrounded us and about a hundred sleepy people were clambering up the dune, whose diamonds of sand were glistening in the morning light. "Tranquil sunrise!" I laughed.

"Let's do it," Jamie said and joined the herd.

I struggled to climb the dune. It was one step forward, two steps back. I kept sinking into the sand: my knee was not strong enough. "Go without me," I shouted to Jamie's back, and I lay down right there, peacefully alone, to watch the sun rise.

"You didn't miss anything," Jamie told me kindly on her return, seeing that I was upset that my knee hadn't been up to the climb. Then she gave me a gentle shove and we rolled down the dune, giggling like children.

After a picnic lunch, we were driven back to town. "Not much to do here but the dunes. Let's go to the ghost town, then I need to get home for work," Jamie said.

"*Kolmanskop was a wealthy diamond-mining town until the mine started to deplete in the 1940s. In 1928, the richest diamond-bearing deposits ever known were found 270 km south of Kolmanskop and the town's inhabitants left in droves, abandoning their homes and possessions.*" I was reading from the guidebook as we walked around the dry, dusty, abandoned ghost town, with brightly coloured wallpaper peeling from the walls of the dilapidated houses, restaurants, and bars, all smothered in rolling banks of sand. It was silent and eerie but you could feel that it was once a hive of activity and merriment.

"Are you looking for diamonds?" Jamie asked, seeing me sieving through the sand.

"Well, you never know," I laughed and continued to check, letting Jamie go on ahead.

"No diamonds then?" she laughed when I eventually caught her up, and we went back to our hotel for our last night together.

~ ~ ~

"Let's get you to the bus stop," Jamie said as I jumped into the truck for the last time. I was nervous, knowing that I would soon be alone in the wilderness of Africa.

We pulled up next to a giant baobab tree and waited with brightly dressed women—kids in their bellies and kids strapped to their backs—surrounded by battered boxes and suitcases. Soon my anxious thoughts were shattered by Bob Marley blaring from a multi-coloured, rusty minibus that was swaying towards me, dust flying in its wake. It was full of people and its overflowing roof had bags, boxes, rice sacks and chickens in wicker baskets hanging all over it. "Will I get on?" There already seemed to be more people than space in the bus.

"Just push through, baby. I'll get your pack on." And Jamie went to the back of the bus.

"Your bag's on the roof." I heard Jamie's voice from outside the rugby scrum that enveloped me and knew I had to get on now. I continued to push forward, managed to secure myself a cramped spot in the aisle and held on tight to the back of someone's seat as the bus bumped and swayed away to the rhythm of the music. Looking back through the cluster of bodies, I caught a glimpse of Jamie waving goodbye.

The open windows provided a warm, sticky breeze but not much relief from the heat, or the sickening smell of body odour, as we passed through tiny villages where people got off, and people got on.

Slowly the bus started to empty and I got a seat. I was relieved to sit down and enjoy the rest of the trip. "First time in Africa?" asked the smelly man, with a big afro, next to me.

"Yes. My first bus ride too," I said as if I had just achieved something big.

"I show you how to greet," he said and took my right hand in a handshake. "This is hello." Then we gripped at the thumbs: "How are you?" Then back to the handshake: "I am fine." Finally, a click of the thumb and middle finger.

"Wow, people do all that?"

"That's the simple one," he told me and started to show me more elaborate ones. I had fun with my new companion as we bumped and swayed through little villages with mud houses and straw roofs. Half-naked children with snotty noses peered in the window, saw me and ran away screaming "Mzunguuuuu!" and making us laugh. Finally, it was his stop and, with an African handshake, we said goodbye.

Enjoying having a seat to myself, I stretched out with a fantastic feeling of freedom. I had no plans, no idea where I was going and no clue what to expect next. I felt entirely alive as I watched the sun go down behind the hills and the sky fill with various shades of red as it darkened and filled with twinkling stars.

By the time we crossed the border into Zimbabwe, it was completely dark so, when I reached the final stop, Bulawayo, I took a room in the first hotel I saw. "You do not go out after dark, OK?" the woman told me as I was checking in.

"But it's dark now and I'm hungry." She just shrugged. Taking nothing with me but a small amount of cash, I ran to the nearest food outlet, bought fried chicken and chips and ran back to my room.

In the morning, with my money belt strapped to my body, and carrying a small bag containing small change and drinking water, I went to check out the city.

"You buy this? I make myself." A wood carving seller beckoned me as I rushed past fried chicken shop after fried chicken shop along a ramshackle road.

"Hey, lady! You want to see my elephant?" another called.

"Come look mine," another.

It was too busy and noisy for me, so I went straight to the bus station and bought a ticket to the mountains.

A bumpy ride ended at a fresh, clean mountain station and I found a tranquil wooden guesthouse in the forest. "What's the easiest walk?" I asked the owner, Dennis, who was from South Africa.

"Follow the path from our main gate. It's all marked but take this map with you also."

A dense forest lay before me as I took off to swim in a waterfall. I enjoyed the fresh, musky smell and the sounds of the birds that were all singing in tune as I carefully stepped over the massive roots that stuck out along the slippery, mossy path.

After five hours, and lots of climbing and clambering through the woods, I hadn't seen anyone else or a waterfall and was utterly lost. My feet were covered in blisters, my knee was swollen and I had run out of water. I started to get frightened: it would be dark soon and I couldn't find any path.

Hearing distant thumping, I headed in that direction, praying for it to be something friendly. Lumberjacks. My saviours! "What you doing here?" A smiley face asked me.

"Looking for a waterfall," I replied, feeling stupid.

"There's no waterfall in the dry season and you're well off the walking path. Let me drop you back to the path. Get on the tractor," the sweaty man told me in perfect English. I climbed over the wheel hub to get in, and he took off back into the forest and dropped me onto a footpath.

"You're about an hour from home. Keep going straight," he told me as I carefully climbed back down onto my throbbing feet. I hobbled straight ahead and finally made it back just before dark, thirsty, hungry and aching all over.

"Where did you go?" Dennis was confused.

"I was looking for waterfalls," I said as I took off my boots to survey my red raw feet that were twice their size and covered in open sores and blisters.

"You won't be able to put them on again for at least two days," he said, giving me a bucket of hot water to soak my feet in.

"Looks like I'm staying here then." I winced as I immersed my feet.

"I hope you like maize."

"What's that?"

"It's like a dumpling. We mix cassava or corn flour with water to make a thick dough that you dip into a spicy sauce."

"Sounds good. Can I have some? I'm so hungry!"

He came back with a plate of white dough that looked like mashed potato, had no taste and hit me in the stomach like a lead brick, but the spicy sauce was delicious.

I relaxed in the garden for a few days while my feet resumed their normal size, then spent a full day and night on the bus ride to Harare. Harare turned out to be scarier, with more wood carvings and more fried chicken than Bulawayo. I got out of there quickly to see Victoria Falls.

I could hear the powerful gush of water, thumping down through a series of gorges into the Zambezi River, as soon as I got off the bus. I will definitely find *this* waterfall, I thought as I headed towards the backpackers, down the town's one road, which was full of restaurants, bars, hotels and tour shops.

The backpackers was lively: there was a party around the swimming pool. I checked in, dumped my bag on my dorm bed, and went to check it out. "Am I still in Africa?" I said to the tiny Aussie girl in a bikini sitting by the pool. I couldn't believe either the luxury or that we could wear bikinis without offending anyone.

"These are tour group people. They come in, see the falls and leave. Go get a ticket so you can eat all you want from the barbecue."

"I hope there's no elephant on there," I said as the sounds of an elephant's trumpet filled the warm night air.

"No, but they roam around the town at night, so be careful not to bump into one or slip over on its shit!" she laughed.

"Thanks for the tip," I smiled. I fetched a burger and sat on a picnic bench watching people dance, my feet still too sore to join in.

The falls were even more magnificent than they sounded and I spent a few days walking along the many paths, enjoying the picturesque gardens and being gently bathed by the freshwater spray. I was immensely grateful to be there.

~ ~ ~

After bumping over craters on another bus ride, I reached Mozambique. It was a relief to get away from the dust to see lush green trees reaching into blue skies along the shore of the Indian Ocean. The clear waters and white sands were seductively cajoling me to join in the play of the waves and I couldn't wait.

I took a boat to an oceanic island, found a beach shack with a hammock and basked in its natural beauty. I was so happy I thought I would burst yet, after a week, it was like something was missing and I found myself craving adventure, so I travelled onward, this time overland to Malawi.

The run-down city of Blantyre looked like a war zone but I fell in love with its happy, smiley people who seemed always to be dancing. Their chilled-out nature made me feel instantly peaceful but, needing to get away from the disarray, I caught a bus to Cape Mclear to enjoy their company in a nicer environment.

When I stepped down from this bus, my breath was taken away by a magical lake lying before me like a sliver shawl, perfectly reflecting towering rain forested mountains. It looked like a tropical island with its sandy beach and palm trees.

I walked to the nearest resort. "Can I get a single room?" I asked the muscular man behind the bar.

"Lake view OK?"

"You have rooms next to the lake? Yes please! Yes! I want one!"

He laughed and led me across the bar to four concrete rooms in a row in front of the lake. Mine was the last one. "There is no electricity but we put on a generator in the evening and you can pump drinking water from the well over there." His deep voice was soothing and he moved like he was gliding.

I quickly changed into my bikini and walked to the lake. "Don't go in. You'll get schistosomiasis," a heavy Glaswegian accent told me.

"What's that?" I asked the blue-eyed beauty who owned the accent and turned out to be occupying the room next to mine.

"It's a disease caused by infection from freshwater parasitic worms. They burrow into your skin and take up residence in your organs."

"What?!" I had no idea what she was talking about.

"Yes. And if it's not treated, it can be fatal."

"This lake can do that?! I don't believe it: it's too beautiful" I got in and floated in the warm, soft water as it wrapped around me as if I was back in my mother's womb.

"You're a bit of a nutcase, ain't you?" She said when I got out.

"Now that depends on what you think is nuts, doesn't it?"

"Aye, true, but going into a diseased lake is a bit nuts, don't you think?"

"Not when you're in it. What's to eat around here?" I asked, since she seemed to know everything else.

"Not much. The restaurant does fish and maize when they managed to catch some fish." I wrapped myself in a sarong and went to get some.

"So you're the woman who swam in the lake?" a skinny, young English boy asked as I tucked into my white brick and fish, enjoying the view of the muscular barman.

"Yes, it's magical."

"Yes, it is. I dive it all day. I'm a dive instructor."

"What about this bug thing?"

"It's no problem. You just take an anti-parasitic tablet and it's cured in two days."

"I'm cool with that," I said between bites.

"If you want to do a dive course, we start a five-day open water course in two days."

"I'll think about it." That hadn't been on my agenda but, after all, there wasn't much else to do.

"I'm Paul and the school is five minutes that way. Just pop in and let me know."

So I signed up for my first ever dive course. To my surprise, I found that learning about the equipment, underwater sign language and breathing techniques that help you dive deeper was exciting. But when it actually came to diving, I realised I was terrified!

Yet when the inevitable day arrived, when I had to flip myself backwards off the boat and down into the lake, I felt light and free, and the silence was heavenly. I found myself in an intoxicating new world, swimming with fish through intricate rock and coral formations. I loved it so much that, when the course came to an end, I wasn't ready to stop so I progressed to the advanced course, which included a night dive.

Seeing this unfamiliar part of our planet was a fantastic experience but wearing all that equipment made me feel like I was intruding into an alien environment and disturbing the marine creatures, so I never dived again.

I wanted to stay by the lake so I took a three-day boat ride to Nakatha Bay, spending it chilling on the deck watching villages passing. I had my own room, with a lock on the door, and a shared bathroom. There was a restaurant, a bar and a few other mzungus to chat to. It was perfect.

As soon as I arrived in Nakatha Bay, I felt at home; almost like I had lived there in a previous life. It had one main dirt road that held a supermarket, a few shops selling dried food and stale biscuits, a couple of backpackers, a few hotels, two bars and a disco complete with a disco ball. Around a big tree in the centre was a vibrant market, where you could get a tasty bowl of rice and beans, and a shake-shake bar. Shake-shake is a cheap fermented maize beer, which is served in litre cartons that you shake-shake to mix. It goes down like porridge and tastes like old socks but it gets you very drunk, very quickly. The best time to go to a shake-shake bar is in the morning, when it's full of happy fishermen who know they have a meal for that night.

I loved the peaceful energy emanating from the people and wanted to stay and be a part of their simple way of life, so I asked around the backpackers and hotels for work.

"You can work the bar here for a free bungalow and a plate of rice and beans a day," the English manageress of Africa Bay backpackers told me. I loved the place and moved in the following day. At street level, there was a kitchen, a few concrete rooms, and some toilets and showers. A network of wooden bridges joined the bamboo huts on stilts cut into the cliff face and the bamboo bar, which was at the water's edge, next to my hut. The place was naturally beautiful and I soon settled into a carefree life by the lake. I would work the bar, swim in the lake—and enjoy my new distraction, my local Rasta toyboy, Winston.

"What the fuck is that?" I asked Winston one night, when we were sitting outside my hut. A big, deep-red ball was rising from behind the lake, bathing everything in a golden orange shimmer.

"It's the moon." His young, innocent face looked at me, confused.

"I've never seen it this big or bright, and especially not red." It seemed like I could almost touch it.

"It's always like that." His beautiful smile lit up his whole face. We sat in each other's arms, watching it rise higher and higher into the star-studded night before we drifted away to my hut.

It was Lariam night, the night for taking my weekly anti-malaria tablet, and I was in two minds whether to take it because of the crazy dreams it gave me and the sickness and depression it left me with in the mornings. "Don't take it," Winston said when he saw me looking at the packet.

"What about malaria?"

"Just put on mosquito spray and cover up at night," he assured me—and he was right. I threw them in the bin and got into bed with my man, safe in the knowledge my sleep would be free of surreal dreams.

I was woken by my usual alarm call of fishermen chatting as they came in from a night's work. I felt fresh with no sickness or depression, and I knew my Lariam days were over. I had a quick snuggle with my man and a swim in the lake, and I was ready for the day's work.

The house speciality was space cake; chocolate and fruit cake made with Malawi Gold weed. Its power was unbelievable. Felix, the cuddly, gay chef, would decorate these cakes according to how much he had eaten, and they were terrific works of art: it was a shame to cut them. Some guests would come for a few days and stay for a week, not even noticing time passing.

I was settling in to the slow pace but I needed to sort out the kitchen: it was just a little *too* slow. "It would be a lot easier if you served the food all at once, and sent it down together," I tried to explain to Felix.

"Um, OK," he answered. But I knew he didn't know what I was talking about so I worked an order through with him: two rice and beans, and one fish and rice.

"So let's make three portions of rice, fry the fish and warm up the beans, and then we can serve it all together." The poor guy was looking confused but nodded as if he understood. Nevertheless, the food still came down one plate at a time. That was African style and that was the way it stayed.

"Can I put a flier up in the bar?" asked one of the five South Africans who had just arrived.

"Sure. Stick it up with the others," I answered while getting them four Carlsberg Green, the only beer in Malawi besides Carlsberg Brown, which is a darker beer but tasted the same to me. *Bob's jump-on-jump-off buses*, the flier read.

"That's us," said Tex as he pinned it to the board. He was a slim man of about fifty. "And this is my son, Jungle Boy." A tall, skinny 21-year-old smiled at me. "This is Bruce, Tony and Jim." They were all in their mid-thirties. They sat on the deck of the waterside bar sipping their beers, telling me about their journey through Africa.

Felix brought down a new decorated cake and I handed him their food order. "Please try to bring it all at the same time," I asked sweetly and he nodded and strolled off up the steps.

"What's that?" asked Jungle Boy.

"It's Felix's special cake," I answered with a wink. That got the others interested and all four of them started asking me questions simultaneously. "Yes, it's a weed cake." One reply answered them all.

"I think we'll have a slice each. We're big boys," Bruce said.

I cut them each a slice of cake then popped up to the kitchen to see why the food order was taking so long. Felix was outside the kitchen, leaning against the wall with his finger pointing to his head, making a crazy sign. He had been at the cake. That meant the kitchen was closed.

Coming back down the steps, I saw Bruce out in the canoe, having trouble steering. "Please make sure he's alright," I asked Foster Fantastic, a local lad who'd been at the special cake himself.

But I was worrying about the wrong guy. While I was still wondering whether Foster Fantastic was cogent enough himself to watch out for Bruce, I heard a bang. Tony had collapsed to the floor and was slipping off the edge of the decking to the rocks below. "Help me!" Tex was shouting as he tried to pull him back up, and I ran over to help.

"He's got a pulse and he's breathing. He'll be fine." I put him into the recovery position. Looking up, I saw Bruce crawling back onto the beach and throwing up, green-faced, and Jim talking to a mango tree. Other guests were also coming up on the cake and starting to get paranoid. Others were waiting to get served. The place was starting to erupt into madness.

At this point, the manageress came back from shopping. "What's happening?" she asked me in disbelief.

"Not much. Felix has just made another cake," I told her and took my chance to exit to my hut for a breather.

"Why you work here? You don't need these problems," Winston said. He was sitting outside the hut, watching from a safe distance. "I know a wicked house in the village. Let me show you." And he squeezed my hand. I looked at his handsome face and agreed, and he took me off to look at it.

From the main road, we descended a staircase carved into a cliff-face to find, sitting alone on the edge of the lake, a small house with one bedroom and a deck area for cooking. "Just you and the lake," Winston said.

"And you." And we made love right there.

Life was peaceful and simple. I sat at the lake by day watching the birds and night, listening to its gentle swirling rhythm. I only went up to the road to shop. Winston would fish and cook on a fire, and some nights he would play the drums. We had everything we needed in each other.

As I floated on the lake one day, I saw a black smoke-like cloud coming into shore. To my amazement, local people were trapping it in baskets on long sticks by waving them over their heads. Eventually, I realised that the smoke was in fact a swarm of lake flies.

As I came out of the water, I passed a man picking at the flies covering his body. "What are you doing?" I asked.

"Dinner," he said, popping a fly in his mouth. I tried some from his basket but found them to be tasteless bits of fluff. Nonetheless, the lakeshore soon filled with people drying flies, mixing them with spices and pressing them into cakes, which turned out to taste better. This local delicacy flew in once a month.

I was content there, happily passing the time until Jamie could join me for Christmas

~ ~ ~

"You're really here." Walking down the steps to my house with her big smile, she was a sight for sore eyes.

"What a journey!" she said, giving me a big hug. "Let's go eat. My girlfriend, Jo, is waiting at the bar." She smiled shyly.

"You got a girlfriend? Wow, we *did* both do our laundry in Namibia," I laughed.

After fish and rice, we went to Africa Bay for a few Carlsberg Greens and some of Felix's special cake.

"That cake is too strong! I have to go to bed." Jo said, her blonde curls flopping over her beautiful hazel eyes that were now all misty.

"Me too. I'm seeing double," said Jamie and off they went, holding on to each other for support.

I went to the disco to see Winston. "That nigga of yours has a wife in the village," some random girl told me as I was dancing to the reggae beat. I doubted it was true but had to check.

"Winston, do you have a wife in the village?"

"No, you're my only wife," and he put his arm around me.

"But she just said you do," and I pointed her out.

Within moments, the three of us were loudly arguing. It escalated to pushing and shoving and I decided we should get out of there. I headed for the door, with Winston following. Outside, the pushing and shoving continued and other customers came out to watch and butt their noses in. As it turned into a scuffle, Winston and I were separated.

The next thing I knew, I was coming round on the road, beaten and robbed. "What happened to you?" a local man was saying, his face close to mine.

"I can't remember," I said, looking around.

"I'm going to take you to the hospital. You're covered in blood. Let me help you up," he said as he put his arms around me for support.

I had internal bruising to my stomach, a cut face that needed stitches, a beauty of a black eye and tooth marks on my chin. They sedated me and put me to bed for the night, and the local man left and went to tell Jamie.

"Fucking hell, babe, are you alright?" she said when she arrived to take me home. I could only nod a 'Yes'. "I've moved you in with us and I think we should leave very soon. Winston's in gaol at the police station for beating you up and looking at two years."

"What? Winston didn't touch me! And anyway, it was just a stupid, drunken fight. Oh God, Winston won't survive two years in a Malawi jail.

I've got to get him out!" I shuffled as best as I could off the bed and into a taxi.

Back at the hotel, I sat on the bed contemplating what to do about Winston. I decided to go to the police station the next morning.

A few people were hanging around outside the small courthouse next to the station. "What's going on?" I asked the person next to me.

"It's the court case today for the guy that beat up the mzungu."

Shit! I hadn't even known it was happening. I had to go in.

As I entered, I saw that the benches at the back were filled with Winston's family and friends, who were all looking at me. I stood frozen until a voice directed me. "Sit here, next to me." It was a police officer who'd spoken. I sat down despite it exacerbating the pain in my stomach.

But what seemed like kindness turned out to be something else entirely. "You're going to be called as a witness but, if you get him off, we will plant weed in your house and you'll be the one going to gaol. This story has been all over the news and it will be bad for tourism if we don't make an example of that nigga," the officer whispered into my ear.

I began to tremble as I realised the seriousness of it all. The police were using him as a scapegoat and had conveniently forgotten to inform me of the court date so I wouldn't turn up to contest their version of events.

The judge entered and called me into the dock. I stood with my bruises on display while he read out the charges. "Is this the man that beat you?" he asked. The room was so quiet you could have heard a pin drop.

I looked at Winston's tired eyes and hunched-up body and said "No!" as firmly as I could. The relief on Winston's face, and the sigh from his family behind me made my fear of the consequences bearable.

I left the courthouse, said a sad goodbye to Winston with a big hug and went back to find Jamie. "I need to get out quickly. I've got him off, and the police are angry with me. There's a night bus tonight and I'm going to jump on it," I said to Jamie and Jo.

"We're coming with you." I was so relieved, I cried.

It felt like a long wait as we sat on a stone bench at the bus station. My heart was in my mouth, worrying what would come first: the police or the bus. "Zanzibar is definitely the best place to heal and forget all this," I said to the girls in an effort to focus on something else.

"Yes. The spice island," Jo said, her blonde curls bobbing with the nodding of her head.

Eight anxious hours went by before a packed bus pulled into the station. We were determined to get on so we squeezed through the crowd until we were wedged in—and stayed like that all the way to the border with Tanzania

At the border, we changed to another cramped bus which dropped us, a bit frazzled and worse for wear, in Dar es Salaam, which turned out to be a big bustling, noisy city. We managed to find a decent hotel, cleaned ourselves up and went out to eat and check out the place. "Nothing to do except climb Kilimanjaro or get robbed. Let's get to Zanzibar," Jamie said.

"Definitely!" I was still battered and bruised and just wanted to rest on a beach.

In the morning, we took a short boat ride across the waves, travelling from hell to heaven. "Look at that. It's a picture," Jamie said, gazing at glorious white sands and green trees as we approached the shore of Zanzibar.

"Can we head north to Nugwi? I heard it's got the best beach and I need to rest," I suggested as we docked in a bustling port.

"Yeah, this is too busy," they agreed, and we went to look for a bus. The cute bus we located gently rocked us along a beautiful coastal road to Nugwi, where we found a small, cheap guest house just behind the beachfront and settled into concrete rooms.

I was relieved the travelling was over and I could rest. I made a shrine in my room and prayed to Buddha to help me stop drinking and getting out of control. Then I went to check out the beach.

I walked a palm-lined path to reach the finest white sand, stretching for miles in either direction and rolling down into the vast expanse of a turquoise ocean. There were about five wooden-shack restaurants and I sat in the first one I came to and breathed in the fresh salt air while my heartbeat slowed in time with the waves.

"You know how slow Africa is? Well, it's completely stopped here," I said when the girls joined me at the table on the sand. "I ordered fish about an hour ago. Then I saw him go into the sea with a spear and he hasn't come back yet," I laughed.

"Well, at least you know it's fresh!" Jamie marvelled, taking a seat.

"I've never seen such a beautiful, exotic beach. I'm getting in that ocean. Are you coming?" Jo said to Jamie.

"Stomach first," she replied and picked up the menu.

Jo ran down the beach and splashed in the ocean. "The water is so warm and clear you can see all the fish swimming. The colours are amazing," she said excitedly on her return, dripping water everywhere.

"I'll go in after this." My food had finally arrived. The girls ordered and we relaxed, looking out at this magnificent gift from nature.

"Right, I'm in," I said after I finished my food, and quickly walked over the hot sand to reach the gentle embrace of the ocean. It was great to let my aching body relax weightlessly in the warm water and I could feel myself beginning to heal though I knew it would be a while before I was dancing.

~ ~ ~

"Merry Christmas!" was the greeting of the day. We were sitting in a beachfront restaurant, enjoying a Christmas fish lunch.

"The Blue Lagoon has a big party for Millennium Eve," Jamie said, reading from a flier a woman had just handed her.

"Then we should start there," I was happy to be feeling better and pain-free, and was excited about a party.

A few hours later, I knocked on Jamie's door with a cry of "I'm ready!"

"You are seriously going out like that?" Jamie was laughing.

"I sure am." I was wearing a pink silk bra with fluffy bits around the cleavage and a pair of red, lacy French knickers, and I had 'Happy New Year' in Swahili henna-tattooed around my belly button.

"Happy New Year!" I shouted repeatedly as I danced on every chair and table in every bar we went to.

"Happy New Year," said Harry, an Aussie guy who was on an African bus tour and who had jumped up to join me. "I've got a bottle of champagne from Australia in my room."

"Go and get it, dude. Go and get it now," I insisted, and he ran off to do so. "Great! At midnight, we're going skinny dipping with that," I said on his return.

The countdown to midnight arrived and the four of us stripped off and ran into the sea with the champagne. It was not long before the rest of the party had the same idea and the ocean was full of party people, all naked and singing out "Happy Millennium."

~ ~ ~

"Good morning," Jamie said as she passed me in at the wooden hut on the beach that served as a local shop.

"Are you coming for breakfast?" Jo asked.

"What? It's morning?" I hadn't realised the time.

"It is indeed. What are you doing?"

"I'm cleaning the shop. I'll be over soon." I always needed to do something when I was out of it, be it dance, have sex, clean something or just fidget. I finished my task, joined the girls for breakfast and ordered a plate of toast and coffee. "Well, that sobered me up. Should I have another drink, find another shop to clean or go to bed?"

"Go to bed!" they both shouted, and off I went.

Jamie and Jo had to get back to their jobs in Botswana so, the next day, we all went back to Dar es Salaam, from where I planned to continue my journey.

At the hotel, I deposited my money belt and other valuables in the hotel safe and went out to party with the girls on their last night before returning to sleep. But I was woken at two am by a loud banging on my door. "Did you leave anything in our safe?" the hotel manager shouted through my door.

"Yes!" I opened the door to see three men looking concerned.

"The hotel's been robbed."

"Shit! All my stuff was there!"

"Is this yours?" He handed me my money belt.

"Yes." I took it and opened it fast. To my relief, my passport and cash card were still in it: only my traveller's cheques and money were gone.

"In the morning, my staff will help you to get your traveller's cheques replaced."

"What about my money?"

"We talk in the morning." And he was gone.

In the morning, I said goodbye to Jamie and Jo and went down to the front desk. A little man in a shabby suit took me to American Express where my traveller's cheques were replaced. When we got back to the hotel, the manager was behind reception. "You have to replace my money," I told him but he wouldn't take responsibility and we got into an argument.

"What happened?" asked a tall, sexy African woman passing the desk. I told her. "Come on. I'll get you a drink." She had a beautiful coffee complexion, big brown eyes and a big white smile. Her soft hand took mine and she led me to a bar across the street.

Her name was Anita and she was from Ethiopia. She sat me down with a cold beer and told me "Don't worry about money. We're alive and that's what important." The men in the bar kept our glasses full and we had a lot of fun joking around and dancing.

"Tomorrow I go to Zanzibar. Come with me." She smiled.

This sounded like a party I didn't want to miss and Zanzibar is such a paradise, it was hard to resist. "But I don't have much money."

"It's OK. We can stay with my friends in Stone Town. I'll show you how to get money." She winked as she wiped the sweat between her nose and mouth with her forefinger.

This sounded like fun. "I'll come," I said with a big grin. The next day we were off.

Anita got busy on the boat chatting with various men and how she made money began to dawn on me. I enjoyed watching her make contacts for future fleecing.

We docked in Stone Town, with its sweet smell of spices, and walked through a labyrinth of narrow cobbled lanes lined with one-storey, wooden houses, bars and restaurants. We reached a short row of houses, and Anita knocked on the door of one. "This is Sandy. He's my good brother." She introduced me to a tall, skinny, coffee-coloured man with a short afro.

"Welcome. Any friend of Anita's is a friend of mine. You two can share this room." He showed us a dinky room with a double bed.

"She was robbed in Dar e Salaam so, tonight, I will show her a good party," Anita said.

~ ~ ~

"You look beautiful." Anita had just finished dreadlocking my long hair and decorating it with coloured beads. I swished it around as I danced in my pretty sky-blue minidress.

"You also look beautiful." Anita was dressed in a golden, backless minidress and red high-heeled shoes, which made her long legs look even longer. "Let's go party." We high-fived and headed for the door.

Anita acted as my guide, leading me through the cobbled streets. "We start here." She pushed open the door to a colourful bar on a corner buzzing with people and funky dance music.

"What do you two beautiful ladies want to drink?" the handsome black man standing at the bar asked as we approached.

"Two Amarulas" Anita took control. "This is marula fruit and cream. It's not strong so we won't get drunk. We just look pretty and fun. OK?" And she pulled me onto the dance floor.

But I did get drunk, and I went home with the handsome black man.

"How much did he give you?" Anita asked when I came home in the morning.

"Nothing. I'm not a whore. I did it for pleasure," I said, shocked at the thought.

"Me too but I got this also." She showed me a sliver bangle and $100. "Still too proud to charge?"

"I'm nervous to." It had never occurred to me to do so!

"Then give it for free but where's your money for breakfast?" she scoffed.

"I hear ya, but I'm uncomfortable with this idea."

She pulled me onto the sofa beside her and looked into my eyes. "When I was a child, I had my clitoris removed by my uncle while my whole family held me down with my legs spread wide. He also raped me most nights. So I feel nothing when I have sex. Anyway, most men are pigs. I hate them." Then she pulled me to the bedroom, lay on the bed and showed me the damage between her legs. I was filled with sadness looking at this pretty woman, her soul full of bitterness, as she showed me her disfigured vulva.

"Now show me yours," she asked and so I did. "Oh, it's so beautiful. I often dream I have one like that and that I experience the pleasure of an orgasm." Now I understood why she liked to take men for all they had —and more if she could. They had robbed her of so much. She was always saying to me, "Watch this stupid man," then leading him to a bar where he'd pay for our glasses to be filled.

I noticed that the men Anita went with treated her with respect and affection and were always looking for her, whereas the ones I went with didn't even talk to me afterwards. I was starting to think she was right.

I enjoyed my time with Anita and her friends and I learned a lot but, after two weeks of partying all night and sleeping all day, I needed to dry out and get healthy so I moved on to continue my journey north, heading to Kenya.

The moment I arrived in Nairobi, or Nai-robbery as most people called it, I wanted to leave. It was rough and I felt lonely, so I called Ann, a friend of Anita's, and introduced myself. "Come meet me tonight in the Booze Bar." I was happy to have a local friend in this big scary city.

The Booze Bar was a brightly-lit, American-themed bar in the centre of the dirty city. It had booths with jukeboxes and framed posters of American idols on the wall, and it mainly served cold beer with burgers and chips. "We need a mzungu around here. You can make big money. I have an Indian guy who wants to have sex with a mzungu and will pay $150," Ann told me as we sat in a booth.

"I don't know, Ann. I haven't done it before and I'm scared."

"You're a virgin?"

"No, I've not asked for money."

"Girl, don't you know you sit on a gold mine? It'll be alright. I'll wait for you outside. It'll only take fifteen minutes and he's so small you won't feel a thing," she reassured me.

Having got to know Anita, I was beginning to think that it *was* stupid not to take money for sex, and $150 was a lot of money in Kenya, so I agreed to do it.

Ann set up the meeting in a hotel and we sat at a table and ordered two beers. "You look good. Here, go wait in room 101." She passed me the key. "I'll wait here for you. If I feel you've been too long, I will come. So don't worry."

I was sitting on a chair in the clean, neat room, wondering what the fuck I was doing, when a potbellied Sikh man came in, removed his turban, sat on the bed and beckoned me to join him. "You are very beautiful," he told me and started to stroke my face. I fell into the part easily and lay back, moaning at the appropriate times. I felt nothing physically or emotionally and didn't even raise a sweat. I was back in the bar in half an hour, $150 richer, having another beer.

"You're good at this. You want me to get you more?"

"Yeah, why not? I'm low on cash and this is so easy." I was pleased with myself.

"Then I need a cut of the money," Ann said. We agreed on 15 per cent and Ann became my pimp. She moved me into a nice room in a mid-range hotel and got me many more clients. Some only wanted to go for dinner. One paid me to take cocaine and drink wine with him. Another paid me to lie on a bed while he wanked over my tits, watching a blue movie. I only had intercourse a few times and, each time, it was quick and I felt nothing.

I was saving a lot of money.

I made friends with other prostitutes and we would hang out at a restaurant in an upmarket hotel waiting for clients. While we waited, we had a few drinks and chatted, mostly about our clients and how screwed up they were.

"Once their dick's hard, you can get anything from them."

"They're just objects to buy you things."

Most of these women had a similar story to Anita's, repeatedly raped by male family members, their clitorises removed when they were young. Just like Anita, they all wanted a look at mine.

"But I still believe in love." I really did.

"Love only happens in the movies. People only want you when you can do something for them. Wake up girl," Ann said.

"So where do you draw the line and have sex for free or even for love?" I was getting confused.

"It's never for free. There's always a price."

"I'm not sure."

One night, we all went out dancing and I pulled a cute English guy and went with him to his hotel. The sex left me feeling robbed for not charging. Yet I knew I'd have felt dirty if I had. My confusion was growing. I wondered if I would ever have sex without charging again.

At the same time, some of the other girls were becoming jealous of the amount of business I was getting, and had started telling clients I had AIDS.

It had been two months since my first customer. I had made a lot of money and lived extravagantly. I had more understanding of these abused women and their limited career choices but I knew *my* prostitution days were over. I took my dreadlocks out, stuffed three thousand dollars in my boots and got a bus to the coast, to chill and become a backpacker again.

I rented a nice little beach hut where the first thing I did was unscrew the panel of the electrical socket, stuff most of my money inside and screw it back on. Then, throwing on my bikini, I went to get in the ocean.

"Hi, how are you?" I greeted the beautiful woman, with long blonde hair and intensely-blue eyes, in the beach hut next to mine.

"I'm bored. Yeah, it's a beautiful tropical paradise but there's nothing to do but sunbathe and swim." She was 21 and on a year's break from university.

"The beautiful ocean never bores me." I came *alive* in the ocean.

"I'm from Denmark. I see the beautiful ocean there."

"You wanna party?"

"Oh yes! Let's do it. I'm Marion."

"Mate, you don't know what I've been up to lately! I could also do with a party." I went for a quick dip before we sat down to make a party plan. We invited other travellers, made a fire on the beach, mixed up a bucket of piña colada, and hollowed out pineapples for cups. People arrived with more drink, and with drums and guitars, and we drank, sang and danced all night.

"Hey, Marion. Check out the monkeys." It was early the next morning, and monkeys were screeching as they swung from the trees and rolled around the floor, play-fighting, while others sat staring into space.

"What happened?" she was as intrigued as me.

"They've eaten the pineapple cups and they're pissed." We laughed at their antics while we ate oranges for breakfast.

"I'm going to go to Zanzibar in a few days. Will you come with me?" Marion said.

"Not sure. I've just come from there and I'm heading north."

"I'm nervous going alone." Her blue eyes filled with tears and I couldn't say no.

A few days later, we left for my beautiful spice island. Giving Stone Town a wide berth, we headed straight for Nugwi. "This is truly the best place in Africa," Marion said as we walked along the golden beach, watching fish jumping out of the water.

"It certainly keeps calling *me* back!"

We passed a few weeks with sun, surf and fun until Marion needed to go back home and I needed to earn money so, instead of heading north, I flew to Cape Town.

As I stepped out of the airport and got into a taxi, I felt that the atmosphere was tense. Through the taxi window on the way to the backpackers, I saw a modern city and noticed there were a lot of mzungu around, and no snotty-nosed half-dressed black kids playing with a tyre in the street. I wasn't sure how much I liked it.

The backpackers was nicely decorated with African textiles and was clean. I was given a bed in a six-bed dorm, and was sitting on the edge of my bed wondering what I would do with myself here when a quiet English voice interrupted my thoughts. "Hi I'm Alice," said the slender girl who'd been lying on the bunk opposite me reading.

"Hi. So what's there to do around here?"

"There's the cable car up Table Mountain. Do you fancy coming with me tomorrow?"

"Yeah, that sounds great. Let's go for sunset." I was pleased to have a friend.

"That sounds even better," Alice said, her petite freckled face, framed by long ginger curls, brightening.

The 30-minute walk to the cable car took us through an immaculate, well-ordered city, where everything was in its right place; pavements free of rubble and dust, working traffic lights, proper litter bins, real bus stops instead of trees that only locals know to wait at. Funky little cafés enticed us with fresh-baked delicacies and various styles of coffee. Most bars were advertising happy hours and live music, and there were lots of enticing shops selling African artefacts and textiles. We stopped for a quick snack at one of the funky cafés and it was great to eat something other than maize. But it felt slightly *too* organised and orderly and I was already missing the African vibe.

The rotating glass cable car took five minutes to glide the 3,500 feet to the top of Table Mountain, giving us the most fantastic view of the mountain range and the city on the shores of the South Atlantic. It was breathtaking. At the top, we bought overpriced beers and sat down to watch the light fade into a deep burgundy and crimson glow.

"Last car going down," an authoritative man told us and we were glided back into the concrete jungle of noise and movement. We checked out a few bars but everything, including the people, felt fake and plastic to me after the open hearts I'd encountered in West Africa, so I went home to chill.

"I'm going to check out the beach," I said to Alice as we ate breakfast in the backpacker's kitchen.

"Can I come?"

"That'd be great!" I was happy to have company as we walked through the plastic Lego town to the ocean.

"Oh my! I can't get in that! It's freezing!" I said, running back from the ocean to our towels.

"It's invigorating," Alice said, wrapping herself in her towel. Her shivering was making me feel even colder.

It was a pretty beach so I contented myself with enjoying the view —until a strong wind came in hard and battered me with sand. "No, I can't do it." Having experienced Zanzibar, I knew it would take me a while to adjust but this beach was not doing it.

"I take it you don't like the beach then?" Alice asked, shivering.

"To be honest, I don't like it here much at all."

"Where d'ya *wanna* go?" She sounded surprised.

"I don't know. You planning anything?"

"I don't have enough money to travel but I wouldn't mind doing something else."

"We could hitch."

"That's a bit dangerous, isn't it?"

"I've hitched all over the world. It's easy and lots of fun. I've heard about this Garden Route that takes you all along the coast. It'd be a fantastic way to check out the country and get out of this toy town." I was starting to get excited.

"It *does* sound like fun." Alice smiled.

"Well, I'm doing it," I told her with confidence.

"Then I'm coming too!"

We left the crappy beach to pack.

The next day, we got a bus to the outskirts of town, and put our bags down and our thumbs out. The Garden Route was a long, beautiful, coastal road with a sea so cold that even I couldn't bear to get in on one side, and open space on the other. Backpacker hostels were not far from the road, making it easy to get to and from our hitching spots, and the interesting stops were only a few hours apart. Most people picking us up were also tourists and there were plenty of them so we didn't wait long for lifts. It was easy and a great laugh.

"I've never had so much fun. What an amazing way to travel." Alice was enjoying the adventure.

"It's the *only* way." We were taking in the beautiful ocean view while we waited for a lift.

"I didn't realise people would be so friendly and helpful."

"They usually are but I do feel an undertone of 'I'm better than you' from these white South Africans."

"Yes, and in the way they are with black people."

"Yeah, it's sad." I hated seeing black people doing only lower status work that white people regarded as beneath them. Even with my limited knowledge of the legacy of apartheid, I could see that white people felt they were doing black people a favour by employing them to do their dirty work, all the time denying them access to opportunities to improve their lives, like a decent education.

"You wanna go into 'black land'?" I was missing it.

"Yes! Let's do it," Alice squealed excitedly. So I made a sign for Lesotho and held it up at the passing traffic.

"I'll drop you at the border but I'm not going in," a big white South African man said, and we jumped into the back of his truck. We knew we were getting close when we turned off the smooth tarred road onto rubble and dirt tracks, and it wasn't long before our driver stopped for us to jump down. "Be careful, OK?" he said before he drove away.

We stuck out our thumbs. "What you girls doing out on the road? You can get killed here for being white! Get in the jeep." A rugged white face was shouting at us.

"We're heading to Lesotho." It seemed innocent enough to me.

"Do not hitch around these parts! It's dangerous. Come and sleep at my farm tonight and I'll drop you to the bus in the morning."

"Great!" And we jumped in the back of his jeep.

After a big meat feed, he gave us a room in the house—and a gun. "What's this for?" I asked, not sure how to use it.

"These blackies will come in the night and rape you or even kill you. You need it." He was spitting venom and I thought he was paranoid, but I put the gun under my pillow anyway.

In the morning, still alive and not raped, we were dropped at the bus station.

Lesotho is landlocked by South Africa and was wild and primitive, just like me. I felt comfortable and at ease there. The local 'blackies' were welcoming, kind and happy and would try to communicate with us using broken English and sign language as we changed buses in small, thatched villages.

We happily bumped along potholed roads, through the rugged landscape, sweeping plateaus, rivers and waterfalls of the Drakensburg Mountains, finally reaching Tsehlanyane National Park just before nightfall to sleep the night in a small family lodge at the bottom of the mighty Maloti Mountain.

"Wakey wakey! We're going hiking," Alice was singing to me, excited like a child.

"Good morning," I called back. It was lovely to wake up in the fresh mountain air.

We hiked all day, climbing over boulders and rocks and wading through streams and rivers to reach the peak of Maloti, 5,600 meters above sea level. There, we were rewarded by finding the prettiest wooden hotel and the most spectacular views of the valleys.

As we pulled open the heavy wooden doors to the hotel, a brightly-burning log fire warmly welcomed us. "Oh, this is so beautiful," Alice said, running over to warm her hands.

"I noticed a wooden cabin out the back. Shall we splash out and get that?" I suggested.

"Yes. We deserve it after that hike!"

We ate dinner around the fire, with a glass of wine, then went out to enjoy the night stars before crawling into our cabin. It snowed during the night and I woke up feeling as though I was on top of the world, in a scene from a Christmas card.

We hitched down the mountain to the bus stop, bussed it through Swaziland's run-down poverty and then headed back to South Africa, finally reaching Durban on the Indian Ocean.

"Yay! Back in the ocean," I sang as I jumped around in the warm water.

"Is *this* beach to your liking?" Alice asked.

"Yes, it is. I like this place. It feels less fake, it's easy to get around and there's a good nightlife." I was happy.

"I'll go and get us a bunny chow." Off she skipped, soon to return with a hollowed-out loaf of white bread filled with delicious curry.

Having seen most of the coast, we wanted to finish in St Lucia so we made our way there before heading to Pretoria to meet Jamie for a weekend of debauchery.

And then I flew back to London. It was great to see my family and friends but, once the merriment of reunion was over, it soon felt 'same-same, *no* different.' I got a lovely flat, found myself a kind boyfriend, took a job as a healthcare assistant in a hospital and another working in the bar in the football club—and went through the mundane motions of life until I'd saved two grand.

Then I was out on a one-way ticket to Mexico.

8. Blown Away: 2001

Travelling solo in Latin America was not as bad as I thought it was going to be. I had heard of women being harassed by macho men, but I used my common sense and kept my wits about me and found it to be a brilliant place to travel.

I flew into the tourist destination of Cancun, in Mexico, and set myself up in a lovely little cabaña, next to a calm, clear ocean that left ripples on the soft white sand. There was chilli for breakfast, lunch and dinner, always washed down with tequila. It was a perfect way to recover from another London work-save-drink-party run-around.

I spent my first day lying on the beach—and burnt myself red raw. "Can you rub this on my back, please?" I asked the scruffy, tubby man sitting in the garden next to my cabaña.

"That's some sunburn you have there, now!" His soft Irish accent was as soothing as the cream.

"Yeah. I'll probably stick to the sheet tonight." I winced as he slathered the cream on.

"Lucky sheet, I say. I'm Mickey. You want to get a drink?" His cheeky smile was irresistible.

"That sounds great. I've just arrived and don't know anyone or anything."

"Well, now, there's a bar over the road that gives you free tequila for just breathing." He winked.

"Let's go!" I ran back to my room and changed into a glittery, blue party dress.

The bar had soft red lighting and was decorated with sombreros and plastic cacti. The ambience was marred by a bunch of Americans loudly doing tequila slammers. I knew that would probably be me later but, sober, I found it intrusive. Luckily the dance music was louder and I sat at a table as far away from them as possible, while Mickey went to the bar.

"Get that down you," he said, placing a tray, with salt, lemon slices and the free tequila, on the table.

A lick of salt, throw back the tequila, bite into the lemon. "Ah! Naughty, but nice," and I chased it down with the cold beer he'd also bought.

"I'll get us another." He was off back to the bar and that was how the night continued. We had a good ol' laugh, dancing and being stupid until we finally staggered home.

The next morning, as I lay in bed staring at the ceiling fan, trying to piece together the events of the night before, I wasn't sure if the banging I could hear was inside my head or on the door. "Top of the morning! Come on, or you'll miss the cheap breakfast trucks." Micky was shouting through my cabaña door.

"I need a quick shower first," I said, opening the door.

"Hurry up." He was still in the same jeans and T-shirt he'd worn the night before, and his short brown hair was stuck sweatily to his red freckly face.

Five minutes later, we were walking along a road behind the cabaña, lined with food trucks giving off mouth-watering smells. "What's good, Mickey?"

"There's chileqiles—fried corn tortillas with spicy salsa—or taco-crispy corn tortilla, filled with beans or meat, and topped with salad, guacamole and spicy sauce—and that fella over there does bowls of chilli meat or beans."

"I'll get one of each." A good chilli was just what I needed to sweat out my hangover.

"That's my girl!"

Carefully balancing paper plates from each cart in both hands, we hurried to a bench, where we devoured the food like a pair of ravenous street dogs, chilli-ing away our hangovers while watching the street fill up with locals in brightly-coloured clothes and sombreros.

"I want to explore some of the Mayan ruins, Mickey. Think I'll get a bus to Tulum next and take it from there."

"Can I come?"

"I'd be delighted to have your company." He was good fun and I was happy to have a travel companion. "Now wipe that chilli off your chin and let's go for a swim."

After a week, we hit the palm tree-lined highway to Tulum, ready for whatever came our way.

As we jumped down from the bus and followed a faded painted sign to the beach along a dirt track, we could see the ruins on the top of the rock face.

We were gobsmacked by the beauty and tranquillity of the beach. The only facilities were a shop in a wooden shack, one restaurant and a few beach huts. We rented a hut each, took a swim and then climbed up the rock face to check out the ruins. "It's magical, Mickey," I said as we strolled around gazing at the ruins and the pristine beach below.

"Gets you thinking, that's for sure but nothing to do here." The big man liked to party.

"Do you fancy Belize? It's cheaper and I can't wait to swim in the Caribbean Sea." I said.

"That sounds like a good plan. When are we goin'?" His freckly face was full of excitement.

"Let chill here for a day and go the next."

"Great. Swim?" And we strolled back to the beach.

We got a bus to the border, were stamped out, took a short walk, were stamped in and we'd changed countries, culture, customs and food.

Another rusty bus took us to crumbling Belize City. "Bejeezus, this is rough." Mickey said looking out the window of the bus, as he flapped his T-shirt to try and cool down.

"No panic, big fella, we're not staying here. We're going to San Pedro." We located the ferry terminal and were delighted to find we were just in time for the next sailing. An hour and a half later, we disembarked onto a sandy street lined with wooden houses, seafood restaurants, bars and dive shops. We burst out laughing in disbelief at its simple beauty.

We got a room each in a charming wooden hotel with a sea view. I was off to swim and Mickey was off to the bar.

This was the first time I had the delight of meeting Garifuna people who live along the Caribbean coast of Central America. One theory is that they're descended from people who swam ashore from wrecked slave ships on their way to the USA.

They lived simple lives and always had time for a chat or if they couldn't speak English, a warm smile. But mostly they loved to dance. They would dance at the drop of a hat. They have a unique dance called punta. I loved it and did my best to learn how to do it. It's so sexy that, I was told, the local government wanted to ban it to reduce the childbirth rate.

We travelled through Belize, stopping off at a few tourist places along the way to drink and dance. I loved the Garifuna people but, if I wanted to communicate with more than just dance, I needed to improve my Spanish. I could speak a little Spanish and had a phrasebook, but it wasn't enough for a flowing conversation. "I've heard of a Spanish school in Guatemala so I'm going to check it out," I told Micky.

"I'm alright to stay here. I'll meet you when you're done."

"Right. I'll meet you in five weeks at The Travelers Lodge, in Tela." I left him at the bar and went off to school.

A ferry, a couple of jostling bus rides and another border crossing delivered me to true cowboy land, surrounded by a volcanic landscape. The men wore jeans with a machete tucked into the waistband, a poncho and a hat, while the women wore rainbow-coloured blouses, tucked into long skirts and long black plaits hung down their backs. I took a room near the school for the month of my course.

No one in the area spoke English so I quickly picked up the basics of the language and felt confident speaking Spanish by the time I took off to Tela to meet Mickey.

"Hey, you bolloxs!" I heard as I jumped off the bus. It was the man himself, sitting outside a dirty, run-down lodge.

"Hola, amigo." I hugged that big fella with all my might.

"We're going to the beach to swim in the Caribbean Sea. There's feck all in this shithole!"

"How long you been here?"

"I've been sitting on this step for five days now."

"Let's go tomorrow, then."

In a town with feck all to do, Mickey and I hit the booze; my first drink in a month.

I had a banging head the next morning as we went to get the bus, but my excitement took over when I saw it was full of Garifuna people, laughing and dancing to the blaring music. Mickey and I grinned as we sat back and soaked it all up.

We soon reached El Triunfo de La Cruz, and I squealed when I saw the Caribbean Sea gently beckoning me to enter her warm caress.

A big cuddly mumma was waiting at the bus stop and greeted us with a big smile. "You need room?" she asked.

"Yes, please," I replied and we followed behind her. She gave me a small room on the beach, with an attached bathroom, and Mickey a room just next door.

"It's beautiful, Mickey."

"That it is. Let's go eat."

There were no restaurants as such, but one cuddly mumma in the house next door cooked us fried chicken and plantain chips. Plantain is a type of banana but these looked like chips, smelt like chips and were very tasty. We sat on a broken wooden bench, with our plates set on an empty Coke crate that served as a table, watching the sea gently roll in over the white sands, and a lone black man on a white horse pass by.

"Feck, this is the bolloxs!" Mickey said, his smile reaching his ears.

"It's fantastic." I was almost in tears of ecstasy.

We settled into a relaxed pace of life, just enjoying the nature around us, and most nights shot pool in the local bar.

"There's a party tomorrow tonight. Let's go and rock the place." Mickey suggested one night. He was always looking for action.

We walked across a field to a barn with flickering lights, entered the big wooden doors and headed to the well-stocked bar at the back. "I'll get the rum in," Mickey said, leading the way, and we sat on empty Coke crates, sipping our drinks, smiling and greeting everyone around us.

Then the music changed and six muscular bare-chested men, with shiny black skin, came onto the stage in ripped knee-length shorts. They started moving in a very seductive way, slowly rocking on their heels and toes, grinding their butts in and out in time with the beat. "You better control yourself there," Mickey whispered into my ear.

"Does it show?" I laughed.

Soon women in long bright-blue skirts and white bikini tops joined the men in an ecstatic union of faster and faster grinding. "You better control yourself." I got him back

"Something for everyone here," he said.

Once the performance was over, the floor was for everyone. It was soon full of beautiful grinding bodies and I rushed to join in.

"How you know punta?" a local man asked when I sat down to get a drink.

"She knows everything," Mickey said.

"Tomorrow, there's another secret punta gathering. Please come and dance with us." I was delighted. My punta wasn't that good but I was well up for practising and learning more.

Over time, we got to meet most of the villagers, who treated us as welcome guests, and we settled down into village life on the Caribbean Sea. It was a delightful break from the macho side of Central America and an excellent opportunity for me to learn more punta moves and Spanish.

Until, "I'm going back to London. I need to get back to work," Mickey said one day and I was shaken awake from my dream.

"I'll come with you to Tela to see you off, and then I'll move on. Otherwise, I might just stay here forever." I was going to miss Mickey, and staying there without him would only make it worse.

"You know, we've been here for three months," he said, scratching his scruffy head.

"Wow! The time's flown."

"It's sure been great," he said, drawing me into a tight hug. It sure had.

I sadly said goodbye to Mickey—not knowing I would never see him again: he died in London a year later, in a car accident.

RIP, brother. XXX

~ ~ ~

Another hop, skip and jump and I kissed the Caribbean Sea bye-bye and entered a new country on the Pacific Ocean, El Salvador.

As soon as I got off the bus in its busy capital, San Salvador, I felt tense and I soon felt fed up with sleazy men looking at me and hitting on me. It was impossible to relax and enjoy the journey, and I missed not just Mickey's humour, company, but his protection.

So I came up with a plan: I decided to shave off my hair and eyebrows! It made me look strange and, with an appropriate expression, I could even make myself appear insane. I liked it and headed out to gauge reactions to my new image. I attracted a few strange looks as I walked down the grimy road, but no one bothered me. Hooray! It worked! Now I was free to relax and enjoy myself.

I joined a tour of the volcano that towered above the city. The climb was spectacular, with panoramic views of the city, and took all day. By the time I returned to the hotel, I was exhausted, with blistered feet, a swollen knee and, because I had no hair, sunstroke—but it was worth it.

A few days later, when I was again fit to travel, I enjoyed the (thanks to my new look) mercifully hassle-free, albeit bumpy, bus rides, and sleeping in random towns as I travelled through undeveloped areas of tall volcanoes and extensive rainforest, to Nicaragua.

I spent a few weeks visiting more magnificent ancient Mayan ruins and temples, built with astounding precision and skill. Some of them were intact and I wandered alone around the lush gardens, meditating in the peaceful, tranquil surroundings. They filled me with awe and gave me a sense of connection that helped me understand why people questioned where the knowledge to build them had come from. It felt like something powerful and mystical must have been involved and I wondered about higher consciousness, parallel universes and aliens.

Feeling a need for solitude to give me the space to contemplate these thoughts, I boarded a bus to Lake Atitlan, which fills a vast volcanic crater in Guatemala. A little boat glided me across the still, green lake, surrounded by coffee fields and pointed volcanoes, and docked me at the bottom of a steep cliff face. After clambering to reach the flat surface at the top, I collapsed to my knees, gasping for breath. Yet, when I'd recovered enough to lift my head, the spectacular view rendered me even more breathless. The big green-blue lake now looked like a mirror and was perfectly reflecting the surrounding green volcanic mountains and the cloudless blue sky.

Eventually, I got to my feet and headed to the nearest guesthouse, where I was impressed with its simple but luxurious style. My tiny room had flowery curtains that matched the bed cover and bedside lamp. The window overlooked both the beautiful lake and a well-nurtured garden, with white iron tables and chairs, where a range of styles of coffee were served in small quaint flowery cups. I sat at one of the tables to enjoy a coffee while recovering from my journey, feeling as though I was in a picture on a postcard.

"You just arrived?" asked a stunning beauty, with jet-black hair and wide green eyes, joining me at my table. She introduced herself as Ruth and told me she was from New Zealand.

"Yeah. Isn't it a picture?"

"If you like flowers," she smiled, showing me her perfect white teeth.

"Haha. It *is* a bit over the top, but so nice compared to the rest of the country."

"Yeah, it's defo been a challenge."

"Indeed it has!" I ran my hand over my bristly head.

"I'm booking a boat trip this afternoon. Do you want to come?" she asked, tucking her hair behind her ears.

"Sound's good. No more walking, please." I smiled as I gently rubbed my knee.

That afternoon, we sat back and enjoyed the rhythm of the boat as it softly cruised over the lake, beautiful green hills rising on either side of us. We docked at a wooden bridge and entered a Mayan village built with wood and mud. The inhabitants were warm and friendly, welcoming us into their homes for coffee. I was delighted to be 'sort of' able to chat in Spanish so I could learn about how they lived so in tune with nature. Then we were conveyed gracefully back across the lake, through a crimson sky, to the guest house.

"Mate, can I ask what happened to your hair and eyebrows?" Ruth asked when we sat back down on the iron chairs.

"I did it to stop the men checking me out." We laughed so much I could hardly stop.

"That's fucking nuts!" She said, then "I got some wine in my bag. Do you fancy a glass?"

"You're travelling these bumpy roads weighed down with a bottle of wine? That's crazier than me shaving off my hair and eyebrows, darling." And we laughed some more.

She came back with a bottle of red and two crazy women sipped wine out of flowery coffee cups, at the top of a volcano in Guatemala, while the stars popped out one by one.

It was nice to have company again and we decided to travel together overland to Costa Rica, otherwise known as Costa Fortune since it had become a holiday destination for Americans.

Costa Rica was beautiful, with a mixture of beach and forest, but hidden taxes made everything expensive so I couldn't afford to stay long. Ruth was happy drinking wine in the bars so, after just a week, we kissed goodbye, and I went back to the Caribbean Sea in Panama.

Panama offered a magnificent cluster of tropical, untouched islands —and good cocaine. To improve my Spanish, I stayed for a month with a local family, and took daily lessons with the lady of the house, but I was often too out of it or hungover to remember my lessons, as most of my nights were spent at my favourite bar.

The bar had a wooden platform that stretched out to sea and I loved to dance above the ocean and under the stars, with cocaine flowing through my veins.

"I want you to be my woman," said the muscular young man dancing with me as he pulled me closer to his body to grind some more.

"Sure," I replied as I stroked his soft skin.

"My name is Ahari, which means 'guardian angel'," he breathed into my ear.

"Well, I need one of those," I said between nibbles of his neck.

He was a kind, easy-going man but I was terrified of his 'elephant trunk' and had to put cocaine around my entrance to numb it enough to enable me to enjoy his punta dancing skills that went beyond the dance floor.

The family I lived with was a friendly bunch but they held racist views which meant they didn't allow me to bring Ahari home. I didn't understand why they held such views but felt unable to challenge them without knowing more. Not being able to have Ahari over was a drag but had the advantage of keeping the relationship casual and stopped him from moving in with me, spending my money and eating my food.

"I want to sleep in your arms," he told me one night, as we kissed good night outside my house. "My family has a house on an island, only a two-hour boat ride from here. Let's go there and be together."

"Maybe." I was wondering how much this was gonna cost me. Something about staying with a family made me suspect they would welcome some financial input.

"Only 15 people live there and you can swim with dolphins and turtles. I will fish and make a fire to cook every day."

"It's only Garifuna people on the island?" It did sound nice.

"Yes, of course."

"Then I would love to go." The next day Ahari organised a boat and we were off across the Caribbean Sea.

"Buiti achuluruni!" was all I could hear as we climbed off the boat and dropped onto the sand.

"That means welcome," Ahari told me.

"Ahari is home!" People were running to the boat.

"My wife," he told everybody. Fuck!

"She can do punta," he announced triumphantly and everyone clapped and hugged me.

"What a wonderful welcome," I said as we were led to a private section of the hut.

"My family, your family. Now you can relax and stop all that cocaine nonsense."

His comment took me by surprise but I knew I could do with a reset and thought his support might help me resist the demon. "Yes, a full detox."

You could walk around the island in fifteen minutes and it held just three substantial huts. It was paradise. Every day, Ahari went fishing while I swam with dolphins and turtles. Every night, we cooked and then, against a backdrop of spectacular sunsets and fabulous displays of shooting and falling stars, exerted ourselves punta dancing, both in and out of bed!

The simplicity was perfect—until Ahari starting becoming overbearing and jealous. There were four married men and two boys on the island—and he accused me of fucking all of them. I felt suffocated and trapped so I asked him to take me back to the mainland to extend my visa. When we docked I arranged to meet him that evening and then I went to my guesthouse, checked out and took a taxi to the airport, two hours away, to book a flight to Quito, in Ecuador, for the following day. I got a room at a hotel near the airport and cuddled up with my thoughts. I felt sad, leaving him like that, but I knew it was over. The way he was behaving, it wouldn't be long before the little slaps started and he put me under house arrest.

On the flight, I met two guys from Australia and it was great to be a backpacker again and trade travel stories. "Want to come to the pub tonight?" Gary, the tall, muscular one said as we shared a taxi to The Quito Backpackers.

"Why not?" I felt like something to help me forget Ahari and Gary was handsome, with big green eyes and tawny, shoulder-length hair.

I checked in, showered, donned a red party dress and found my catch waiting in the TV room. He looked fresh in a pair of jeans and a green checked shirt.

I enjoyed the brisk 10-minute walk in the fresh mountain air that took us to a lively pub, where people and noise surrounded us. The walls were painted black and draped in rainbow coloured sheets, the music was good and people were dancing. "We needed to catch up fast," I said tapping the side of my nose.

"That's my girl. I'll go see what I can score," and I watched his checked shirt disappear into the crowd.

On his return five minutes later, we went into a cubicle in the women's toilet and took a big sniff each. It was good coke and all my senses came alive. We could not stop talking and snorting.

"Time to dance," I announced. I had so much energy I almost broke the toilet door off its hinges as I pushed it open.

To our surprise, the bar was empty and the only door out was locked. "Whoopee! A free bar!" I jumped behind it and started making cocktails and we sniffed the last of the coke. Gary found the sound system and put on some dance music and we boogied away until the coke wore off.

At which point, we realised we were stuck in a bar, tired, cold and wanting to sleep, with no bed and no blankets. "I can't find a key anywhere," Gary said, searching around the cold, damp bar.

"It looks like we're here for the night." And I tried to find something warm to put over my simple cotton dress. Gary took the rainbow sheets off the wall and we huddled together to keep warm, playing 'I spy with my little eye...' until sunrise.

"I'm hungry," my stomach was growling.

"There's a slit in the front door for the mail. I'll see if we can get someone's attention."

He yelled through it until the waiter in the restaurant opposite heard him and came over.

"What's going on?"

"We're locked in, mate. Do you have a number you can call?" Gary called through the slit.

"No. I don't know anybody from the bar but the manager arrives at six pm." It was only noon.

The waiter found our situation so funny that he brought all the restaurant's customers and staff out to peek at us through the slit in the door!

"Can we get a couple of burgers, chips and coffee squeezed through this slit?" Gary asked.

"Sure!" The waiter disappeared back into the restaurant, returning half an hour later and passing us everything through the slit in the door.

"We'll just have to sit it out," I said as we enjoyed our meal. Then we waited until a noise at the door heralded the arrival of a tall, confused-looking man.

"What you doing in here?" he said as he entered, glancing around at his bar that was now looking like a campsite.

"You locked us in," I said as we legged it out the door and back to the backpackers to get a shower and some sleep.

The next day I said goodbye to Gary and jumped on a bus to Baños, where I was looking forward to floating in a natural hot pool.

It was a grubby town but the hot pool provided the perfect way to revitalise my aching body after the back-breaking bus ride which had been scheduled to take three hours but in fact took six. I floated, mesmerised in the hot pool that was surrounded by the soaring Andes. In the distance I could see women in flowing skirts and beautifully-knitted jumpers, with long black plaits down their backs, and men in woollen ponchos and pork-pie hats, manoeuvring across the rocks. It all looked like a movie set and I relaxed, happily enjoying my part.

Back at the backpackers, I was sitting in the TV room wondering where to go and what to do when a short, bald man, with big dancing blue eyes and deep red lips, came in. "Who wants to travel to Mancura?" he asked the room, grinning cheekily at me.

"When you going?" He looked like a fun companion.

"There's a bus at nine tomorrow morning," he told me and introduced himself as Delo, a DJ from Leeds, in the UK.

In the morning Delo, a Belgian couple and I jumped on the bus to reach that beautiful beach town, and checked into a friendly hotel with clean rooms set around a tropical garden, just one street back from the ocean.

Just as I was getting out of the shower, there was a knock at my door. "Wanna get some coke?" The cheeky grin of Delo beckoned me.

"I could do with a break. I'm trying to sort myself out and have some kinda profound experience, but I keep getting into all sorts of shit," I told him.

"The owner of this place said he'd do us half an ounce for $50. We could split it between the four of us." He was nodding an excited 'Yes, let's do it' at me.

"What a guest house! Pick up your coke with your keys," and we both started laughing.

"Come on! It'll be fun," he winked.

"OK, I'll make this my last blowout," and I handed over my cash. Ten minutes later, we were splitting the bag into four portions.

"I don't want any of mine left for tomorrow otherwise the session'll go on and on and I'll get worse and worse. I'm gonna do the lot tonight," I stated to Delo's shocked amazement.

"Don't fucking OD!" he called as I headed to my room.

I snorted a fat line up each nostril, and put some in a fag and smoked it. My room now felt too small as I walked up and down, working my mouth, so I went to find the others. "Let's go to the bar," I said to Delo, who was sitting in the garden, riding high and full of energy, playing an imaginary drum kit.

"Yes. There's one round the corner." And he was up from his chair like it was on fire. "Come on, you two," he called to the window of the Belgian couple and they came out with their mouths rapidly opening and closing without me or Delo being able to make out what they were saying. Ready for anything, we walked briskly to the bar, all talking at the same time.

The doors of the small bar were wedged open and we tried to pile through the gap simultaneously, like one big human ball. Eventually making it through, we walked past the few tables to the bar at the back. Most of the customers were also off their heads and there was a great, vibrant atmosphere. I sat on the bar counter and joined straight in with the madness, singing along to the jukebox and knocking back cold beer after cold beer.

After a while, I got chatting with a cute, longhaired man who took me off to a dance club. I signalled to our cocaine dealer, who I'd spotted sitting at a table near the dance floor, and he motioned me to follow him to the toilet. "You like it, baby?" he said as he cut up a couple of lines on the window sill and gave me a rolled-up dollar note to sniff it up. "Just give me ten bucks for this." And he handed me a wrap.

"You've had enough of my money today," I said as I slipped the wrap into my jeans and started to leave. He pulled a gun out of his pocket and put it against my head. "I don't care." I was too off my head to be afraid.

"I blow you away," he said, pushing it harder against my temple. I shrugged and just looked into his eyes and, after a long minute, he lowered the gun. He opened the barrel to show me it was loaded, but I was still unimpressed so he put it away.

"You tough cookie, eh?" he said as he cut me up another line on the window sill. "Now give me back my wrap and my dollar," which I did. Then I returned to the dance floor to find my long-haired man.

I came to my senses a few days later, in my bed with the long-haired guy. My head was pounding, my jaws ached and I was utterly fed up with myself. Again, the familiar questions tortured me.

Where have I been?

What did I do?

Who do I have to say 'sorry' to?

Why am I so easily persuaded?

Why do I do it?

Why do I go completely off the rails?

Why can't I stop at one?

I went for a shower and looked in the mirror. Bloodshot eyes looked out from black sockets sunk into my spotty hollow cheeks, the effect exacerbated by my face having no hair to hide behind. My skinny, bruised body felt like it had been through a mangle.

Rather than face the music of my antics over the last few days, I packed my bag, sneaked out and got a bus to the border. I slept cramped up on a rickety seat for the whole bumpy ride until I had to get out to get my passport stamped. A wobbly walk across no man's land, another passport stamp, another sleep on another rickety bus, then a change of buses in Lima to get away from the bustling city's noise and commotion, and I finally stopped travelling in Huacahina, a desert oasis with a lagoon said to have therapeutic properties.

When the bus stopped in the tiny village, I was thrilled to find a hotel right next to the palm-fringed lagoon, below the high, rolling dunes. It was the perfect place to recover from my hangover from hell and pull my addled body together. After a week, I felt cleansed and fresh, and ready to take the night bus to Cusco, the gateway to Machu Picchu, an ancient Incan city high in the Andes. I always got goose bumps when I heard about this place: my connection to it felt so strong that, when I saw pictures, I almost cried. Now I was going there, it felt like a chance to reconnect with my spiritual ancestors. Maybe some time with them would help me make sense of things.

Cusco was a vibrant city but my eagerness to see Machu Picchu took me directly to the bus station to get a ticket to the start of the trek. I was surprised that the rickety old bus, that tugged and clunked its way along a rubble road through the massive green and yellow mountains, made it to the top. Getting out of that shit heap, I felt light-headed, breathless and cold and my backpack felt like it was full of bricks. The thin, high-altitude air made the short walk to my hotel an ordeal as I attempted to lift legs of lead over the potholes in the lane. When I finally reached the hotel, I felt like a sick old lady so I spent the rest of the day in bed, acclimatising.

I felt a little better the following day so I checked out the hillside town and realised my 'ol' knee' would not be able to manage the four-day hike up to Machu Picchu, so I booked the train ride instead, for the following day.

Descending from the train, I understood why Machu Picchu was regarded as one of the Seven Wonders of the Modern World. The Incas must have been extremely advanced in technology to be able to build this empire of dry stone walls, which aligned precisely with the planets, naturally blended in with the surrounding space and seemed to be one with the high peaks of the mountain backdrops. The community was self-sufficient and able to communicate by smoke signals as far as Lima. Maybe the Incas simply declined due to the invasion of the conquistadors but people told me they mysteriously disappeared overnight. Some say they attained 'rainbow body', dissolving their physical forms into higher consciousness. The sacred atmosphere of the place made me believe it!

I followed its stony paths for hours, lost in thought and admiring the remains of this magical kingdom and its panoramic views, until I found a temple that I resonated with. There, I sat down to meditate until it was time for the last train back to town.

I had a night of beautiful dreams and spent the next day walking around, looking in wonder at the beautiful old colonial buildings lining the narrow roads.

The next day I took the bus back down to Cusco and the backpackers. "You fancy getting locked in a bar with me?" a voice whispered into my ear as I was checking in.

"Gary!" What a lovely surprise!

"There's a funky bar across the road. Do you fancy a beer?" he winked.

"As long as it's just beer. I've got a bus in the morning."

"And I'm doing The Inca Trail, so it won't be a late one."

After a few beers, we were on the dance floor, but this time the door was open, and we left to go to his room.

Feeling restored by my night of passion, I caught the bus to Nazca's desert to see another intriguing mystery; The Nazca Lines. A series of enormous geoglyphs, sketched into roughly 200 square miles of desert, they can only be seen from above so I had to fly over them in a small aircraft. The flight was an experience in itself as we glided over the reddish-brown trenches, forming the unmistakable shapes of birds, animals, flowers and trees. It was awe-inspiring.

No one knows their meaning or purpose but one theory is that they are linked to the heavens, with some of the lines representing constellations in the night sky. Another is that you can reach a sacred place, such as Cahuachi with its adobe pyramid, by walking across them.

Still reeling from this magnificent site, and wondering if I'd left my stomach in the aircraft, I jumped on a night bus to Pampas, along with some other travellers I'd met, for a jungle tour.

The tour began with a boat ride through wetlands and rivers to reach our campsite for the night. "I am the jungle man of the Pampas," our guide told us as he went off to catch an anaconda python and bring it back to show us. I did not sleep well that night!

Another bus ride took me to the world's highest navigable lake, Lake Titicaca, on the border between Peru and Bolivia. This expanse of water reflected the surrounding grassland like a mirror and I sat beside its calmness, listening to the various bird songs and reflecting on my journey around Latin America.

Another border crossing and a short bus ride took me onto La Paz, surrounded by snow-capped mountains, and filled with appealing, bustling streets leading to colourful markets. It's the highest administrative capital in the world and didn't my lungs know it! I was freezing and could hardly walk for lack of air. I had to stop every ten minutes just to regain my breath. I would wake in the middle of the night gasping for breath, feeling like someone was choking me. In the morning, before I did anything else, I had to trickle water into my eyes so I could open them, and into my mouth to unstick my encrusted lips from my teeth. Following local advice, I constantly chewed on coca (cocaine) leaves to increase my stamina, combat altitude sickness and open my airways, but it didn't seem to help. I felt exhausted so I had to move on, though I decided to visit Salar de Uyai, to see the world's most extensive salt flats before I descended to sea level.

In the thin air, my skin was as dried up as the lake, which was so white it looked like snow. Though I was almost breathless at the sight of its salt rock formations, cacti-studded islands and pink flamingos, I was truly unable to find enough air to breathe through my cracked lips, so I had to leave. I wanted to stay longer in the Andes: the people and places were spectacular and beautiful. But I was so cold and altitude sickness got the better of me so, after only three months, I had to leave just to be able to breathe again. Nevertheless, despite all the challenges, it had been worth it.

Ironically, as soon as I reached sea level, and without taking any drug, I felt the highest I had ever been. I could breathe, blink, smile and walk again. I could hardly control myself, and was laughing and dancing when I got off the bus in Paraguay. It was wonderful to have energy again.

I did a quick jaunt to Iguazu Falls, the powerful waterfall bordering Brazil and Argentina, then bussed it through Brazil and Uruguay to chill in Buenos Aires, the city whose name means 'fresh air'.

I loved it as soon as I arrived. It was a fresh, clean, modern city that was easy to get around, with a lively and vibrant energy and plenty of good bars and restaurants. The men were sexy, and hungry for fresh meat, so I took my pick of the crop, taking advantage of the abundance of love hotels.

Love hotels offer rooms by the hour, equipped with everything you might require for a sneaky quick one, including an enormous bed that sits below a mirrored ceiling. As soon as you put your keycard in the electricity slot, soft music and dim lighting comes on, creating a romantic mood. The bathroom contains soap, shampoo, a razor, aftershave, perfume, a comb and a hairbrush, and there's an iron and its board in the wardrobe. So after you've had your fill, you can clean up and leave any trace of a quickie behind you.

I was tired of getting on and off buses, so I took a simple room in the backpackers, and set myself up to stay for a while.

"Do ya wanna come to San Telmo on Sunday?" Muriel, an Aussie girl, asked. She looked like she was off to the office, in a black trouser suit, with neat short brown hair and manicured nails.

"What's that?" I was cooking lunch in the kitchen.

"It's a funky neighbourhood, the birth place of tango, and there's loads of bars and street entertainment." She was excited just talking about it.

"Sounds like fun."

"It is and, because of the financial crash, the exchange rate's through the roof, so everything's cheap. I've bought loads of clothes" She posed for me in her suit.

Sunday came and we walked down a cobbled lane, past colonial buildings, to reach the main square, which was buzzing with street art, lively entertainment and people dancing tango. "This is the best bar," Muriel said, pulling me excitedly inside and to an empty table. We ordered chicken asado and two beers, and watched a dancing couple glide across the stage. "You can take lessons if you want," she said, running both hands through her short hair to ensure it was still in place.

"Not today." I was busy tucking into my barbecued meat.

It was a lovely day and I behaved myself, having only a few beers and heading home for bed early, so I'd be fresh for job hunting in the morning.

For a week, I was on the hunt, checking the papers, making phone calls, filling in application forms and checking windows for 'help needed' signs.

"Did ya find work?" Muriel asked when she joined me in the pub to watch England play Argentina in the World Cup, on a big screen.

"No, and I'm getting bored of looking now," I told her. I was more interested in the game, in which England was doing OK. In fact, to my delight, they did better than OK, winning the game. "That's it. I'm off to Brazil for the next England game!" I said as I knocked back my cold beer.

"Jeez mate, just like that?" She didn't believe me.

"Yep, just like that. I've eaten and drank myself stupid, visited lots of love hotels and learned the tango. It's time for something new. Maybe the Amazon will offer me something deep with more flavour."

I booked a flight to Rio de Janeiro, and the next day I was in a new backpackers, in Copacabana, heading straight to a bar to watch the game. "You should try a caipirinha," the barman said as I sat on a barstool, not knowing what to order.

"What's that?"

"It's a cocktail made with sugarcane liquor, sugar and lime; Brazil's number one drink."

"OK, I guess I should get in the flow."

England were playing poorly and, after a couple more caipirinhas, I forgot all about the game and went off dancing. It was a whole *new* ball game on the dance floor as I went from tango to salsa. I watched and quickly learned the basics but, as the caipirinha flowed, I couldn't handle all the spinning my partner was making me do, so I let go of his hand, closed my eyes and just did my own thing. I was not surprised when I heard we had lost the game, and I was happy for Brazil.

I woke with a hangover and needed the beach. It was next to the main road; nothing private or pretty about it and the waves were big and dangerous, so I was nervous about getting in. Unimpressed, I found a piece of unoccupied sand and lay down to sunbathe, jumping into the water only briefly to cool off or pee.

"No nudity, ma'am," said the police officer standing over me. I wasn't naked: I had a G-string on so I was a little confused. "Put your top on or $50 fine," he looked serious.

"Honestly? But this is Brazil!" I looked up and down the beach and noticed that the other woman had little straps covering their nipples, so I picked up two seashells and placed them over my nipples. "Is this OK?" But he wasn't amused, so I put my top on to continue my laze on the beach, watching Brazilian beach life.

As the sun was setting, I noticed a gathering of people making strange movements to music. It was amazing how they moved their bodies so I joined the crowd to watch. "What is this?" I asked the guy standing next to me.

"Capoeira," he told me, explaining that it's an Afro-Brazilian martial art that combines elements of dance, acrobatics and music. It was developed by enslaved Africans in Brazil at the beginning of the 16th century, to disguise martial arts.

"Wow! It's impressive." I was mesmerised, watching muscular bodies gently glide around in perfect synchronicity.

"You should go to Salvador. It's bigger there." I made a mental note of that.

There was no other action besides this, so I went home to see if anything was happening at the backpackers. "Want to go watch the game tomorrow?" I asked two blonde girls from England sharing my dorm. Brazil and Germany were playing in the final.

"We're going to watch it on a big screen at Copacabana beach. Come with us."

The game was taking place in Japan and kick off was at eight am Brazil-time, yet the beach was packed. Everyone, including the dogs, was dressed in the colours of the Brazilian football team, and all you could hear was the chant 'Bra-zil! La la la la la la la la!' The excitement and energy flowed through everything. Even the food and drinks were in the team's colours. When Brazil scored, the crowd went wild 'Bra-zil! La la la la la la la la!' The people in the building across the street from the beach threw torn-up bits of newspaper out of the window, to fall like streamers. The atmosphere was intoxicating and, when Brazil won, the crowd went bananas, and the party began. There was live music on the beach, and lots of dancing in crazy, flamboyant costumes. Dancers on floats in a Gay Pride procession blitzed the place with sequins and glitter. Drinking stalls were popping up everywhere, ready to blend tropical fruit and liquor into a creamy shake. I was swept away with the excitement and enjoyed all of it on full power until someone grabbed me to salsa and started spinning me around this way, then that way, then this way again—and I threw up all over the place and had to go home.

"Where did you disappear to?" I asked the blonde duo in the morning.

"We came back to sleep, to be fresh for the parties."

"What parties?" They'd never invited *me* to any parties.

"Usually, the parties start at midnight. Brazilians sleep after work, then they go partying and just catch an hour or two of sleep before going to work the next day," the friendlier of the two said.

"We didn't want to wake you up. You looked deep in sleep," said the other with a smirk. It was pretty apparent that two was company but three was a crowd, so I left them to it.

I adapted to the Brazilian lifestyle and culture quickly and learned most of the moves of the dances, which are such a huge part of Brazilian life. Even though I couldn't speak much Portuguese, I could dance so I was ready to go party in the streets of coastal Salvador.

Salvador was full of Afro-Brazilian people, and there were loads of parties on its cobblestone streets, from which alleys branched off to large squares with colourful buildings and baroque churches. With the caipirinha flowing and the cocaine blowing, I was out every night, shake, shake, shaking.

One morning, with a heavy hangover and knees and hips swollen from dancing, I realised I needed to rest, so I took the three-hour boat ride to Morro de Sao Paulo and got a cabin near the beach to chill.

On my first evening, after a big, healthy feed, I went to my cabin for an early night but distant music came bouncing off my walls, calling me to come out to play, and I couldn't resist.

Walking onto the beach, I saw an enchanting, colourful bar, with a few tables and chairs and people dancing. The music drew me in and my legs auto-piloted me to the bar. "Oh no! I meant to say 'Coke'," I told the sexy bare-chested barman who was passing me a cold beer.

"Baby, wait until I've finished. I've got the best coke," he winked.

I considered my options. Should I go back to my room or finish my beer? I knew if I finished the drink, another would follow and then what? Well there was nothing to do back in the room, so I finished the drink and hit the dance floor.

The next day, I came round in an unfamiliar room, surrounded by a crack pipe, cigarettes, beer bottles and used condoms. Shit! where was I? I was weakly attempting to sit up when the bare-chested barman came into the room, gave me a smile, lifted a floorboard and pulled out a bag of coke. Trust me to pull the dealer as soon as I arrived! I came here to chill! What was his name again?

I had a quick wash, dressed and opened the door to leave. The barman was sitting outside with some people. "See you tonight," I threw over my shoulder as I walked away, knowing that was a lie.

Later that day, I sat alone on the beach outside my cabin feeling exhausted, sick and depressed. I was a prisoner of my addictions with no control over, or connection between, my mind and body. My mind was up for anything and everything even though my body was screaming 'No!' Then as soon as the first drink went down, I had no control of either. One's too many, and a thousand is not enough. I didn't know who I became and, half the time, what that person did. All I knew was I didn't like her and she got me into a lot of trouble. I thought, maybe, if I take a load of coke, I'll get bored and stop. No, that wouldn't work. If it was going to, it would have done by now! But I had to change something.

After a few days of self-hate and shame, I went back to the mainland. I sat alone on a dorm bed in a backpackers in Salvador, questioning my life. "I'm 39 years old, with no intention of marrying, having babies or building a career. I have no real friends or a boyfriend, and I've travelled everywhere I want to go. What now? The only time I've ever felt right is when I'm travelling. Maybe I should go back to nature. How about the Amazon rainforest? After all, that's what I came here to see."

I stopped at a coastal town on the way, where I met Samuel, the Rasta-Amazon jungle man, selling amazingly-intricate jewellery on the street. "Can you teach me how to make it?" I asked him in my limited Portuguese one evening as we sat on the street corner.

"You pay me?" he shrugged.

"I can rent a house in the village for a month, buy all the materials and cook the food. You just teach me the jewellery."

"I know a place," he smiled.

We rented a simple house in a beachside village, next to a pretty, deserted beach, with a backdrop of high sand dunes. For a few days, we worked quietly, with no distractions. He taught me techniques for twisting metal into shapes, fastening them together and adding beads, to fashion beautiful pieces of unique jewellery.

Then one day, "You capitalist pig!" came out of nowhere while we were sitting making jewellery on the front balcony. "Your jewellery is shit!" He picked a piece up and threw it. "You think you can buy me." And he walked out.

I had no idea what had sparked him off but, over the following days, I came to realise that I could never be sure what would come out of his mouth next. Life became tense and I was sinking into misery. However, over the two weeks we'd spent together, I had learned enough to practice and develop my own style so, for my sanity and safety, I decided to leave. With my stock and tools, and a new way to make money, I sneaked out and jumped on a bus.

I felt relieved to have got away from that abusive man as I sat on a bus through vast dunes on one side and wild beaches on the other, to reach the tourist resort of Jericoacoara. I found a lovely guest house and headed to the beach, with my jewellery on a board. To calm my nerves, I had a swim in the freshwater lagoon then walked along the soft, untouched, natural white sand to the crowded part of the beach, where there were a few restaurants with tables outside, to try my luck.

"That's a nice piece," a Brazilian woman said, having called me over to her table.

"I made it myself," I said more confidently than I felt.

"Where are you from?" she asked me in response to my accent.

"England."

"You're from a rich country like Great Britain, where work and money's easy to come by, and you're doing this?" she laughed.

"What?" The man with her exclaimed, looking at my board. "I'll take this piece for my niece. She'll be delighted to have a piece of jewellery made by a girl from Great Britain!" News went around that a British girl was making jewellery and selling it on the beach, and business was good.

Until, "Why you come here and take our business? You can work in your own country," an angry seller said to me one day.

"I'm not taking your business," I told him.

"Yes, you are. The people buy from you because you are from a rich country and then they don't buy from us." He spat on the floor.

"I don't force them to buy from me," I said, defensively.

"Stay off the beach or I will call the police. I bet you don't have correct work papers."

He was right. In fact, my visa was due to expire so I went to the nearest city to extend it. "You've overstayed your visa. This is a severe case," the officer in the immigration office told me.

"I have not! It's for three months." I showed him the three in my passport.

"That three means thirty days. You have seven days to leave the country, and you must pay a $500 fine," he told me authoritatively.

"Shit! Where do I pay the fine?"

"Either here or the airport."

"OK, I'll pay at the airport."

At the airport, I had two choices. Pay now or pay on my return. I chose 'on my return', knowing that probably wouldn't be in this lifetime.

I flew to New York to try for work there. But it wasn't long after the September 11th terrorist attack so it was hard to find a job without a Green Card. Selling jewellery on the street seemed like hassle so I went home to good ol' London to see my family and friends and get a job there.

Of course, the excitement soon wore off once I had caught up with everyone. They were still doing the same ol' things, and most of them were miserable and too busy to meet up with me as often as I'd have liked. Bored and lonely, I could feel myself being drawn into the type of drunken mess I was trying to avoid so, after just two weeks, I was on the road again, to meet Muriel in Portugal so we could travel through Morocco together.

9. Nothing But Hassle: 2002

"It's so great to see you again. You saved me from getting stuck in London," I said, hugging Muriel having got off my flight to Portugal. In a pair of combats and a T-shirt, she looked more casual than the suited girl I had met in Argentina.

"Well, there's nothing much to do here. Do you wanna head straight off to Morocco tomorrow?"

"Sure." I wanted to keep moving.

As soon as we docked in Tangier, the contrast with Europe was tangible. Almost every man was dressed in a dirty djellaba and staring at us as if we were naked, even though we were covered from head to toe.

"Fuck, it's tense here," I said.

"Fuck mate, look at him!" said Muriel in horror, pointing to a man shamelessly stroking his balls as he stared at us.

"Let's get out of here," I said, leading us to a bus stand.

We were quick to jump on a dusty bus to Larache just as the muezzin's call started, and men ran towards the sound. Sitting on the rickety bus, I was happy to be back on the road, even if that road was a potholed mess, the ride was accompanied by screeching music and I felt like an exhibit in a museum. After an hour of this, we reached the almost-modern port town, Larache.

The bus had hardly come to a halt when the doorway filled with dirty, dusty men looking to see what they could fleece from the white women and Muriel and I looked at each other like soldiers about to go into battle. Suddenly, I noticed someone had collected my backpack from the boot and I jumped into action and pushed through the men at the door. "Hey! Leave my bag alone!" I shouted. I knew he only wanted a tip for carrying it but it made me nervous that it would get stolen.

"Payment, payment." He had his tobacco-stained hand out.

"What payment?" I said, pushing him away and taking my backpack back.

"Porter," he insisted.

"You just took it out of the boot, now fuck off!" His dirty, stained teeth and grubby hands were making me feel sick.

We pushed through the touts and walked briskly up a dirty, dusty street to a beachside hotel. It was well-maintained compared to the street outside, and we got a nicely-decorated twin bed room with a sea view. We dropped our bags onto our chosen beds and I opened the balcony doors to a beautiful ocean, licking the yellow sand that wrapped the rocks and boulders like a soft blanket. "This beach is beautiful." I began to strip off so I could shower the predatory glares off my skin along with the dust.

"Fucking hell, mate! It's a nightmare out there. Sexually frustrated little pricks, or what?" Muriel said, lying down on her bed.

"I know, but would *you* fuck the ugly fuckers?" I laughed as I got under a hot shower.

"Maybe it's more chilled on the beach," she said hopefully.

We each scrubbed our bodies and clothes with vigour, covered up in trousers and T-shirts, with only our arms showing, and ventured back out along the short path at the side of the hotel, to the beach. We set ourselves up next to a giant boulder and sneakily stripped to our bikinis, trying to blend in with the boulder as much as possible. "I think that guy behind the rock over there is wanking," Muriel said.

"He fucking is! This is too much!" Disgusted, I quickly covered my body with a towel.

"Looks like the beach is out. Let's go to the ancient Roman ruins." Muriel proposed and I agreed.

The uphill climb was hard work in the stifling heat, and it was irritating having to avoid stares and catcalls all the way. But the ruins were pleasant and peaceful and the picturesque view over Loukos estuary made it worthwhile. We enjoyed a quiet stroll along grassy paths through the ancient site until, a couple of hours later, Muriel said, "I'm hungry. Shall we brave the market?"

"Well, we gotta eat!" And back down the hill we went, keeping our eyes straight ahead, as though wearing blinkers, to avoid attracting male attention.

In the bustling market, we found many little shacks selling everything but their mother. We followed our noses, allowing mouth-watering spicy aromas to lead us to a stall displaying a row of tagines, with their cone-shaped clay lids. "This one looks and smells the best," I said as I lifted its clay cone to reveal layers of aromatic meat and vegetables.

"Yeah, I'll go for that," Muriel said, drooling.

"Two of these and a pot of sweet mint tea," I told the guy behind the counter, and we sat down in a corner to enjoy the delicious food, ignoring the gazes of everyone that passed by.

"Wow! With food like this, I can put up with the lascivious stares," I said as I mopped up the sauce with a hunk of bread.

"It doesn't seem to matter what we wear, mate. We're just gonna have to get used to it." And she was right.

A quick stroll took us back to our hotel, where the manager greeted us with a big smile. "If you stay two more nights, I give you a big discount." He was in his mid-thirties and casually dressed in baggy pants and a long, flowing shirt. Having enthusiastically accepted his offer, we went to our room to gaze at the ocean from the safety of our balcony, with no sex shows.

We spent the next few days sneaking swims in the early morning, eating tagines and drinking herbal teas.

"I make you a farewell party," the manager of the hotel said as we were going out for lunch, on our last day.

"OK. We'll be back by four," and off we went into the bustling marketplace. On our return, the manager was waiting for us in the lobby with two cans of beer.

"One each," he smiled, showing his black-stained teeth.

"Thank you," Muriel said, taking her can, and we all sat down on the armchairs in the lobby.

"You can have mine as well," I put mine on the table. I knew one would fire me up into a search for more, and I didn't want to become that girl here—or ever again if I could help it.

"I don't have a wife and I lonely. You stay longer. You can have the room for free," the manager offered, adjusting his balls.

"We have to meet friends," I lied, giving Muriel a 'don't you dare agree!' look, and went off to bed.

In the morning, we took a beaten-up bus to Rabat. We were not even out the bus door before someone was at our luggage. "I'll take that, thank you!" I said, taking my pack back. We booked in at the first hotel we saw, then went for a walk in search of a tagine, the only pleasant thing we'd found in this country so far.

Rabat was a sprawling city and quite pretty but, having been constantly hassled for sex or money, we left the next day on the morning bus to Casablanca—where we experienced even more hassle.

Even though we dressed and behaved appropriately, we were treated like whores and, no matter how hard I bargained, we were always overcharged. Honestly, Moroccans would charge you for the air you breathe if they could—and then return with a tax bill.

Needing to relax and wanting to enjoy our trip, we headed to Marrakesh, thinking it might be more touristy. It turned out to be colourful, with a maze-like medieval quarter, and a central main square that transformed into an evening market alive with street entertainment.

"This is better, Muriel," I said as we walked a beautifully-tiled lane, with hanging baskets of flowers, to our hotel.

"Indeed it is." Her relief was evident. "Oh my! This it's like a palace," Muriel laughed in delight as we walked between tall pillars of a gleaming white arch to the reception desk of our riad, where pools, fresh flowers floating on their surfaces, lined the walls.

"It's amazing!" I was also stunned as we walked through another tall arch to the rooms. The rooms were set around a lily pond, surrounded with decorative textiles, pottery and stone benches. We passed through the carved wooden doors of our room into an opulently-decorated paradise, with a capacious four-poster bed in the middle. "Finally! Civilization," and I lay down on the comfortable mattress, giggling gleefully.

"Let's hit the market tonight," Muriel said, pulling a pretty top out of her backpack.

"Yes, about time we had some fun!"

We excitedly walked around the market, with its pretty, colourful twinkling lights and buzzing music, checking out bright clothes and knick-knacks on the stalls—until the smell of the spices got my tummy rumbling, and I couldn't resist a delicious bowl of couscous.

I sat down on a stone bench, enjoying the aromatic flavours while watching the bustle and listening to the music. "How's your couscous?" asked a half decent-looking guy that came and sat next to me. I was not in the mood for men so I just nodded, but Muriel started a conversation.

"Mohammed has invited us back to his house and he's got beer and wine. Come on. Let's go."

"I could do with a drink." The journey so far had been disappointing, we hadn't had much fun since we arrived and my self-control was wearing thin.

"That's the spirit," she smiled, and we were off.

Mohammed had a lovely house and seemed genuine, so we relaxed on his roof, drinking wine and smoking a spliff to the accompaniment of the call of a muezzin.

"Come again tomorrow for good home cooking," he said as we were leaving.

"Sounds cool," we agreed and walked the 10 minutes to our luxury hotel to spread out in our clean bed.

The next day, we walked around the maze-like medieval city, with its thriving markets, mosques, palaces and gardens, at a more leisurely pace. "This is better," I said as we stood watching a snake charmer with his dancing cobras. We were constantly stared at but had hardly been groped or pestered.

"It still has to be the craziest place I've ever been!" And we found ourselves laughing uncontrollably as all our pent-up frustrations came out. It *was* mental but, underneath it all, I did feel relatively safe.

We went to a rooftop restaurant and sampled an assortment of kebabs while watching the crazy show below, before going home to shower and dress for our home-cooked dinner at Mohammed's.

"Quite the party man," I said, as we sat on his roof surveying his supply of puff, coke and Es, without a sniff of food. Muriel and Mohammed popped an E while I tucked into the coke. "I guess these are our starters. I wonder what's for the main course," I said in a low voice when Mohammed went to get cold beers. He came back with a beer each and invited Muriel to accompany him to another room. I entertained myself with the supplies and dancing.

Then Muriel burst into the room. "Let's get out of here quick while he's in the toilet. He's spiked my drink with another E. I could see it floating in the glass. I don't know what he's up to but it feels dodgy." Her words were all falling over themselves and she looked bombed and scared.

I grabbed the puff and we darted out the door and back to our hotel. Sitting at the lily pond, I rolled a spliff and we chilled out. "That was a nice dinner," I said and our laughter danced around us, echoing off the marbled walls.

After a smoke and a long calm moment, "Shall we get moving tomorrow?" Muriel's voice broke our stoned silence.

"Yeah, I don't want to see Mohammed again. Let go to the desert."

In the morning, we managed to book a night train to Fez before returning to our room to pack and check out. Leaving our bags at the hotel, we went for our last walk around the crazy city, eating little snacks from the stalls, with our eyes peeled for Mohammed.

The train was shiny and clean and, having settled into our carriage, we nodded off for a few hours.

When we arrived in Fez, we were delighted to hear no 'honk honk'. It was a car-free zone—but not a hassle-free one. The city is enclosed behind a high stone wall, and we entered through its imposing wooden gate. All eyes were on us, looking for something, as we walked the narrow, winding labyrinth lined with stall after stall of colourful pottery, carpets, and leather goods, looking for our hotel.

"Get the fuck off me!" I shouted at a man, reeking of tobacco, who was either trying to grope me or rob me.

"Fuck! There are touts, pickpockets and perverts on every corner," Muriel was horrified.

"Let's just book the Sahara desert tour and get out of here." I was exhausted by all the attention.

The next day, we were off in a jeep. Surrounded by the Atlas mountain range, we drove for 10 hours through the desert's vast plains and sun-baked dunes. When we reached the end of the dirt track, we climbed on waiting camels and took off to our campsite, to sleep under the stars at a Bedouin camp. Our guide showed us our tent, which contained a sizeable mattress and woollen blankets, then took us to the master tent, where we were served a delicious tagine with sweet mint tea, while being entertained by traditional Berber music and dance, as a golden sun set over the dunes.

"What a beautiful evening," I said as we snuggled down for a peaceful sleep.

Our guide woke us early to watch the sun rise over a sea of orange dunes, while we were served breakfast of bread and sweet mint tea. Then he took us on a camel ride across the golden desert and over the dunes.

A quick lunch of bread and cheese and we were back in the jeep. "That was beautiful," Muriel said as we bumped our way back along the dirt track.

"It was a wonderful and hassle-free time, alright."

Back in Fez, we got a bus to Chefchaouen, a city in the Rif Mountains. We rented a room in a hotel on the main square of the old town, next to the red-walled kasbah and a mosque. The area was enchanting, with blue-washed buildings and steep, cobbled lanes lined with leather and weaving workshops. This hidden little town is a global hashish manufacturing hub so, because most of the ball-scratchers were stoned, we were left alone and finally started to enjoy ourselves both in and out of the few restaurants that looked out over the main square

~ ~ ~

"Happy birthday," Muriel greeted me one morning.

"Fuck! Forty and still no sense," I laughed.

"All that's on offer is a tasty tagine, apple tea and a game of scrabble," she told me as she gave me a little kiss on my head.

"That will do me. I'm just happy I'm still alive."

We sat at a table outside our favourite restaurant in the main square and ordered a tagine and a pot of apple tea. Despite what I'd said earlier, I was edgy and grumpy because, in truth, I wanted a real party, and my mind kept wandering as I tried to work out a way to get some booze. This was my first birthday without a big party in twenty years.

"Can we join you ladies?" said a chunky Spanish man.

"Sure! We love entertainment," I said, nodding at his guitar.

"This is Pedro and I'm Marco," and he sat down and started to play Spanish classical music while Pedro got busy skinning up.

"More apple tea, please," I asked the waiter and the alcohol-free party began.

I woke the next day with no strange man in my bed, no hangover, no memory loss, no one to say sorry to and no bruises. "I feel great! I'm alive and I'm sober. I don't have to be drunk to have a good time," I sang out the window in the morning. It made me realise that what I needed to do was shift that thought 'It's boring without a drink' that was so embedded in me, and my habit of filling time with sex, drugs and rock 'n' roll.

~ ~ ~

Ramadan had started and I knew it was time to get out. "I've experienced Ramadan three times before; in Egypt, Israel and Zanzibar. It's not pleasant," I told the others as we sat playing cards after breakfast.

"Why not?" asked the innocent Marco.

"People can't eat, drink or smoke during the daylight hours. And they cannot have sex for the whole month. They get very aggressive."

"I did see people arguing today," Muriel piped up.

"Yep, and it's only day two." I was ready to leave.

"I'm driving back to Spain in a couple of days. Come with us?" Pedro said.

"Excellent." I looked at Muriel, and she was nodding a big 'Yes!'

As we crossed the border out of Morocco, Muriel and I guessed something was up because Pedro slipped money to the customs officer. We pretended we didn't see and said nothing. Then crossing the border to entered Algeciras, in Spain, a customs officers pulled us over, and the car was unloaded and searched.

They found nothing.

One went off and came back with three sniffer dogs. Still nothing.

But they were not giving up. Another brought a screwdriver and started to dismantle the car's boot. "What's happening?" I asked Pedro who just shrugged.

The officer removed a panel at the bottom of the boot and, revealing it to be a false bottom, found forty kilos of tightly-wrapped hash, covered with mint.

"Oh, *that's* what happening." Apart from on the telly, I had never seen so much hash, I was mesmerised.

"Can I take a photo?" Muriel asked.

"I don't think that's a good idea," I told her.

Until then, it had seemed like a laugh but, when the police slapped handcuffs onto our wrists and put us into a cold cement cell in the police station at the port, we realised we were in trouble.

"Please don't worry. I'll admit it's all mine and you were just getting a ride," Pedro told us through the bar of his cell as we watched a comedy show play out. The officers were so excited at having made such a big bust that they did not know what to do with themselves. One paced up and down, giving a nervous twitch that made his whole body jump every couple of seconds, while smiling gormlessly at us. The other two were falling all over each other, copying each other's antics that involved moving things around on a desk.

The fourth officer was a woman who just seemed to be in the other officers' way. "You've had it now," she smirked.

"I need the toilet, please," I told her for at least the tenth time.

"No toilet for a drug dealer." Oh, she was a bitch.

"OK, I'm going to do it right here," and I started to undo my jeans. She grabbed me and took me to the loo, where I had to pee with the door open while she watched. Then she pushed me back into the cold, damp cell, and I continued to watch through the bars as other busts were brought in. Hash had been stuffed into shoes, empty shampoo bottles, toothpaste tubes and cameras, and the other two cells at the station were now packed, mostly with Moroccans. They were observing Ramadan, and it was time for them to eat. "Allahu, Akbar," they shouted continuously through their bars.

We finally got an interview with the Chief of Police and were taken to his office. "No comment. I want a translator," I told him.

"Tomorrow translator coming," he told us, before taking us to an interrogating room, where we were searched several times, our jewellery was removed, our fingerprints were taken, we were photographed, our stomachs were X-rayed and we were given identity numbers. Slapped back into handcuffs again, we were put into a police van, transferred to a prison on the other side of town and placed in a cold cell with flea-ridden blankets, and graffiti all over the walls.

"I'm busting to poo," I told Muriel as I checked out the hole in the floor that served as our toilet. There was no toilet paper and no water to flush with or to wash your hands.

"Oh, just do it," she said.

"This cell is depressing and smelly enough without me adding to it." I sat tight.

The following day, back in handcuffs, we were put into the same police van and taken to court.

Upon arrival, police officers grabbed us and pushed us into another cell, with no toilet, where we stayed for four hours. I got escorted to the toilet by a police officer and tried to do my poo, but I couldn't do it with her watching so I just had to wait it out with my swelling aching stomach.

In court, Pedro admitted it was his hash and they let us go. I think Pedro got four years.

We kissed Marco goodbye outside the courthouse, hitched a lift to Valencia and booked into a nice hotel—where I finally had my poo in private!

"I've showered and scrubbed my body three times, and it still doesn't feel clean," I said to Muriel as I washed my clothes in boiling water.

"I need a drink," was all she could manage to say.

"Me too." We dressed in our best clothes and went to the nearest bar. It was a lively bar playing funky music, full of young people, and I couldn't wait to get into the groove, so I headed straight to the bar for a well-deserved beer.

"If you could have any drink you wanted, what would it be?" the bald guy next to us asked as we sipped our cold beer at the bar.

Muriel and I looked at each other, and said in unison, "beer."

"Come on, girls! I'm only in town for tonight and I'm alone. I would love a night out. Don't worry about the money. I'll put it on expenses," he said, a big grin spreading over his round face.

"Brilliant! We just got out of gaol and need a piss up. But no sex!" I told him.

"Gaol?! You'll have to tell me all about that. Let's get on the slammers and have some fun." And fun it was. He sure picked the right people to show him how to spend money and have a good time. We went everywhere and drank everything, until the early hours of the morning. When we couldn't find any more alcohol places open, we went to Moneybags' posh hotel and raided the minibar until it was time for him to leave, giving us money for a cab home before he did.

Soon after that, we took a bus to Barcelona, where it rained all the time, which was not our favourite weather.

"I'm going to Thailand," Muriel announced one day. The lure of Thai food, culture, beaches and men meant that I wasn't far behind her.

10. Bucket Power: 2002

"Sawadee ka," I greeted the immigration man as he stamped me in for thirty days. It had been five years since I was last here, and I had forgotten how much I loved the place and the people. It felt like coming home. Tears of ecstasy filled my eyes as I walked through the arrivals gate and got a bus to the port, to catch the boat to my favourite island, Kho Chang.

The size of the ferry was my first clue that things had changed. When I first came to Kho Chang, eighteen years before, a small boat dropped you as close to the shore as possible, leaving you to wade your way to land with your backpack over your head, colourful fish darting around your feet.

Now there were three piers and no fish, and the small bamboo paradise that I remembered so well was a concrete jungle, full of hotels, bars showing English football, restaurants with English food, ladyboys and whores. Surely there had to be an area better than this!

"Keep driving," I told the taxi driver and we continued along the bumpy dirt track alongside the beach until, eventually, I found a less developed beach, which had only three resorts and one bar. A construction company was making a mess in the middle of the beach, building a big, concrete hotel, but it was as good as I was going to get, it was getting dark and I needed a shower and something to eat, so I got out of the taxi.

The beach huts were all occupied so I walked into the jungle, found a resort with just one hut left available and took that. It was small, and next to the smelly communal toilet, but it would do for one night. Tomorrow, I told myself, I'll get up early, walk around and find a nice place to sit still for a few months. After travelling the last fourteen months, I was tired and needed money, so a few days chilling out on the beach was just what I needed while I made a plan.

The following day, I walked along the beachfront, enjoying the fresh sea breeze and the sand under my feet, until I reached a resort with an open-plan restaurant that looked out to the ocean.

Between the restaurant and a row of beachfront huts, a palm tree-lined path ran to the main road through an area of grass, interspersed with flowers, banana trees and papaya trees. Another row of huts run along this path. I noticed someone coming out of a beach hut with a sea view. I wanted that hut!

Approaching the middle-aged Thai man behind reception, I pointed it out. "Is that hut available?"

"Yes, but we need to clean. Come back later." But that made me too nervous that someone else might get it, so I paid for a week right then, went and got my luggage and sat in the restaurant to keep an eye on it.

"A vegetable rice soup," I told Ying, the pretty Thai girl behind the counter and savoured the smell of Thai food while I pulled my jewellery out to check it was intact after the journey. My rice soup arrived, smelling delicious, and I was quick to remove three of the metal lids of the glass condiment set and add a spoon each of fish sauce, chilli flakes and vinegar with crushed chillies. The top of the sugar stayed on. Satisfied with the taste explosion, I spooned it in until my mouth was on fire and my eyes and nose were running.

"That's unusual jewellery," the guy sitting at the table next to me said.

"I made it in Brazil," I replied between sniffs.

"How much is that necklace?" He picked up a bamboo piece.

"I don't know. 100 Baht?"

"I'll take it." I couldn't believe I'd made a sale so easily! Maybe this is what I'm going to do, I thought, as I finished my soup.

My hut was ready and I climbed the four wooden steps to reach my balcony and enter. There was just a bed with a mosquito net, a few nails in the wall to hang your clothes, a western toilet, a sink and a cold shower. I opened the two windows, put the fan on and unpacked my backpack. That was my home sorted: now to sort out my work.

I found a piece of cardboard, covered it in a red velvet vest and hung my last ten pieces of jewellery on it. Feeling nervous and unsure, I took a deep breath and set off for the beach. My head was preoccupied with questions as I walked out of my resort and along the beach. Is my jewellery good enough? Will people like it? Will the police arrest me? Will locals harass me?

I kept going until I noticed a closed bar. A small tree grew beside it, providing shade, and I propped my board against its trunk. "It's OK I sell here?" I asked a Thai vendor, who was walking up and down the beach with his board of jewellery.

"No problem. Not same mine." And he sat with me for a while and reassured me I was fine and my jewellery was beautiful.

I was still unsure until I sold two pieces to a young girl passing by. Excitement ran through my body and I celebrated with a swim. My job was sorted!

My hands could hardly keep up with the speed at which my jewellery sold but soon my board was full of exotic designs and colours.

~ ~ ~

"I found ya!" It was Muriel, who'd been travelling up north and had come to visit me. "You want a beer?" And her slender body disappeared into The Nature Bar next to my tree, which was preparing to open for sunset, and returned with two cold Chang beers. These of course, led to another each, and another and into the bar.

It was a simple wooden bar, under a palm-tree roof. On the sand were tables on plastic mats, surrounded by a few cushions and with a candle in the middle. Muriel and I reclined against cushions and supped our beers while watching the sunset bathe everything in a lavender glow. Once it was dark, three sexy, bare-chested Thai boys came out and performed a fire show. I think every girl watching that had a fire show of her own going on in her pants!

A group of young Thais, with a bucket drink, joined our table and the sexy one, who had shoulder-length black hair and shining eyes, sat next to me and passed me the bucket. "You like?" I wasn't sure if he meant himself or the bucket, but the answer was 'Yes' to both.

"I like." I took a big suck on that straw.

"My name Chai," he told me in the softest voice. "I work there." And he pointed to the construction site between the bar and my hut.

"You wanna dance?" I asked and he was up in a flash, pulling off moves so sexy I felt compelled to take him home to groove in my bed.

"I go work now," he told me the next morning. "I come tonight." My heart melted as I watched his hairless muscular body as he put his shirt on and walked out the door.

"He's fit!" my neighbour said as I opened my window.

"I know, but Thai men are like chocolate cake: they look good and taste good, but they are very bad for your health."

"Haha! You've been there before, then?"

"Yeah. They can't keep their dicks in their pants, they tell lies and they're possessive, but I can't resist them. They're just too sexy!"

"I know what you mean!" she laughed. "I'm Sarah. Catch you later." She headed to the beach tossing dreadlocks that were as thin as her anorexic body.

I was so happy I could hardly contain myself and sung as I showered. I had everything: a home; a job; a beautiful lover and friends, all on a tropical paradise. I practically danced along the beach on my way to my tree to set up my board, and I sold plenty again.

Making enough stock to keep up with demand gave me backache and blisters, but I carried on, improving my twists of metal and becoming more adventurous until I had a wide variety of designs and needed a bigger, better board.

"Can you bring me four pieces of plastic piping?" I asked Chai as I passed the building site on my way home. That night I made a four-foot-by-four-foot square, covered it in black cloth and hung my jewellery on it. It looked great. In the morning, I went to the beach with my easy-to-transport shop, leaned it against the tree and chilled out.

"You can use my bar in the day. It's no open, so no problem," Lek, the manager of Nature, told me.

"Maybe later." I felt shy but he picked up my board and moved me in there.

Now I had a shop in the middle of the beach and business was great. My shop became the beach's meeting spot and girls would gather to hang out and make plans for the night. It was great for custom but having to act as agony aunt to emotionally-incontinent western women, moaning about their Thai boyfriends, was a nightmare.

He will not let me out.

He will not let me drink.

He will not let me talk to her.

He beat me.

He's shagging another woman.

Then leave him! It seemed like the obvious solution to me.

~ ~ ~

"Look behind that palm tree," Muriel said. She was hanging out at the shop and had spotted Chai hiding behind it, spying on me.

"Yeah, he does that sometimes. The funniest is when he uses binoculars to spy on me from the roof of the construction site."

"Why's he spying on you?" She knew I was besotted.

"Ask him. I haven't a clue." He'd been the only one in my bed, night after night, for the last three months, but he always thought I was cheating on him.

"I find it freaky. Let's get in the water."

As we swam out to sea, I watched Chai go back to work.

~ ~ ~

"I have to leave the island," Lek said one day when I was at the shop. "Three of my girlfriends are all here, right now," he explained while checking whether any new girls were alighting from the taxi that had just pulled up at the next door resort.

"Why don't you settle down with a nice Thai wife?" I asked.

"Thai women don't want a beach boy. We have tattoos, long hair and dark skin from the sun. They like farang."

"But farang go home."

"They like white skin and money," he laughed.

"Is that why there are so many skin-whitening products?"

"Yes. And they keep their body covered when they're in the sun." Then he noticed a young girl getting out of the taxi and was off after the fresh meat.

~ ~ ~

I woke one morning to find a dead dog lying on my balcony. Its furless body was covered in open sores and it looked like it had been beaten. The stink was bad. I went to reception and asked for help to bury it. Ying came out from behind the bar and we went back to my hut and tried to move the reeking carcass.

But then I saw it breathe. "Wait! It's not dead!" I cried.

"I don't know any doctor here for dog." Her big black eyes were full of concern.

"I guess we'll have to leave it here and see what happens." Leaving bowls of rice and water beside the dog, I went to work.

To my amazement, when I got back, she was roaming around looking for food. "It's a miracle! She's alive!" I said to Ying as I passed the restaurant on my way to my hut.

"Not for much longer if the Cambodians who work in the kitchen get her," the manager said.

"What do you mean?"

"She was disturbing the guests at the dinner tables and she smells no good." He screwed up his face.

"Please don't kill the dog. I'll take care of her until she gets better," I begged the kitchen staff who reluctantly agreed. Despite her condition, the dog had a beautiful face and love in her eyes. I had to help her. So I now had a dog, who I named Smelly.

~ ~ ~

Christmas came and so did the parties—and the weirdos. Who knows what stone was turned up to let this lot out. Hippies, new-agers, cowboys, kilt-wearers, rockers, ravers, dopeheads, pillheads, pissheads and me! On Christmas Eve, my little beach hosted twenty-foot speakers and sound blasted everywhere.

I was so excited to party that I bought a new pink miniskirt and a red halterneck crop top, blow-dried my now shoulder-length hair into a tidy bob, and put glitter around my eyes, on my chest and on my legs. I was ready to rock this party!

"Fancy sharing an E?" Muriel said as we approached the celebrations.

"No, you're all right." But when I looked around the party and saw the state of everyone else, I thought, why not? If you can't beat 'em, join 'em. "Go on then, gimme that E," I said as we headed to the bar, and I popped it in my mouth.

We sat on a mat and toasted Christmas, watching girls dance on top of the twenty-foot speakers.

"I can't get up." I wanted to join in on the speaker action.

"Then don't," Muriel said, patting my knee.

"But I want to dance up there with them!" I managed to get onto my knees and starting crawling around on the sand.

"Just sit still." Muriel pulled me back to the mat.

"I can't. I'm full of energy. I need to swim." But I couldn't move my legs.

"Chai," Muriel called over to the mat next to us. "Sit with her. She drink too much." And she pulled him onto our mat. Unsure how else to stop me crawling away out of sight and into trouble, Chai tied my foot to a tree with a six-foot-long piece of string. Then he sat with me, sharing buckets.

I came to in the Thai/Cambodian tin-shack village on the construction site, with Chai and his friends sitting around a karaoke machine doing loud, out of tune 'sing-song'. "You do carrot cake?" one asked.

"Maybe. Let me see cake." I wasn't sure if I fancied cake right now.

"English song." He passed me the mic and *We wish you a merry Christmas* blasted out of the machine. I kept looking for the carrot cake —until I realised he meant karaoke! I took the mic and sang along.

Eventually, "We go room now," Chai said and he half carried me back to the hut, where he washed and dressed me so that we could go to meet the others already partying on the beach.

"You were wild last night," Muriel said as I joined the party.

"I feel like shit and don't remember a thing," I confessed as I gulped down a cold beer.

"This'll sort you out," and another E was down the hatch.

This time, I woke in my hut, nude, surrounded by empty beer bottles, five naked Thai men—and no recollection of how I got there or who the men were. "You OK in there?" Sarah was calling through my window.

"What happened? Who are these guys? Where's Chai?" I was bewildered.

"I haven't seen him. I just heard some kind of a party here last night but I was pretty out of it myself," she told me as she entered my hut. "You can all leave now," and she gently pushed the Thais out, with their clothes in their hands, and sat on my bed to offer me a bottle of cold water. "Drink this."

"I'm so ashamed of myself. I need something stronger than that."

"Why? So you can go and do something worse to cover it."

She was right. My whole body ached and I had chest pain and a sore throat. "I need a swim to sort me out," I said and I pulled on my bikini, sheepishly left my hut and headed to my shop.

Passing the construction site, I saw Chai. "Finished. I no more love you," he told me in disgust. The day seemed to get more confusing every second. What the fuck happened? Where was Chai last night? Who were those guys and how did they get into my hut? It was obvious Chai had made his mind up. Tears pricked my eyes at the thought that our relationship was over. "I will always love you," I told him. And it was true.

I continued onto the bar to put my board up. Feeling even more like shit and ready to cry, I went for a dip in the ocean. I floated on the calm, warm water, trying to get some normality back into my body. I had hit rock bottom and I needed a new direction.

"Hey, get over here. I want to talk to you." The Dutch guy from the dive shop called. Oh shit, what now? "You know, last night you tried to drown yourself?"

"What?" I didn't believe him.

"You'd've succeeded if I hadn't seen you out there. I had to swim out and drag you in, resuscitate you and put you in your hut. You were out cold."

"I don't remember a thing." But then I had a flashback and horror filled my body. I remembered feeling fed up with myself and my addictions, and swimming out to sea and asking the ocean to take me. The Thai men must have seen it all happen and, knowing I was out cold in my open hut come in for a free for all with my unconscious body.

"You got a big problem, lady. You'd be dead now if it weren't for me," the dive guy said, shaking his head.

"I'd probably be better off dead," I told him and I meant it.

"You need to stop drinking. I bet you can't stop for a week."

"Of course I can."

It sounded easy enough but it wasn't. Parties were everywhere and all anyone talked about. I went along to the bars ordering just water but, after an hour, I would start to get irritated by everyone around me talking gibberish, laughing at nothing funny and telling me to 'Go on! Have a drink.' I refused the drinks and would go home feeling lonely and sad. I had trouble sleeping and, when I managed to drop off, nightmares would wake me. I'd lie there in a cold sweat hearing music from the parties, and people laughing and singing. But I was determined to win the bet.

And I did.

In fact, I won more than just the bet. I won my life back. After that week, I didn't want to get drunk anymore. I had seen the ugly side of party life and realised that half of my life had been spent either in a drunken haze or sleeping off a hangover. As for my poor abused body, it was battered and my brain was fried.

Without booze and drugs to numb me, it was becoming increasingly difficult to ignore the pain from my knee. It stopped me sleeping, prevented me from dancing and made it hard for me to get about. I kept hearing the voice of that doctor back in the UK, *"You're going to need a knee replacement in the end"*. The very thought of the operation and its long recovery time horrified me. I saw myself stuck in dreary old London, hobbling around on a stick. But more than that, what if it didn't work or I didn't make a full recovery, and I became even more disabled? I'd managed until now with sunshine, massage, swimming and the occasional painkiller. Would I still be able to travel and explore with a piece of metal as my knee? At the same time, now that I was sober, my days felt long and empty. I needed something to fill the time I used to spend drinking and recovering.

Then like a miracle, two yoga teachers moved in next door to me for a month. They looked so healthy, fit, and happy. "I want to be healthy like you," I said to Ellie as she sat next to me at breakfast, her toned body glowing.

"Come do yoga with us tomorrow morning," her radiant husband, Texas, said.

The following day, I joined them on a platform that looked out to the sea. I felt inadequate, stiff, overweight and stupid as I struggled with the postures. I couldn't even sit up straight. "Just do what you can. It's not a competition." Ellie lovingly guided me through the moves. I tried my best to bend and stretch into the postures, as I watched the ocean coming and going and the party people staggering home.

As the days passed, I felt so relaxed and blissful after a session that I even started to like myself and knew that I didn't want to hurt myself anymore with the stupid things I did when I was drunk. I would find myself smiling for no reason. Ellie and Texas also taught me an effective relaxation technique to help me sleep. I had something to get up for and was ready for yoga every morning.

After a month, I was starting to build a little muscle, develop a waistline, and my stomach was becoming flat and toned instead of wobbly. But more than that, to my amazement, my knee was less swollen and more flexible. It no longer hurt so much when I bent it. Could this be the alternative to surgery I'd dreamt of?

"What will I do without you? I'm petrified I'll start drinking again and I want my leg to keep getting better." I said as they were preparing to leave the island.

"I'll draw you some pictures, and you can do it by yourself," Texas offered.

"That'd be great! Can I also tape one of the sessions with my Dictaphone?" I had brought with me the one I had used to record patients' care plans, and was using it to record poetry that I spontaneously composed.

"Yes, of course."

The day they left, I was terrified of being alone on Party Island with no yogis. It was up to me alone to keep up my practice.

Over the next few weeks, I hung onto my Dictaphone like a life raft, sleeping with it next to my pillow. As soon as I woke, I would press Play and Ellie's voice would fill my hut and my heart. "We will start with a breathing exercise," she would sing out of the machine and I would jump out of bed before I had a chance to think about doing anything else.

Some days, my mind was willing but my body was tired and I didn't want to do it. Other days, my body was willing but my mind was tired, saying, "I don't have time. I did it yesterday." I was searching for the intellect in the middle, where willpower and dedication lived but for now, at least I had the willpower to press that play button every morning, and jump into yoga action.

That hour and a half session became my rehab for one year. I couldn't do yoga with a hangover so, every time I was tempted by a drink, I thought about my morning yoga, and yoga usually won. It is not easy to give up the habit of an adult lifetime but I had a strong tool to help me develop a new lifestyle and interests.

The next stage was to get off the beach where temptation surrounded me.

"I have a spare bedroom in my house in the fisherman's village. It's just local people and there are no bars or restaurants," Lotty, a French girl, said to me while we were sitting in my shop. "Do you want to rent it?" Her big grey eyes were enticing me to say yes.

"Smelly?"

"Of course! Smelly's welcome." Her pretty smile almost reached her ears when I nodded in agreement.

The house was open plan and on stilts, set back from the road in the rainforest, surrounded by banana, papaya, mango and coconut trees. The central area was for sitting and cooking, and there were two partitioned-off bedrooms. The toilet and shower were in an outhouse just a few seconds back into the jungle. A five-minute hitch, or about a thirty-minute walk got me to the beach and my shop. The journey was easy during the day but dangerous in the dark. I was nervous about snakes, drunk drivers, getting attacked, maybe even being raped, and not stupid enough to think I'd encounter anyone sober to give me a lift. Which was great because it kept me home, listening to the night calls of jungle animals and getting to bed early. It was the perfect place to keep away from temptation while I adjusted to my new lifestyle of yoga and meditation.

~ ~ ~

"What the fuck is that?" I asked Lotty at six one morning, as I was putting my yoga mat down on our back platform that reached into the jungle.

"That's the neighbours' 'sing song' machine. Here, do this." The switch for their electricity supply was in our house and she flicked it off.

Silence.

"Just flick it back on in about half an hour when they've gone to work."

I settled in nicely but jewellery selling was hit and miss and I needed some backup money. So when the rainy season came, I went back to London and got a job as a healthcare assistant in a hospital. I did agency work so I could choose my shifts, days and wards, and avoid getting involved in workplace politics. I kept head down, working as much as possible and spending my days off with my mumma. Knowing that soon I would return to my beautiful house in Thailand, Smelly and my jewellery business kept me sane.

When I arrived back in Thailand, Lotty and I got busy cleaning up our house after the rainy season and transforming it into a beautiful home. "It looks magnificent. Let's go dance," Lotty said excitedly.

"I'm trying to stay clean but I guess a little welcome party will be OK," I agreed. We went to The Sunshine Bar, in the forest. It was buzzing with people when we arrived, and the music was lively, so I went straight onto the dance floor while Lotty settled down onto the big slumber cushions with some Thai boys, to get stoned.

"I'm going to go home, Lotty, so I can do yoga in the morning." I'd been dancing for over an hour and was tired.

"I'm going to stay." She gave me a subtle wink.

It felt good walking the jungle road home, sober, with Smelly, snuggling into bed and falling asleep.

I was jolted from sleep by the glare of motorbike lights through my window and the sound of giggling voices, and then kept awake by music and voices blaring from our sitting area.

In the morning, after I'd cleared away empty beer bottles and overflowing ashtrays, the house felt clean enough for me to do yoga and I unfurled my mat to stretch and welcome the new day.

"What was all the noise, last night?" I asked Lotty when she emerged from her bedroom.

"I have a naked Thai man in my bed," she whispered.

"Which one?"

"Kit." The barman from The Sunshine.

"Ooh, enjoy!" And I went off to sell jewellery, hoping this wasn't going to happen every night. I had gotten deeper into yoga and meditation and was going to bed at ten to get up early and practice as the sun rose over the jungle.

But, as I feared, every night Lotty and Kit would wake me up when they came home. Often, there would be a random person or two sleeping in the sitting room, all stinky and sweaty from a night of raving. My life was becoming miserable due to sleep deprivation and reeking hungover Thais in my yoga space.

The only peace I could find was when working at the beach, and with Smelly, and even that was starting to change. Wooden shacks were popping up all over the place, to host 'ladies'; in other words, prostitutes. Naturally, they attracted sex hunters looking for pussy, and the police had started to visit regularly to take other vendors and their jewellery away. It made me nervous since I didn't have a work visa.

"It OK. You sell here. I say it's mine," Lek said, but I wasn't sure it was safe. My little paradise was changing and I had a feeling that I should leave. But then my Smelly got pregnant and I was not going to leave her alone.

On New Year's Eve, I went to the beach party but something told me to go home. When I got there, Smelly was lying in my room, not moving. She was in labour but something was not right. She had a puppy stuck inside her.

I opened her legs and helped her get it out. I did the same for the second puppy but, after four hours of trying, I still could not get the full body of the third out. My increasingly desperate calls to the island vet went to voicemail, probably because she was still partying, or sleeping off the night before.

After what seemed like forever, the vet picked up and she came and gave Smelly an injection to induce her, but the pups still would not come out. "She needs surgery. You'll need to take her to the mainland," the vet told me. "I'll call around and see who's open." And she got busy on her phone, while I comforted Smelly, who must have been in agony.

"I've found one that will open. Go now or she will die," the vet said urgently.

"I need a driver. Can anyone help?" I asked into the space around me.

"It's New Year's Day. The whole village is drunk," Lotty said, more interested in the spliff she was rolling.

I managed to get Smelly and the two puppies down to the road and tried to hitch a ride to the ferry. "You give me money, I take you," a drunken fisherman said.

"OK., OK. Let's go! Fast!" And I got in the back of his truck with Smelly and her two baby boys.

As it turned out, the four puppies still inside her were dead, but beautiful Smelly and the two baby boys I delivered survived. I found two Thai friends to take the pups once they were old enough, and let them choose names. The firstborn became Pee Mi (New Year, in Thai) and the second, Elvis.

Until the pups went to their new home, we would all hitch to the beach to set up shop. Usually, I would get a truck and jump in the back with Smelly and the two babies but, sometimes, I would fit the four of us on the back of a motorbike. Pee Mi and Elvis enjoyed the beach, and I would take them for a swim to give Smelly a rest.

One day Lotty came to the shop and sat down with me. "My friends are coming to visit from France. I hope it's OK that they stay with me at the house." Did I have a choice? "You will love them," she reassured me. "Jonathan is gay and Lilly is a cross-dresser. They're adorable."

"Well, as long as I have my own room, I guess it doesn't matter how many people are sleeping all over the sitting area and kitchen," I said, reluctantly. I was getting fed up living in a shelter for the lost and bewildered.

"It's not for long and you'll love it!" That big smile was not convincing me.

They arrived with all the drama that a certain type of gay man can bring, making their grand entrance into the wooden house as if it were the stage for their grand finale at Gay Pride, peeling off their clothes and dropping them randomly everywhere, until they were in tiny Speedos and ready for the beach.

I left them to it and tried to stay out of the way, just going to the shop and coming home for shower, bed and yoga.

Valentine's Day came, and the beach was abuzz about the party. I thought I would go as I hadn't been out for a month or so. Returning home from work, after sunset on the day of the party, I climbed our wooden steps to see Lilly sitting on the floor, all her stuff strewn about her. "This nail polish matches my shoes," she told me excitedly as I carefully tiptoed my way across the minefield of clothes. "And I think this top because it matches my violet eyes." She held up a glittery vest.

"You will party with us tonight, please, please!" Jonathan emerged from the hammock and strutted up and down in his tight jean hot pants in the limited space available.

"Yes, tonight I will come out to play. But it's a one-off, OK?"

"Yes!" And he clapped his hands.

I went to the outhouse for a shower and, on my return, found Lilly all sequins and glitter in her pink stiletto heels that matched her nail polish. Jonathan, in a pair of skin-tight spandex shorts and a leather belt, was dancing around a load of Thai boys and Lotty. "You're coming to party with us tonight, I hear," Lotty said, all excited.

"Well, I'm not getting any sleep or peace in this house, so I may as well jump on this crazy train." I was up for a big night with the wild bunch, so I put on my pink miniskirt and red crop-top and joined Lilly to use her makeup.

We went to Lottie's boyfriend's bar. "It's Thai culture, Lilly. You must take off your shoes when entering a building," I told her as we were entering the bar. I was already barefoot as I knew shoes often went missing outside bars and restaurants.

"No, they go with the outfit, darling. I cannot." And she strutted up the wooden steps to make her grand entrance.

Everybody else in the packed bar was barefoot so a stocky ladyboy in stiletto heels, treading on people's bare feet, was causing a few problems. Bang! A Canadian redneck, had punched her in the face and she was on the floor. She took off a pink stiletto and started smashing it at anything that moved. All hell broke loose.

"Lilly, come over here!" I grabbed her arm to pull her away and, before I knew what was happening, she lashed out and bashed me on the head about four times. Lottie's boyfriend grabbed my hair and started kicking me around the bar. There was not a lot that I could do about it as I was already down.

Somehow I managed to break free and, with blood pouring out of my head, I went home to be with Smelly and her pups.

Finally facing up to the fact that this house was hardly the right place for spiritual enlightenment, the next day I packed my backpack, rehoused the pups and left Smelly with the Thai boys at Nature Bar. With an aching heart, I left for Bangkok to arrange my visa and flight to India.

I found a cheap deal which involved a two-hour flight to Bangladesh, a stopover in a hotel and another two-hour flight, putting me in Delhi the following morning. All I had to do until the flight left was wait five days for my visa.

Sitting in a filthy, dingy, cramped plywood room in Bangkok, I felt lost, lonely and depressed. My dream life had crashed around me before it had even started. No house. No dogs. No jewellery business on the beach. No friends. It was all gone. I thought, "There must be more to life than all this suffering all the time. Even when I live in paradise, I'm not happy and, even when I try to go sober, there's bullshit." Maybe I would find the answers in India.

Part Two

Introduction

It was time to let go of that life, use ancient wisdom to reprogramme a lifetime of habits, turn inward and seek out the self. It would take discipline, hard work and practice to apply these tools to my life, but I was ready to do whatever it took.

1. Om Sweet Om 2004

The first thing I saw when I entered the airport was chaos at the check-in desk. There was no queue; potbellied men with macho moustaches, and round women in saris, were pushing, shoving, shouting and checking-in all types of electrical equipment, oversized suitcases and themselves. I got behind the smallest group of people and waited my turn.

The smell of unwashed bodies and curry began to make me feel sick. Plus, I was the only white person in the cluster and many people were staring at me. Then I realised I was showing my shoulders and quickly put a T-shirt over my vest, pulling it down over my jeans to cover my arse and fanny.

"Where's your husband?" the man next to me said, picking his nose.

"I'm meeting him in Delhi." It felt safer to say I was married.

"You have children?" he enquired, his breath gusting over my face.

"They're with my husband." I could almost taste his lunch and it made me heave.

"Where are you from?" The way he looked me over repulsed me and I tried to turn my back on him, but I was lodged between all the other sticky, smelly bodies.

"UK." I answered. Then, "please step back," I asked the man behind me who was pushing his body against my back.

"Sorry, sorry. What's your good name?" He didn't move away.

"Fuck off! That's my bad name." I gave him a shove as I moved to the side of him. That stopped the questions and I managed to get some peace through the rest of the airport security madness and make it onto the plane.

In all my years of travelling, I had never seen an aeroplane in such bad shape. The battered, ripped chairs had no tables on their backs and my shoes stuck to the carpet as I walked down the aisle to my seat which, of course, didn't recline. I was in shock as I watched the wobbling fat people in front of me fight over seats and locker space. "Why did I buy such a cheap ticket? Am I sure I want to leave Thailand?" I thought as I looked out the dirty window at Bangkok airport.

"Looks like they put the only two white people together," said a bulky old man, his bright-red face full of broken blood vessels, as he tried to squeeze into the seat next to me.

"Oh, yes," I said, relieved that he wasn't stinking of curry.

"I'm on my way back to Germany. I need to rest now after fucking all the pretty girls for two weeks." His hands cupped his cock, and he gently stroked it like it was a sick child. Speechless, I turned my head away to look back out the window. "One night, I brought a girl back to my room, and she turned out to be a boy. I refused to pay the full price but, once I covered his lap with a cloth, he looked like a little girl, so I let him milk me," he told my back in triumph. That was the reminder I needed as to why I wanted to get away from Thailand.

The pig next to me was woken by the chaos heralded by mealtime. Cabin crew call bells dinged merrily as people helped themselves from the food and drink trolley while others walked up and down the aisle, pushing the trolley and cabin crew out of the way. One guy even started a fight. "I'm glad this lot is not drinking," I said to the pervert as I accepted my tray of salmonella.

"Look!" he said, pointing to a bottle of whiskey being passed around in front of us.

"Thank fuck it's only a two-hour flight," was all I could say.

Finally, an announcement told us to fasten our seat belts to prepare for our landing in Dhaka. But no seat belt was equal to that landing! As we bumped up and down, and swerved off the runway, I was thrown around in my seat, and the Cockstroker ended up in my lap. Some of the other passengers jumped out of their seats and shouted at the cabin crew.

"Sit back down and remain calm. There will be a delay as there has been a problem with the brakes," an announcement told us as we came to a halt on a grassy bank. I pushed the Cockstroker off me and closed my eyes to avoid any more disgusting conversation about his sex life.

After half an hour, an announcement told us we could leave the plane and a tidal wave of potbellied people started pushing, shoving and shouting as they tried to fit through the tiny slit of a door. They almost knocked over the army and police officers who were waiting on the ground to cram us onto a bus to the airport terminal and transit desk.

As we piled through the door to a grubby little room, a police officer took our passports to ensure we didn't try to escape into Bangladesh. Then we had to wait for the staff to sort out who was going to which transit hotel.

Four hours later, I finally got to my hotel. The room was en suite and clean, with a kettle and a TV. I had a lovely hot shower and settled down for a few hours' sleep.

In the morning, I went downstairs for my complimentary breakfast to find an empty restaurant of just six tables, each covered in a stained tablecloth, cutlery and a vase of plastic flowers. I took a seat by the greasy window and watched a tall, skinny man, in a stained white shirt and crumpled shiny black trousers approach. "What would madam like for breakfast?" he asked in a heavy accent, pushing back his oily black hair.

"Fried eggs on toast and a tea, please," I smiled.

"And lunch?"

"I don't need lunch, thank you. I'm in transit. My flight to Delhi is in an hour," I said with confidence.

"Your flight is delayed while they repair the plane, madam."

"Fucking hell! I hope not with glue!" He just wobbled his head and walked off.

I was starting to feel nervous about this cheap airline and my situation.

After breakfast, I went back to my room and flicked through the TV channels to find something in English. I found a crappy movie which I half-watched to get some kinda respite from my mind, which was continually criticising me for taking a cheap flight just to save a few quid.

Five hours later, there was a knock on my door. "Plane big problem, madam. When there is a flight, I tell you," the same head-wobbling man told me.

"Do you know how long?" There came the wobble again and he walked off.

Two hours later, I was finally on a grubby minibus through Dhaka, on my way back to the airport. I looked out the dirty window, both horrified and excited as the slowly-moving bus crawled through a never-ending stream of traffic. Colour, movement and a symphony of noise swirled around a sea of rubbish.

When we pulled into the airport, I was thrown back into chaos. A throng of unwashed, potbellied people, with oily black hair and moustaches, engulfed me, dragging me from the bus to armed police, who escorted us into a small room with a few metal chairs. In front of the exit door was a desk protected by a dirty plastic shield. Behind it, a guard with a waxed moustache that reached up to his eyebrows, in a faded brown uniform with shiny buttons, stood proudly holding a battered tin box that contained our passports.

He would call out the name on a passport and that person would push through the crowed to stand in front of him. "Name?" Hadn't he just called it out?! He would look at the photo, then at the person, several times before handing over the passport. Reuniting each person with their passport took a full 10 minutes. I was the only European and the only woman but, twisting his moustache, he still went through the whole procedure, making me wonder if I would make my flight.

But finally, reunited with my passport, I boarded my connecting flight to Delhi.

This flight was just as chaotic and I was grateful when I landed at Delhi airport in one piece. But I was horrified anew when I saw passport control. The queue should have formed an S-shape but the people had taken down the ropes and were clustered around the passport check desks in a disorderly mass.

Well, I wasn't standing there all day! With elbows out, I went into the mass, pushing and shoving with the rest of them while elbowing and kicking off the gropers. I finally made it to the other side, feeling like I had just woken up from a nightmare, only to re-enter it as soon as I walked through the exit.

It had been eighteen years since I was last here and it had not changed at all. It was still a great, big, noisy, polluted, grey dustbin.

I pushed quickly past the other people at the prepay taxi stand, paid for my ride, got my ticket and jumped into a taxi to my guesthouse. Staring out the taxi window at what looked like a war zone, with half-dressed, disfigured people dragging their bodies around, I wondered if I had made the right decision to come here. It looked rough and dangerous.

My taxi pulled up at my guesthouse and to save coming out again, I dived quickly into the clothes shop next door, away from the hustle and bustle. "Any discount if I buy three?" I asked the shopkeeper, holding up a long skirt that looked like it would suit my grandma better than me.

"No, this is the best quality cloth, madam, but I give you a shawl for free."

"Great." Happy to have some tent-like clothes, I went to my guesthouse to shower and sleep.

In the morning, dressed as an old lady from the '50s in my new long skirt, baggy T-shirt and shawl, I stored my backpack at the hotel and got ready to brave the streets to the train station. I was going to Rishikesh to look for a yoga ashram, a centre for spiritual learning and religious practice.

Outside the hotel, I stood under a grey, polluted sky, lined with a mass of crisscrossed electricity cables on which monkeys swung. On either side of the narrow, cramped, noisy, potholed street were hotels, restaurants and shops that looked worn out, sad and in need of refurbishment. On every bit of space in front of these were stalls selling food, fruit, veg and clothes that hung from the crossbars. In the middle of all this madness, multitudes of people, motorbikes, bicycles, cows, dogs and ox-drawn carriages, full to the brim with colourful things, moved in every direction. The noise was deafening.

I took a deep breath, kept my focus and, like a warrior going into battle, fought my way through scruffy, dirty people trying to sell me all sorts of junk; through pickpockets, scammers and even snake charmers moving around me in every direction. I looked straight ahead, trying not to inhale the smell of shit, stale piss, exotic spices, deep-fried oil and petrol, or to catch the haunting, hollow eyes of maimed and disfigured beggars of all ages, dressed in rags. The lepers seemed to be little more than open sores with bits of flesh hanging off them, where the flies were feasting. When they saw me, they followed, asking for money in a constant whine, pulling on my clothes or grabbing my feet or hands. One snotty kid gestured that she needed food while grabbing my hand. I felt her trying to pull my ring off my finger, so I pushed her away as I dodged another on a makeshift skateboard, whining beside me, not giving up.

I was relieved to reach the train station and stood against a greasy wall to recover and brave the next step; buying a ticket. I was pleasantly surprised to find a tourist ticket desk and, within a few minutes, I had a ticket for a train that night.

With ten hours to kill, I went back into the asylum, found a juice bar, and sat on a stool outside to watch this dance of constant movement accompanied by its cacophony. I had just ordered a pomegranate juice when I heard a voice over the commotion. "What you doing in Delhi?"

"Waiting for a train to Rishikesh. What are you doing?" I said to the attractive young Indian man who sat next to me.

"I'm waiting for an interview for a job in Australia," he explained, introducing himself as Raj Kumar. He was smartly dressed and spoke good English.

"Nice place to wait," I smiled.

"I've nothing to do and you have nothing to do. Do you want to go be tourists?" He nodded to encourage me to say yes. I shrugged, as I wasn't sure of him yet. "I have a motorbike and I can show you around the city," he was still nodding encouragingly.

"OK." I had nothing else to do.

After a few hours dodging in and out of noisy traffic through an overpopulated, polluted city, looking at dusty dilapidated buildings, I was sweaty, hot, dirty and overwhelmed. "You are a guest in my country. I must show you great Indian hospitality and get you a room so you can clean up for your train journey," Raj said.

"That sounds like a great idea." He had been sweet and kind all day, not letting me pay for anything, and I felt I could trust him.

"This room is easy for you to get the train," he said as he checked us into a mid-range room opposite the train station. After a hot shower, feeling fresh, I was ready to leave.

"Please stay the night with me. Please," he begged.

"But I have a train to catch!"

"Go tomorrow, please. We can go get your bag and you can rest here for the train." The look in his dark eyes was so desperate and sad that I felt sorry for him, plus I felt I could do with a bit of loving after that flight and entrance to India, so I decided to stay.

We got room service and had a lovely time together. I only left the room once—to rearrange my train ticket—until I left to get the train. My first, and only, 'Indian takeaway'.

Leaving the hotel, I was submerged back into the freak show outside Delhi station. "Hey! You come here. Go there. Want a hotel? You need rickshaw? Come with me, I have discount ticket." I pushed past them, suppressing the desire to punch them in the face. I needed to learn patience but with the overwhelming noise and big black eyes watching my every move, I had none.

I reached the entrance and negotiated an obstacle course of bodies, sprawled-out on the floor with their luggage, trunks, bags and suitcases, to the display board to identify my platform. Some people were cooking, while shooing away the dogs and beggars that roamed around in search of crumbs. I was scared but also excited, with my senses coming alive as I stood looking up at the giant cracked board that told me my train would depart from platform eight. It was lucky I had a backpack because there was no lift and I had to climb the stairs, along with a mass of others going in every direction.

To my relief, I spotted another white woman through the mass on the platform, and I pushed my way to her. She was short, and looked approachable behind her outsize black-rimmed glasses. "Hi. Where are you going?" I asked.

"Rishikesh," she told me in an American accent. I felt she had come to guide me.

"Me too. Can I tag along with you? It's my first time going there."

"Sure. I'm Nancy. What's your plan there?" she smiled, revealing a perfect set of white teeth.

"I'm looking for an ashram to do some yoga." The words sounded strange to me: I still couldn't believe I was going to do this.

"I work in the office of an ashram. Come with me if you want."

"Thank you. I will." This was the sign I needed. Everything started to feel alright. We had seats in different carriages so we agreed to meet on the platform when we got off.

I squeezed through the train door into the packed sleeper-class carriage and was instantly gasping for breath due to the overwhelming smell of fart, masala and unwashed bodies. I carefully stepped around and over the people and kids that were already sitting in the narrow aisle, eating, burping, grunting, farting and snoring, looking for my seat. It was like a bustling market as vendors pushed up and down selling tea and snacks. "Chai, cutlet, samosa," they sang in a monotone as I tried to squeeze past them to find my seat, while others pushed me out of their way looking for theirs.

I finally found my section, which consisted of three sets of bunk beds. Two sets of three were opposite each other, perpendicular to the aisle which ran along one side of the train. They were separated by the length of the third set, this time of two bunks, in the aisle itself. I had a top bunk.

"Excuse me. I think that's my seat," I said to a man lying up there, showing him my ticket. He got off with a grunt and squeezed into a space on the floor below, among all the other people and luggage that couldn't fit under the bottom bunk. I threw my backpack onto my bunk and climbed the thin metal ladder to the few inch gap between the bunk and ceiling. I slithered along the dirty plastic bed with my pack and lay down under a rusty tin fan that struggled to move the hot air around. I was content and felt alive as the train gently rocked me to sleep, along with the sound of "Chai, cutlet, samosa."

At four am, I got off in Rishikesh, feeling like a survivor of a great battle. "I'm here!" Nancy called across the many greasy black heads. We got a rickshaw as the town was woken by sunrise, and the sound of bells and pujas from the temples and ashrams that run along the edges of the vast, sacred Ganga River, dividing it in two.

The rickshaw dropped us off at a long metal suspension bridge. As I walked across that bridge, which wobbled beneath my feet, over the sacred river with the sunlight shimmering over it, I felt like I was leaving my shaky life behind and entering my new life.

We carefully dodged the cows, bulls and dogs that were looking for food, along the clean, narrow lane, which passed the Ganga on one side and was populated with restaurants and shops on the other.

The sweet smell of chai was irresistible. "Please, let's get one," I said, and we sat on a metal bench and watched the vendor add tea, sugar and spices to the boiling milk in the burnt-black saucepan. Pouring it from a great height, he filled our two glasses. The warm sweet liquid refreshed my body, and I felt revitalised and ready to continue our walk.

Outside the ashram gate, I admired a big, blue, concrete Shiva, sitting majestically before a beautiful Himalayan backdrop, in the middle of the river. Then after a deep breath, I entered the gate to my new beginning.

In front of me were a few buildings, painted in soft pastel colours, and soothing music was playing. I followed Nancy to the office, along a paved path with neatly-trimmed hedges on either side. Pretty flowers, mature trees with colourful blossoms and little temples, with brightly-coloured statues of deities and gods doing various activities, dotted the well-kept lawns. "This is a breath of fresh air. I love it," I told Nancy. I felt like I was in a fairy tale; my fairy tale.

"Happy you like it. This ashram prefers recommended visitors so I'll say you're my friend," she smiled.

If I had got the train the day before, I would never have met her and would never have entered this ashram. I knew she had been sent to guide me and bring me here. No matter what, I thought, I'm going to stay.

My room was big, clean and airy, with a comfortable bed and hot shower. It was luxury compared to Thailand. I unpacked and made it cosy within minutes, then went to check out my new environment before lunch.

Just behind the dining room, I found the yoga hall. A class was about to begin and they let me join it. It was a small group who had come to India with their teacher from Los Angeles. The teacher sat on the stage, dressed in white, with a big purple stone in the middle of her turban. Her face looked frozen from one Botox too many as she stared into space.

I copied the others, as we did a single movement for ten minutes or more before changing to another action. The grand finale was a dance and song about love. While everyone was singing and embracing each other, I made a dart for the door. I wasn't ready for that kind of yoga yet.

I crossed the well-maintained garden to the other side of the complex, where there was an orphanage for street boys. If they became monks, the ashram provided them with a home, food, and education. "No women allowed here," a monk gently told me, pointing me in the direction of the dining room.

"Sorry," I said and headed where the finger pointed. It was a medium-sized dining room, with grey plastic tables and chairs down either side of a whitewashed wall, and a big white table at the back, holding serving trays and spoons, buffet-style. There were potatoes in a bland sauce, dal and rice, and I spooned a dollop of each onto my tin plate. (I soon found all meals were in the same style and I could see my slim bikini body slipping away). I could not find any cutlery so I sat down on a chair to eat with my hands in silence.

After washing my plate, I left the ashram and walked along the little lane. One side now had a line of sadhus, in orange robes, waiting for free food from the ashram next door. Foreigners with yoga mats walked urgently to or from class. Continuing past the suspension bridge and the pastel-painted buildings, I saw a chai shop on the bank where, sitting quietly, I asked the sacred river to help me make the changes I needed to make to my crazy life, and to find the discipline to stick with them.

Returning to the ashram, I noticed a gathering on the steps that led down to the big, blue Shiva, that sat in the middle of the Ganga. "What is this?" I asked a man, who was removing his shoes at the top of the steps and depositing them into the shoe house.

"Aarti. You must come and get a blessing," he told me as if it was the most important thing on earth. Then I saw the ashram's resident guru arrive and enter the crowd. He was a big man with greased black hair tied in a topknot, and a long, black beard, and was dressed in traditional orange robes.

I quickly removed my shoes and sat in a vacant space at the top of the steps to check out what the fuss was all about. There was a roaring fire on the platform at the bottom of the steps and a few people were throwing seeds into it, symbolising that they were burning the seeds of their ignorance. The orphans, all in traditional orange robes, were sitting around the fire. Behind them, in a pecking order, flowing up and around the steps, sat the other people from the ashram. In the middle of this gathering, I saw the guru sit down amongst the musicians.

As the sun started to set, the chanting began and the guru went to the fire and lit four or five aarti. The brass candelabra, filled with purified butter, then passed from person to person. As each person received it, they held it in front of their chest and turned it clockwise, signifying om, which denotes the origin of all, and offering light back to the sun that has provided light for us all day. Then they passed it to the person next to them.

The energy level rose as people started pushing to reach the aarti, or get to the Ganga to bless themselves with, or drink, the sacred water. A few monks appeared and started to bless people, placing a red dot of powder, or tilak, on their foreheads. The crowd began to head towards me, to collect their shoes from the shoe house. I jumped up quick to watch from a safe distance as they all tried simultaneously to get their shoes from the one shoe attendant. I was indeed seeing a whole new way of life and could not wait to be part of it. Content and eager to start my new beginning, I went back to my room and slept soundly.

I woke excited and walked over to the yoga hall for the eight am class. As I passed people bowing and making offerings to the many concrete idols and trees around the garden, I started to smile from my heart.

I felt nervous as I entered the spacious hall and saw that the students were already warming up on their mats. But the petite 78-year-old teacher who soon walked in seemed normal and down to earth. "Good morning." She greeted us in an American accent, unfurled her mat and got down to business. She was gentle, understanding and caring about my disabilities and took time to teach me how to use props to enable me to get into the challenging postures. She made me feel loved and worthy.

After a few of her drop-in classes, I knew she was the teacher for me and I signed up for her four-week intensive course, which was due to begin in three days. "It will run every day from six am until five pm and it includes pranayama, two yoga asana classes, yoga philosophy and group discussions. Aarti is optional," the skinny man in the office told me.

"It sounds amazing!" I was smiling despite my inner fear of this strict schedule. I knew I would need a lot of discipline and control to stop myself from running away. But if I wanted to turn my life around, I also knew I had to stay so I picked up the pen and filled in the form.

"It's good if you don't leave the ashram for the next two days," he told me as I wrote.

"Why?" I'd been planning to check out the town before I got stuck into the course.

"Because it's Holi, ma'am."

"What's that?"

"It's the festival of colour that we celebrate every spring, to signify the triumph of good over evil."

"Maybe I would like to see that," I told him, and he just smiled.

Stepping outside the ashram gate, I was astonished to see colourful powder all over not just the road but also the cows and dogs. Groups of people were dancing along the lane with small packets of the stuff and smearing it all over each other. Others were spraying each other with water guns.

I immediately got hit by a colourful blast. The cool water was lovely in the heat but my new white ashram pants and shirt were now multi-coloured. Well, it couldn't get worse than this, I thought, and I continued walking, soaking wet and looking like a rainbow. Then, dropped from a rooftop, a balloon full of coloured water exploded on my head. Now I looked like a painting whose oils were melting in the hot sun. Stunned into immobility, I was looking out for more missiles when a group of boys surrounded me and smeared coloured powder all over my body and face. It smelt toxic and tasted bitter.

Realising I had made a mistake, I briskly walked back to the ashram!

Passing the office on the way to my room, I saw the skinny man laughing and had to join in. After three soapy showers, I still couldn't get the paint off my skin or my hair. As for my new ashram clothes, they were never white again.

My first lesson at the ashram: listen.

Once the course started there was no time for anything else. I didn't even have to think about food, since the ashram provided it. It was time to let go of the outside world and throw myself entirely into the routine of class, class and more class. My mind absorbed information like a sponge and my body felt like spaghetti as I learned ways to get into postures with the aid of props. Some days were more challenging than others but, mostly, emerging into spirituality and the bliss of yoga, study and worship was brilliant. With the teacher's love and kindness, and the other students' support, I battled on and took pleasure in my new spiritual friends and simple ashram life. I felt grateful for everything, especially my past, which kept me 'real' and grounded.

So what did I learn?

Yoga means 'to join'. Join what? Body and consciousness.

The body consists of six elements: earth (bones and muscle); water (fluid); fire (heat); air (breath); space (emptiness within); consciousness (mind, ego, and intelligence).

Yoga asana (body postures) and pranayama (breathing technique) help you to still the turbulent movement and fluctuation of the egoistic mind. The egoistic mind likes shifting and sorting, which disturbs the consciousness. It works with memory, I, me and mine, loves the past and fantasies of the future, and has plenty of tricks to keep you under its control.

And didn't I know it! My mind would always be thinking about an exciting life outside the ashram but, whenever I went to check outside, I realised the most exciting thing right now was the positive change in me.

Consciousness works with intelligence and can freeze-frame the flow of mind's endless thoughts to perceive the present moment. Because the breath is constant and happens naturally, it is the best tool.

Inhale divinity; rest. Exhale ego; rest.

The momentary rest creates a pause for you to be in the present moment, with no past and no future. The correct momentary perception and correct action join in a peerless moment, slowing down your response to every situation. No longer swept along by the movement of time, you experience a series of discreet and present moments, and can channel and transform the six disturbing emotions: ignorance; desire; anger; pride; doubt; wrong view.

Untransformed, they are the enemy of spiritual growth and deny you life's freshness and the ability to see what truly is.

I found this breathing technique incredibly helpful, especially as I was in a country where nothing worked, nothing was on time, nothing was available and everything I saw and was doing was new. Most days, I was overwhelmed by the never-ending discoveries and experiences that were transforming me, and knew I was sitting at the most critical crossroads of my life. At the end of the course, would I return to chasing fleeting moments of self-gratification and cheap thrills, or would I embrace the opportunities afforded by this new-found knowledge?

It was time to let go of that life, use ancient wisdom to reprogramme a lifetime of habits, turn inward and seek out the self. It would take discipline, hard work and practice to apply these tools to my life, but I was ready to do whatever it took.

It took a lot of self-study and reflection for me to find flexibility in my conditioned mind. I had to learn to accept the flow of life, with its inevitable challenges, ups and downs, sorrows and joys, without running away or hiding in sex, drugs and rock 'n' roll.

By the time the course drew to a close, I had a new perspective and I no longer wanted to seek oblivion, smoke, eat animals or be abused by men. I now had the confidence to walk down the road holding my head high, knowing I had not disturbed anyone or done anything shameful. But most of all, I knew that I deserved to be happy and I deserved to be loved. I was starting to find the inner peace and everlasting happiness that I had always yearned for. It was the start of a significant transformation and I knew, this time, I was on the right track. I surrendered right there on the bank of River Ganga.

Nevertheless, where there is light, there is darkness.

A resident monk was caught having an affair with Maria, a woman who was on my course. In response to the scandal, the ashram was arranging for the monk to be moved to another ashram the following day, to enter a solitary retreat, reflect on his actions and either redeem himself or give up the robes.

"We have to get married. Please can you help me?" Maria's green eyes shone out of her innocent, freckly face despite her desperation, as we left the morning yoga class.

"I'd love to." I had never been to a Hindu wedding before. We arranged that she come to my room at two am. She arrived at my door looking excited, holding her traditional flowing wedding dress, red with gold trim.

"Your dress is beautiful," I told her as I wrapped her up like a Christmas present, squeezed her hands into glittery red and gold bangles and applied her makeup. She looked stunning, with her curly ginger hair framing her pretty face, and her animated luminous eyes.

When we got to the altar, we found only the monk, a priest and Nancy. "Is it just us?" I asked Nancy as Maria rushed to her lover and touched his feet.

"Yes. This marriage is not allowed. She thinks if she marries him they won't send him away," she whispered.

"Why is it not allowed?" I was clueless.

"Because he's a monk! To tell you the truth, he's probably just looking for a passport out." She looked at me as if I was stupid not to realise that, in a country without social benefits, some men take the robes solely because it ensures food, shelter and education. "She is a deluded young girl." It didn't occur to me to wonder why, if she felt like that, Nancy was helping the lovers.

We sat on the floor and the ceremony began. It took about half an hour, then the couple disappeared and I went back to my room for a quick nap before the morning yoga class.

Later that day, the guru found out about the wedding. Nancy must have been keeping the administration informed even as she pretended to help the pair. Their wedding didn't change anything. Maria had to leave the ashram and her husband was sent to his retreat.

On my first free day after the course, I woke to the usual sound of puja bells and did an hour and a half yoga session all by myself. I felt it was time to let go of the life-transforming tape that I had held onto like a life vest for the last year and a half, and to practice yoga in silence, guided by my own body.

I went for a stroll along the Ganga, passing begging sadhus, and sat on a rock to contemplate. Like the Ganga, my mind was turbulent and in continuous flow. As I tried to fit all this new information into slots inside my head, I thought I might explode. Although I felt I had developed some awareness of my many triggers, and that I had tools to change thought processes that led to wrong action, I knew I needed to go deeper if I was going to transform them. As I continued to watch the river's constant flow, I knew it was time for me to move, but to where and to do what?

I returned to the ashram for my usual potato lunch and chatted with Tina, a petite middle-aged yoga student from Switzerland.

"I'm getting a taxi to the Himalayas. Do you want a lift?"

"What's there?" I was intrigued.

"Snow-capped mountains, Buddhist teachings and enlightened beings," she said blissfully.

"That could be just what I'm looking for." I couldn't believe my guidance had come so fast but, just a few days later, we were in a taxi to the Himalayas.

Sitting comfortably in the back of the car, during our 12-hour ride, Tina told me about our destination. "The local population is mainly Tibetan refugees. They walked from Tibet to escape the Chinese occupation."

"Why do they escape?" I was completely ignorant.

"Because they want to be near their spiritual leader and away from Chinese rule," she said as she put her long grey hair up in a bun. "Leaving their families behind, they walk to Nepal, which takes them between thirty and forty days. When they arrive, some of them are suffering from frostbite, snow blindness, blistered feet. Some of them don't even make it."

"That sounds extreme!" I was shocked.

"It is." She looked sad and we sat in silence as the taxi took us through rough mountain roads.

We arrived at night. I went to a guesthouse and Tina went to stay with friends.

The fresh, cold mountain air woke me early. I drew my curtains and gasped at my first sight of the immense snow-covered Himalayan range against a clear azure sky. Pulling on a jumper, I went to the roof to do yoga where I could breathe and stretch with the ancient mountains looming over me. It was fantastic. I felt happily in tune with my surroundings, and ready to let the day unfold naturally.

Later, I stood in the morning sun on the little dirt track outside my guesthouse, wondering which way to go and watching maroon-clad monks and nuns, with shiny, smiling eyes and malas in their hands, pass by mumbling mantras.

I chose 'up' since that would be my direction from that moment on.

Following a tiny trail cut into the mountain, with houses and monasteries on one side, a vast valley on the other, and the sound of puja drums, bells and chanting coming from almost every window I felt like I was in a peaceful dream. I didn't recognise the new me, but I liked her.

When I reached the main road, I was bombarded with the sound of beeping horns and the sight of a crush of moving people. I slotted into a space and continued my walk. On either side, Tibetan people were setting up handicraft stalls outside the tightly-packed abundance of hotels and restaurants. The smell of food made me hungry, and I chose a restaurant with a big window overlooking the main square.

Perusing the menu, I realised that, after almost two months of eating rice, dal and potatoes in sauce at the ashram, I wasn't sure what to order. "Banana porridge," I said eventually to the sleepy waiter, whose hair fell over his face. He grunted and disappeared.

As I waited for it to come, I spotted a poster on the restaurant's noticeboard advertising a ten-day silent retreat, in a Buddhist centre, starting in two days. "Is that place far?" I asked as a hot bowl of creamy porridge, with sliced banana on top, was put in front of me.

"Just 15 minutes' walk up that hill," he replied with a sweet smile.

Fifteen minutes if you were a mountain goat.

It was a steep rubble road cut into the side of a mountain, with dense forest on either side, and I could feel myself developing muscles on my muscles as I breathlessly huffed and puffed my way upwards. The Himalayas would pop in and out of view through gaps in the trees, in which aggressive-looking monkeys sat like gangsters, pondering whether to rob me. I dodged their gaze and kept huffing up the hill.

Finally, I reached the entrance of the retreat centre and sat at a chai shop just outside to catch my breath.

Unsure whether I was ready for this, I forced myself to walk under the placard above the gate, exhorting me to 'Silence', and down the dirt track, with the Himalayas watching from each side like guardian angles. At the bottom of the track I found, shimmering in the morning sun, a pretty golden Tibetan temple, and I took a moment to admire it before going inside.

I pulled open the big wooden door to be greeted by a peacefully smiling golden Buddha. My heart started pounding, my legs began to shake and tears fell down my face. Overcome by having actually brought myself here, I crumpled to the floor beneath the statue.

It was some time before I got to my feet and went in search of the centre's office. I felt like a fraud and an interloper and was so sure they would ask me to leave that it took all my strength to walk the few steps to its door and enter. Inside, a Tibetan nun was sitting behind the desk chanting mantra. To my surprised relief, she greeted me with a smile. "I'd like to sign up for the retreat, please," I asked in a shaky voice.

"You are lucky: we just had a cancellation," she answered, in perfect English.

"Great! Can I take it?" I asked, though I still wasn't sure if I was ready.

"You are welcome. Please put your name on this list." She handed me a clipboard. "It's a fantastic program involving meditation, Buddhist teachings, yoga and a one-hour discussion group each day."

"It sounds amazing but, please, can I have a single room? I'm new and have a lot of stuff to deal with without anyone else in my space." I did not want to be disturbed, and I wanted to practice yoga in the mornings on my own.

"Yes, we have one free," and she put my name next to it.

I was delighted and, with a fantastic sensation of freedom, and happy simply to be alive, I skipped back down the trail to the town, laughing and singing.

Two days later, I returned to start the course. My room was just a few steps down from the golden temple, where the day started at six with a guided meditation. And it had a magnificent view of the valley, where it lay enclosed by the snow-capped Himalayas.

The silence was calming. Only natural sounds accompanied me to the temple, where I removed my shoes and entered. Again, at the sight of the peaceful, serene golden Buddha, my heart busted open. It felt as though emotions poured from me onto the floor, and I fell onto my knees crying. "I'm so sorry I got lost and mistreated myself for so long, and for all the terrible things I've done. Please forgive me. Please accept me." I felt like a rebellious teenager coming home from a big night out. As I took a seat, tears were still rolling down my face. I couldn't believe I had made it this far, or even that I was still alive.

I had to keep going on this spiritual journey: finally, I was starting to love and care for myself, something that didn't come easily to me.

A nun, sitting on a chair under the golden Buddha, sounded a gong to begin the meditation. I embraced the silence and searched inside myself for the root of my self-destructive behaviour. The experience was dark and intense so I was glad of the opportunity the discussion groups provided to get stuff off my chest, and of the teachings that gave me tools to make progress.

I was beginning to transform: I was ready for a guru, to guide me and show me the guru inside myself. A true guru is an embodiment of love and compassion. They guide you and give you meditation tools to enable you attain enlightenment. Though they can't do it for you: you have to apply the teachings, trust your guru and surrender.

They have the wisdom, and maybe even clairvoyance, to recommend the most appropriate practice, and teach you in different ways, time and time again, until you get it. It can be painful but you can't overcome your barriers without recognising them yourself and working through them to transform them.

When I left the silent retreat centre, and had set myself up in a room in town, I called my mumma, to thank her for having me. She'd been my first guru. Now I needed to find my spiritual one.

I heard about a reincarnated monk, who had recently escaped from Tibet and gave public audiences three times a week at the monastery where he was residing. The monastery was only a short bus ride from town, so I decided to check him out.

I was full of excitement and fear as I jumped down from the bus at the monastery's golden-gates, and gazed over the sprawling complex. Feeling like an imposter, I gathered my courage and set off along a paved path, flanked by beautiful manicured gardens. I climbed marble steps towards the red and yellow monastery, which looked magnificent against a backdrop of snow-clad mountains and the cloudless blue sky.

I was surprised to find armed police and army personnel in the courtyard at the top, alongside people who were walking around the monastery clockwise, mumbling. Others people were standing around looking lost, damaged, mentally ill or at least as though they weren't managing life's challenges. I felt like I had walked into an open-air mental institution and wondered if the police and army personnel were there in case the residents got out of control.

Confused, I asked a monk 'why the guns?' and learned that the reincarnated monk, known as The Boss, had been under police protection since he'd escaped from Tibet to India. Out of my comfort zone, I thought, "What are you doing here? You don't belong here. Get out, now!" Yet my feet took me to a group of people looking up at the monastery's balcony.

"What's happening?" I asked one girl though she seemed neither friendly nor interested in helping me.

"That's where The Boss lives," someone behind me offered. He had two tiny rooms, each giving onto the balcony, and the small crowd was waiting for him to come out.

"Is this a public audience?" I asked the woman who'd spoken, thinking perhaps he would come out and wave to whoever was waiting, like some rock star.

"No, you need to go register." She pointed to a small window, just under the balcony. A long queue of people were chatting excitedly about meeting The Boss, how many times they had met The Boss and how many pieces of red string they had.

I learned that the pieces of red string were blessing cords, bestowed by the guru. Devotees either tied them around their wrists or hung around their necks for protection from negative forces, and as a reminder of dharma.

I joined the queue and, on reaching the window, was asked to show my passport. Then I was allowed to approach the monastery door and join another queue, this time for a body search, before entering the monastery.

The sweet smell of incense engulfed me as I stepped inside. In silence, I walked towards the shining Buddha statue and took a seat beneath it. I was carrying a white, synthetic, scarf-like cloth called a katha, to offer to the guru, for him to place around my neck. The aim of this Tibetan tradition is to ensure that everyone can afford to offer something to the guru. An offering be it practice, money, food or service, is an important part of the Buddhist tradition. It helps you practice generosity and generate merit.

The room fell silent as The Boss glided in, surrounded by monks, men in suits and security guards. His presence oozed peaceful tranquillity and the hollow space inside me filled with a potent, blissful sensation that I instantly recognised as oneness in a world of duality. I felt calm, protected and loved.

People started jumping up to perform three prostrations, to show reverence to the Buddha, his teachings and the spiritual community; but I couldn't move. I was mesmerised, stunned that someone this beautiful was alive, on this planet and standing before me.

My bubble was popped by a security guard pushing me to join the queue that had formed behind me. People were lining up to pass the guru, and receive his blessing and a red cord. I took my place at the back of the long queue and, in a dream-like state, shuffled forward, my now sweaty hand gripping my katha. The only sounds were the clunking of mala beads, the mumbling of mantras and my thumping heartbeat, as the maroon-robed monks herded me forward until I was in front of the guru.

I froze. I wasn't sure if I wanted to poo, pee, vomit or run. In fact, I stood transfixed, looking into his radiant eyes. I felt I had found what I had been searching for all my life. I could feel him looking deep inside me and recognising the goodness. "It's over now," he said in a resonant, hypnotic voice, as he handed me a blessing cord.

But I knew it was just the beginning.

The Boss gave public teachings in the shrine room, at two in the afternoon on Saturdays and Sundays. I was always there by 12:30 to pass security, and be ready when the doors opened at one. I soaked up every drop of his wisdom like a giant sponge.

There was always a long queue outside the shrine room, usually made up of women who were renting houses nearby. They were a friendly bunch, but protective of their guru, their space in line and their seat inside. It was obvious they didn't like an outspoken, rough-and-ready woman, joining their flock. We would exchange polite greetings but I tried not to get caught up in their competitive talk.

"I had a private audience yesterday and he remembered my name," said a woman in her fifties who was sitting beside me.

"Maybe that's because you see him every week," an older woman sneered at her.

"He always smiles at me," another chirped.

I found it discouraging but held strong. I understood that they were working through their own stuff. Besides I didn't know where else to go for the teachings I needed.

I was captivated by the guru's presence and his words.

The four noble truths:

The truth of suffering.

The truth of the cause of suffering.

The truth of the cessation of suffering.

The truth of the path that leads to the cessation of suffering: I wanted and needed to walk that path.

One day, as I left the shrine room after a talk, I felt a pat on my shoulder. "Hey! So you found the best place." To my delight, it was Tina, wearing a blue tracksuit and matching headband.

"I sure did, mate! He's the bollocks. I'm finally starting to get it, though I'm going to need to stay for a while for it all to penetrate. It's best I distance myself from friends that don't understand my new life and want to pull me back into a life of debauchery. I think people miss the entertainment of my drug and drink-fuelled behaviour. It's strange how they see me trying to dry out and clean up and they want to pull me back in."

"Good idea. You'll find new friends here." She hugged me. "I've got a taxi. Do you need a lift to town?"

"That'd be great." I was glad of the alternative to the bus ride, which was so bumpy it made me travel sick. As the taxi swerved and swayed its way up the hills, we continued our conversation. "People think I'm going through a phase and I'll get over it, but I know with my whole being this is it, this is the meaning of life that I've been searching for, for so long."

"Just keep looking at the guru, with the teachings in your heart, and keep going forward."

It was good advice.

I felt my next step would be to take refuge in the Buddha, dharma and sangha so one weekend, after the teachings, I asked The Boss's attendant if I could have a private audience, and was pleasantly surprised to be given a day and time.

There are two types of refuge:

External refuge gives a sense of direction or goal.

It might take the form of: The Buddha; the dharma (path); the sangha (Buddhist community).

Internal Refuge is your true nature. Everybody has this nature, or inner guru. It is the ultimate refuge. It helps you free yourself from suffering and fear, to achieve the pure, free and beyond-conception awareness, compassion and wisdom of enlightenment.

To prevent obstacles or detours from our true nature, we need to develop Bodhicitta, or loving-kindness and compassion.

Whatever is practised, be it generosity, effort, samadhi, sadana, meditation or wisdom, it is to help all beings to recognise their true nature, or inner guru.

I knew almost nothing about the refuge ceremony except that I felt compelled to do it. I turned up like a bewildered, lost child.

After the usual security procedures, I joined a queue of the other people fortunate enough to secure a private audience. The queue consisted of three small groups—and me.

"Follow me." A security guard led us up two flights of stairs. "Wait here." Outside the door of the guru's receiving room door, on the balcony everyone stared at. I felt out of place and unworthy. My stomach churned. I held my katha in my clammy hands, fighting the urge to run away. Where would I run to? Back to the bar? Back to the drugs? Back to the endless men? I knew this was it: I had to keep going forward. Behind that door was the man that held the key to my new beginning.

"In you go." My thoughts were interrupted by the security guard and the door was open. I took a deep breath and entered what turned out to be a medium-sized room. The Boss was sitting behind a desk at the back but his presence filled the room and I froze, captivated.

"Come and sit down." The translator's voice snapped me out of my trance.

I was trembling and found it hard to walk those few steps. Then The Boss smiled at me and I relaxed enough to make it. I performed three shaky prostrations and offered him the katha, which he placed around my neck and then I melted to the floor before him. Every inch of my body seemed immersed in a sea of bliss, and my mind became empty and still. Then my heart exploded with boundless love and devotion as I felt my consciousness merge with his.

In a mumble, I echoed his triple declaration, in Tibetan, of the refuge's vows and received my Tibetan name, Karma Tswang Yusho, life's power in a turquoise ocean.

Afterwards, I wrote him this poem:

You are a beautiful flower in life's tangled mess;

You shine like the sun and the moon;

You are my breath.

Past lives, this life, future life;

I follow you, my master, 'til death.

I was now a Buddhist, with a guru but, to see him privately one had to make an appointment, and even when I got one, it always felt rushed. At the teachings, monks and nuns sat at the front, so he was far away on his throne. For public audiences, he was surrounded by security, and I was shoved along so fast, I got little more than a glimpse.

In that one timeless moment, all past and future joined in one breath. My experience was beyond words and that bliss stayed with you. But I needed more than bliss. I needed someone I could talk to directly, someone who would personally guide me along this bumpy path.

Then, one day, I saw a poster in town advertising teachings by a rinpoche at a nearby monastery. In Tibetan, 'rinpoche' means 'precious'. It's an honorific given to a spiritual teacher held in high regard, one who can control their consciousness at the moment of death so as to reincarnate repeatedly, to benefit beings.

The poster told me that the rinpoche's teachings were running every afternoon from Monday to Friday. Every week there would be a different topic, with a question and answer session and, after class, you could see him privately to discuss your practice. I was amazed at what I was reading. It was just what I needed; someone I could talk to without all the nonsense I had to go through to see The Boss. It also fitted nicely with my schedule: yoga in the morning; rinpoche teachings in the afternoon; The Boss at the weekend. I felt I was being guided. I was ready to let go and let this river of dharma wash over me.

So I huffed and puffed up the hill to the monastery where the rinpoche was residing. Arriving, I headed for some foreigners who were hanging around, outside a room on the roof. I entered a kitchen that led to a small, cold, damp room and, on a wooden bench, which looked like it was also his bed, sat a humble monk in meditation. Some people were already sitting quietly, on cushions, so I sat down on a free one. I was surprised to see how basic the room was with just a couple of thangkas on the wall and a few shelves of texts and books. I was impressed by his modest style of living: no throne; no attendant; no police; no security; no entry fee.

And when he started chanting, I was blown away. His hypnotic voice sounded like it was rising from a canyon as he recited ancient words that seemed to emanate from all over his body, creating goose bumps all over mine.

Although he taught through a translator, he was precise and ensured everyone understood what he was saying. I felt he was the real deal and I could trust him, so I started going to every class.

Yet I still felt unworthy, unpure and that I didn't belong. I needed support and guidance. Instead, it seemed to me that some of his followers were neurotically possessive about their seats and their guru. I felt they made it evident they didn't want this newcomer in their flock, and I couldn't handle feeling excluded as I negotiated such a transformation. I stopped attending.

"Now, what do I do? I *am* a Buddhist but I don't fit in here," I said to Tina one day when we met for lunch.

"What do you mean?"

"Well, everyone seems very cliquey and caught up in themselves. I just feel excluded."

"Yeah, the guru brings all your hidden shit out, darling, and some people can't handle it, so they throw it out on others. Maybe what you're experiencing is something coming from you. Why don't you go to Bodhgaya, where Buddha attained enlightenment under the sacred Bodhi tree? You can practice there."

Instead of going straight there, I went on a random tour of India, going with the flow and ending up at various ashrams, attending yoga teacher training programmes, learning a variety of yoga techniques and visiting holy sites for blessings.

Eventually, I arrived in the small town of Bodhgaya. It was more of a freak show than Delhi, and even noisier. All of life was lived in the open, along one dirty, dusty road. Every type of vehicle went every which way, honking their horns and rattling my nervous system. Deformed people grabbed at me, chased me or hung off me, begging. I'd never seen anything like it; polio, elephantiasis, one leg, no legs, one arm, no arm, no eyes, even just a torso on a skateboard.

A mass of half-animal, half-human skeletal bodies spat, snotted, pissed and shit all over the place. Frightening eyes, needing something from me, looking out of hollow faces. Everywhere I looked, I'd see a man with his cock out, pissing among starving cows, oxen and donkeys, and deformed, scabby dogs and puppies. Rising from the ubiquitous litter, next to restaurants, hotels, guesthouses and lavish monasteries, were houses made out of cow dung, congregated iron, cardboard and plastic.

I was terrified until, in the distance, I saw a magnificent, grey stupa-like structure reaching to the sky. Then everything seemed to go quiet, as I slowly walked towards an 11-meter high pink wall, built in the style of Indian temple architecture, which surrounded the complex. I walked through the open arch, and found myself at the top of two flights of wide, marble stairs leading down to the entrance of a magnificent, 55-meter high tower, representing the eightfold path. On each of the four corners, was a miniature stupa, representing the four noble truths. It was incredible.

Removing my shoes, I descended step by step, almost in a trance. I passed a grassy sloped bank, with a small stupa on my right and a few small temples on my left, reached the inner path and entered the temple.

The musty smell and murmur of mantras were enchanting. At the back, in a glass case, a three-meter high golden Buddha statue, dating from the 10th or 11th century, was sitting peacefully on a patterned cushion making the earth-touching gesture, by which Buddha calls the earth goddess, Paṭhavi, to bear witness to his enlightenment.

I approached it feeling like a naughty schoolchild going to see the head teacher, and sat at its feet in admiration and devotion.

A nun sitting next to me increasing the volume of her chanting snapped me from my trance-like state, and my eyes rested on the pedestal below. There were five niches, divided by small pillars. The two outer niches on one side contained lions and the two on the other elephants. In the central niche, Paṭhavi, the Earth Goddess, was represented rising from the ground, holding a vase of jewels and witnessing the Buddha's victory over ignorance.

It was breathtaking and it was a few minutes before I could get up and walk around the inner path to the back of the temple, where I found the sacred tree where the Buddha sat and attained enlightenment. Its thick trunk was behind a golden fence. Its branches spread high and wide, some so long and heavy they were supported with iron pillars.

Sitting around the golden fence were monks, nuns and laypeople, meditating, chanting, praying or standing waiting for a leaf to fall. Unfortunately, it seemed some of them believed Buddha to be deaf: they were chanting their prayers through megaphones or portable speakers. It felt more like a busy market than a place of tranquillity.

The inner path was surrounded by a pillared stone wall and four openings led to the middle section. I walked through an opening onto a grassy area, where a prayer festival was taking place, again with loudspeakers. A guru was sitting under the tree, on an elaborate throne, surrounded by his entourage. Almost every bit of grass was taken up by monks, nuns and lay practitioners, chanting peace prayers or doing prostrations on a board. Further back were lots of stupas where people under tented mosquito nets were meditating, praying or making offerings on oversized cushions, while others went around offering them food and money.

It was a big celebration of dharma in a little village.

I walked up a few steps to the outer path, with its marbled floor, and joined the crowd of devotees, tourists and seekers doing kora, each with a mala or prayer wheel in their hands. On one side of this path, was a pretty flower bank; on the other, a row of prayer wheels, which I gently spun as I enjoyed the aerial view of the temple grounds. Turning a corner, I spotted a picturesque meditation garden. Continuing my kora, I descended marble steps to a waterhole, in which a giant Buddha statue sat under a giant cobra. I took a seat and tried to take it all in. Finally, resuming my walk, I passed two gardens with butter lamp houses and then I reached the exit gate back to the street.

Although the temple was bustling and noisy, it had a peaceful, blissful energy. That disappeared as soon as you stepped outside. Two very different worlds were separated by the temple wall. I had never been surrounded by so much suffering or noise and I just wanted to get out.

I was constantly harassed by people looking for anything they could get, while I carefully manoeuvred over the abundance of human and animal shit, and rubbish. There was a constant whine from the beggars who followed me, or blocked my way to shove an empty, battered tin bowl into my chest. People were trying to get me into their shop to sell me something I didn't need or want. The loud horns of rickshaws, motorbikes and taxis seemed to run up my spine. Rickshaw drivers almost ran me over, in their enthusiasm to insist I wanted them to convey me to another place. I began to think they were aiming to damage my legs so that, unable to walk, I'd have to take one to the hospital!

Walking to the temple involved running the gauntlet of a profusion of noise, filth, and pollution that I didn't want or need.

Feeling that I had still not found my feet, I decided to go to Tibet. Since that was where my guru was from, maybe I would find the peace to practice there.

2. Top Of The World: 2004

In all my years of traveling, I'd never before been interested in going to Tibet. Its mountainous location put me off, I still remembered my experience of altitude sickness and freezing weather in Bolivia. I was a beach baby.

But, if I was to learn about Tibetan Buddhism and culture, I knew I had to go.

"Another shit 'ole," I thought as I surveyed Kathmandu. The Himalayan city was an enormous rubbish tip, with open sewers that flowed through the busy potholed streets, which had colourful shops on each side, selling the same junk as I'd seen elsewhere.

I went to a guesthouse in a funky part of town and took a basic room. There was a double bed, a bathroom and a window overlooking the distant mountains. I put my bag down, did my usual trick of hiding my valuables somewhere in the room and went out to book a tour to Tibet.

"You can get a seven day or 21-day Tibet pass and we have a five-day jeep journey to Lhasa leaving in two days," the unwashed man in the tour shop told me.

"I'll take a seat and a 21-day Tibet pass please." I was delighted.

I whiled away the two days before my jeep-trip checking out lavish monasteries, which lay down dirt tracks and potholed lanes littered with rubbish, shit and piss.

The jeep was a rusty, old, battered tin can and it took me on a hardcore ride through some of the best of nature's beauty. The imposing Himalayas stretched far and wide into the bluest, cloudless sky. Wide waterfalls plummeted into rivers that flowed onto wide-open plateaus. I had never seen so many different shades of green. We stopped only to go to the toilet and to sleep in damp, dirty rest houses, which served thukpa, Tibetan noodle soup.

"I have a big headache and feel dizzy," I told the jeep driver when we finally reached Lhasa.

"It's altitude sickness. Just rest and drink lots of water."

My guesthouse room was adorable, with a little bed, a big duvet and a brightly-painted bedside cabinet. All I could do was lie down. It wasn't easy to gauge the time because the clocks were set to Beijing time, the light was all wrong and the nights were bright. I just rested until I felt better.

Hunger finally drove me into the fresh air and I was surprised at how modern the town was. Paved roads had restaurants, shops and tour shops, all covered in flashing neon lights. It reminded me of Hong Kong, except for the mighty snowy mountains jutting into the cloudless sapphire sky.

In a dream-like state, I walked to Barkhor square, a pedestrianised market area. Maybe it was the altitude or maybe it was lack of sleep but I felt relaxed and peaceful in this exciting, high-energy market. Pilgrims and other people had gathered to socialise, buy and sell, or do kora around Jokhang Temple. Jokhang is the home of the Jowo Rinpoche, the most sacred and revered Buddha statue of the country. Tibetan folklore regards it as a true image of Buddha Sakyamuni at the age of twelve, blessed by the Buddha himself and, at over 2,500 years, the oldest Buddha statue in existence. Tibetans sometimes make pilgrimages from their nomadic villages to the sacred Jokhang, and many significant events have taken place inside.

I yearned to go in, so I reluctantly paid the entrance fee and drifted through the wooden gates into the ancient stone temple that smelt of yak butter and incense. The Jowo statue smiled peacefully at me. Overcome, I fell to my knees in devotion and made many resolutions. With tear-stained eyes, I got up from the cold, cobbled floor and went to the roof, where I could see over Lhasa to the Potala Palace, the home of the Dalai Lama.

I never went inside the Potala. It didn't feel right to go into the Dalai Lama's palace while he was in exile in India. Instead, I did kora around it and sat at the river, meditating and absorbing its peaceful energy.

"Where are you from?" a Tibetan man, who smelt strongly of yak butter, asked.

"I'm from the UK."

"Come. I show you," and he briskly walked off, with me following, to a run-down building. When I entered, the familiar smell of incense and yak butter greeted me, as I noticed beautiful thankas on the walls. A radiant monk in maroon robes sat on an elaborate, golden throne in front of a Buddha statue, surrounded by people reciting mantras.

Out of the blue, a monk pushed me to lean over a long tin bath filled with saffron yellow water, and another poured the thick yellow liquid over my head. Then they gently pushed me to sit down among a group of Tibetan people on the sticky, yak-buttered floor. The mumbling of mantras and clicking of mala beads were peaceful and I relaxed. The people's faith and devotion was so affecting that my heart seemed to burst. I sat, thoroughly blissed-out, until it was over.

The man who'd invited me suggested I return the following morning but, although I knew it was the real deal, I didn't go. Morning was yoga time.

I wanted to explore away from the bustle and the MSG food that always made me sick. I tried to board a bus but was not allowed because it did not take foreigners and there were checkpoints along the roads. My only option was to book an expensive tour and buy a Tibet pass from a tourist shop.

"Can I book the day trip to Sera and Drepung monasteries?" I asked the muscular-looking woman behind the desk in a tour shop.

"Yes, I can organise everything for you." She booked it for the next day. The extortionate price included my Tibet pass, which I never saw: tour shops almost certainly inflate the prices of these passes.

Sera Monastery was a short picturesque jeep ride from Lhasa. We bounced through rugged, rocky, grey mountains to reach a big white building, with a red and gold trim. A few monks were sitting in the dusty garden as I walked up the steps to do kora around the cobbled path, and we smiled at each other. Entering the main hall, I smelled the ancientness of my surroundings and felt the energy of the numerous prayers that must have been made there. Slowly walking around, looking at the faded thangkas and shiny statues, I heard a little voice from a crack in a wall.

"Hello, hello," it whispered. Peering closer, I saw a brown eye looking back.

"Dalai Lama, OK?" he said.

Oh, bless him. He was hiding but needed to find out if I had any news of his guru.

"Yes. Yes, alive and well," I whispered back. I caught a glimpse of unkempt teeth as he smiled. Then he disappeared.

The jeep then drove me through a spectacular green and yellow range of mountains with brilliant white snow caps and waterfalls gushing into clear running rivers, joining the birds in a song symphony. The majestic monastery, with its unique architecture, lay on top of the highest peak, seeming to be one with the mountain.

Relishing the cold fresh air, I climbed a rugged path to reach the monastery doors. The view of the stunning Lhasa valley mesmerised me, and I walked around in peaceful silence.

The next day I wandered around Lhasa, trying to work out why I was still in a dream-like state. Then it dawned on me; no crowds, no honking horns, no shouting, lots of space. Everything was moving in peaceful silence. It was like a dream.

I was sitting in a restaurant, on a wooden bench covered in a colourful blanket, waiting for thukpa, when I saw a leaflet on the wall—and my heart skipped a beat.

Samye.

The first official, and most influential, Buddhist monastery in Tibet, built in 762. It covers more than 25,000 square meters, is in the shape of an oval to symbolise the centre of the universe, and is famous for a great debate between Buddhist schools from ancient India and China.

I couldn't finish my soup quickly enough so I could get to the tour shop and book a visit.

The next day, I bounced along in my jeep, through the rugged landscape, until I could see the magnificent white walls of the monastery. It sat majestically on the top of mount Hepo Ri, its shining gold roof shimmering in the sunlight, against a cloudless blue sky. It looked like something out of a fairy tale and I could hardly believe little ol' me was there.

We parked by the river, and ordered steamed momos and Tibetan butter tea from a wooden shack, before taking a boat across the turbulent river.

Standing at the bottom of stone steps to the entrance, I felt immense gratitude for life. I floated up them to do kora around the beautifully-symmetrical mandala. As I entered the main hall, the monks were doing puja and the drums and cymbals thrummed through my body, connecting me with the universal vibration. I sat in a peaceful state of oneness with everything around me.

When the puja finished, I climbed the 30-minute trail up the mountain, admiring the beauty of my surroundings, then sat spaced-out by the panoramic views.

Finally, feeling overcome and sun-stroked, I found my driver in time for the last boat back to the mainland.

When I got back to my guesthouse, three lads were outside having a cigarette so I joined them.

"We're doing a two-day tour to Namtso Lake tomorrow. Do you want to join us?" Gary, the very confident Aussie asked.

"It's the highest saline lake on our planet," John, who was from the UK, added. He was travelling with his brother, David, and they'd met Gary along the way.

They seemed like nice lads, I had nothing planned and spending the night at a magical lake seemed like a fantastic idea. "Yes, I'll come."

"Meet us here at four am, tomorrow," Gary said with a cheeky wink. No, Gary! Not a chance.

The six-hour drive took us through spectacular natural beauty, and we stopped only once, for thukpa and momos.

Finally, with dizzy heads, we reached the lofty altitude of 4,718 meters and were blessed by the stunning beauty and pure water of Namtso Lake. Its sparkling, sapphire waters, seagulls hovering above, were hugged by the imposing Mount Nyenchen Range, and other distant, snow-capped mountains. On the open grassland, yak herds and local nomads went about their business under a clear sapphire sky. It was sublime.

We camped in a Mongolian tent at the edge of the lake and I was quick to drop my bag on a bed and go off to do kora on a peaceful walk around the beautiful lake. As the sun was about to set, I saw a small monastery embedded in the rock face. I didn't have a torch with me so I decided to explore it in the morning.

I sat contentedly outside my tent, watching the colour of the snow-capped mountains transform into a deep orange and red that reflected flawlessly in the lake, then ate a bowl of thukpa and went to bed. I wanted to get to sleep so I could get up early to visit that monastery before we left but, despite wearing all my clothes and being wrapped in three blankets, I was freezing and couldn't drift off. Then, I heard an out-of-tune rap song coming towards my tent. The lads were on their way back from dinner.

"What a great laugh, what's that drink called again?" Gary was giggling.

"Chiang. It's fermented barley," slurred John as they stumbled into the tent and crashed onto their beds.

I was happy to be sober and finally fell asleep to the sound of Gary making up rap songs about Chiang.

Morning came and I jumped out of bed and jogged around to defrost so I could do yoga at the lake as the sun rose. Stretching on the lakeshore, as the clouds lifted from the mountains and everything was bathed in shimmering gold, I felt at one with the universe.

When I went back to that little monastery, I discovered it was tiny by comparison to others I had seen. But it was beautiful and had a Buddha statue and a photo of The Boss on a shrine. I sat happily on the freezing, sticky, yak-buttered stone floor until a nun came in. Her short, plump body jumped with surprise when she saw me sitting there, and she stopped mid-mantra. Her brown eyes shone through her well-worn, weather-beaten face, as she gave me a loving smile, then proceeded to her business of cleaning the butter lamps.

All Tibetan monasteries have these copper lamps, which are offered to the Buddha and help focus the mind for meditation. In silence, I joined the nun removing the burnt wick and washing the lamp, ready for it to be refilled with fresh yak butter.

Although I felt lost in time, I knew it was getting late, and I had to leave. I got back to the camp to find the lads and the driver waiting to leave, so I had no time for breakfast. "Are you a rap artist, Gary?" I asked as I was getting into the car, and we laughed.

"Lads, on the way back, could you please drop me at Tsurphu monastery? It's the main seat of my guru and I'd like to spend my last days there."

"Sure. We'll come with you and have a look around," John said.

The Boss' monastery was in a vast valley next to a river. I went to book a room for a few nights while the lads explored. I met a monk who showed me a bare, dirty room containing nothing but a bed. As I entered the room, he shut the door and tried to touch my tits. Horrified, I pushed him off me and ran out to look for the lads. "I'm coming back to Lhasa with you," I told them, and we jumped into the jeep for the bumpy ride back.

Despite my experience in The Boss' monastery, there was so much more to see of Tibet that I did not want to leave, but I could not get a visa extension on my Tibet pass. So, to milk the most out of my 21-day pass, instead of doing the five-day jeep ride back to Nepal, I flew, passing Mount Everest along the way.

It was the perfect end to a perfect trip.

3. A Devastating Loss: 2005

My mumma, Joyce, was born in the 1930s, in Notting Hill, and grew up during World War Two. Her father, Danny, was a bare-knuckle boxer and a rag-and-bone man. Later in life, he bought a fruit and veg stall in Portobello Market. Her mother, Dolly, was a housewife who loved to dance. There was not much money about and times were hard, but everyone stuck together, helping each other out, and her childhood was happy.

My mumma never recovered from my father's death. At the age of fifty-two, while they were shopping in Notting Hill Gate, he dropped at my mumma's feet, dead from a heart attack.

To overcome the shock and for comfort, she started drinking more whiskey than usual. She was a lively, lovable drunk and was always singing, telling jokes and offering advice to anyone who asked.

She was, and still is, the best friend I have ever had, even though she did not understand the new, clean yoga-me.

"I've packed up drinking, smoking, sex and meat, Mumma," I told her on my return from India, to get a job and renew my visa.

"You may as well pack up living then, girl!"

"I believe in this Buddhist stuff. If you think it's mumbo jumbo, prove me wrong when you die. Come back and let me know what goes on. If you don't come back, I'll know I'm wasting my time, and I'll go to the pub and drink a large one to you."

"Alright. If I can come back to tell you, I will."

"You promise?"

"I promise."

We were spending the summer together in London. Without support or understanding, New Me was struggling with the temptations around. My friends only wanted to meet in pubs and, when I went, they would encourage me to drink, so I didn't enjoy going. I went for meals with my mumma instead and took all available shifts at the hospital.

When winter reared its head, I knew it was time to get out. My leg was starting to play up from both the cold and the walking my nursing shifts entailed. I had saved enough money and India was calling. It was hard to leave my mumma, but she knew I was miserable in London and sent me off with her blessing.

Although I missed my mumma immediately, it was wonderful to arrive back in India. I headed straight to meditate at Kanyakumari, the magical southern tip, where the Bay of Bengal, the Arabian Sea and the Indian Ocean meet.

It was beautiful to sit where the three oceans merged but I felt a need to go deeper, and thought it would be better to go to a meditation centre where everything would be taken care of, and I could focus on meditating. I had heard about a place in Kodaikanal so I booked a bus for that night, which of course left late. I called my mumma while I was waiting for it to leave.

"Hi Mumma. How are you?" My heart ached to be with her.

"I've had a bit of a cough and a sore throat," she croaked.

"Please go and see the doctor."

"If I don't feel better tomorrow, I will."

"The bus is leaving. I have to go, but I'll call you tomorrow."

"I love you with a thousand hearts," she told me.

"I love you with a million hearts," I replied and then boarded the bus.

On 23rd November 2005, I arrived in the fresh mountains of Kodaikanal and, after sorting out a room and breakfast, I went to check email and look for a phone to call my mumma. I felt carefree and happy as I walked through the mountain village. Little did I know it was to become the worst day of my life.

There was an email from my elder brother saying that my mumma had died that morning. I must have read that mail 50 times before it sank in.

Wanting to believe it was all a mistake, I phoned my mumma's house but, when a police officer answered, I knew. My mumma was dead.

I felt life drain out of me at the realisation that my best friend and confidante was gone, and I was now alone in the world. I wanted to die right there, right then. How would I live without my mumma?

I knew my sister would not manage this terrible loss well so, in a haze of disbelief, I flew back to London. I was there within 24 hours of getting the news.

I felt as if I was in someone else's nightmare as I walked around my mumma's house. I could feel her presence in that empty house that held so many memories, and kept expecting her to appear.

To feel close to her, I slept there and, before I fell asleep, spoke to the open space, telling my mumma everything I needed to say.

I went to the undertakers to kiss her body for the last time—and left my heart there, knowing I would never be the same person again.

To stop myself from falling apart, I kept myself busy by cleaning up the house for the wake. "Dust doesn't show once it's an inch thick!" I could hear her saying. She hated housework.

People came and said nice things and left, but I could not feel consoled no matter what anyone said so, with my fake smile, I went through the motions of polite conversation and making tea.

I just wanted to take my empty shell of a body back to India and The Boss.

Sitting in my mumma's house a few days after the funeral, I could feel grief taking over my whole body, and I knew I needed to be alone and do a puja for my mumma. In Tibetan Buddhism, death is considered to be the gateway to another life determined by one's karma, and I wanted my mumma to have a safe journey.

I booked a flight back to India, took some of my mumma's ashes and, on arrival, went directly to Varanasi to put them in the sacred Ganga River.

Varanasi is in the northern Indian state of Uttar Pradesh and has been regarded as India's spiritual capital since the 11th century BC. Manikarnika Ghat, which has burned continuously since it was first lit, is one of the holiest cremation grounds along its sacred riverfront. People come from all over India to this holy place, to die, to be cremated on the ghat and to have their ashes thrown into the sacred river. Men carrying dead bodies wrapped in red shrouds on stretchers chant their way to the fire day and night.

Unsure what I was going to do, I walked along the banks of the river and bought flowers and candles to perform a ritual and put her ashes in the water.

"What are you doing?" asked a man sitting with four other men on a platform on the river bank. They were all dressed in white.

"I have my mumma's ashes and I want to put them in the water."

"We can do a puja for you. We are Brahmin." Brahmin are priests and teachers who maintain sacred teachings across generations.

"Yes, please." I removed my shoes and joined them on the platform.

He took the little box of ashes from me and placed it on the floor, lit a small fire and performed an hour-long puja, with prayers, water and incense. The next stage was for me to take a boat out on the river, carrying my mumma's ashes on a plate surrounded by flowers. I had to throw it behind me and not look back. When I came back to the shore, the Brahmin poured water over me as a symbol of rebirth, and that concluded the ceremony. It was one of the most beautiful things I had ever done, and I could feel my heart healing.

I craved the comfort I felt in the presence of The Boss, and wanted to ask him to perform powa, a tantric practice, to transfer my mumma's consciousness to the Buddha's pure realms.

The Boss turned out to be in Bodhgaya, presiding over the annual prayer festival. Oh no! Not that shit 'ole! But I needed to see him and it was only a four-hour train ride away—that's if your train is not fifteen hours late!

I gave The Boss a photo of my mumma and he performed powa for her and told me what prayers to do at the temple. Only his presence and the need to do prayers for my mumma kept me from running away from that shitty little town.

For ten days, I saw him every day under the Bodhi tree, and every evening in a monastery where he was teaching. It helped ease my pain and my loneliness but it did not fill the space in my chest where my heart used to be, or remove the sinking feeling in my stomach.

My mumma was my life.

Once The Boss had left and I'd finished my prayers, I couldn't wait to get out of Shitsville, but I didn't know where to go. I definitely wasn't going to look up at a balcony with the mental cases or go to get bullied at the rinpoche class.

Then I heard a story about a sixteen-year-old boy who, in 1896, had challenged death by a penetrating inquiry into the source of his being. Later hailed as Bhagavan Sri Ramana Maharishi, he revealed the direct path of the practice of self-enquiry and awakened humankind to the immense spiritual power of the holy Arunachala Hill, the spiritual heart of the world. I liked the sound of this. It felt like the ideal place for me to go and heal.

I took a smelly train to Tiruvannamalai, a small town in Tamil Nadu, in south India. It was a sleepy, peaceful town, whose one main road, that had a few restaurants, chai shops, and fruit and veg stalls, circled the holy hill.

The Bhagavan Sri Ramana Maharishi Ashram was small, with peacocks roaming the well-kept gardens. There was a puja hall, a meditation hall where I felt peaceful as soon as I entered, and the room where Ramana died, which had his photo on the bed. It was the perfect place to practice self-enquiry and breathe fresh air.

On full moon days, I would walk 14 kilometres around the hill, a beautiful walk populated with sadhus and pilgrims. I would stop at little chai shops on the way and make the most of the ambience.

I rented an apartment next to the holy hill, on the ground floor of a three-storey house. As it had a private gated entrance, I made a hammock and hung it on the balcony. It made a quiet, secluded place where I could study, practice, contemplate and heal.

On the corner of my road was a small ashram that sold delicious thalis for less money than it would cost to cook them myself. I ate lunch there every day and met interesting, friendly people to guide me.

I rented a bicycle to visit temples around the hill. On one of my excursions, I stopped off at Karnapa Temple. A short walk along a dirt track through the forest, with wildflowers, and trees full of birds and monkeys, brought me to its entrance on top of a hill.

I climbed 15 steps, bowed to the few Hindu gods inside, dressed in red cloth, and sat at the back of the temple out of sight. An orange-clad sadhu was sitting there in meditation. He looked peaceful and I sat near him to get on his buzz. All of a sudden, his deep hypnotic voice broke the silence. "What is your question?"

"Who am I?" I was not sure if whether or not my question related to self-inquiry.

"You have another question," he smiled at me.

I wasn't sure what he was on about but, after a few minutes in deep thought, it came to me. "My mumma said she would contact me after her death, but it's been ten months and nothing."

He went into meditation. "Your mumma cannot reach you because you are grieving too much. You need to do tapas. Come here for ten days from six am to nine am and meditate, I will be at the gate." And he went back into meditation.

For ten days, I got up at four am to do yoga and then cycle 30 minutes to sit at the back of the quiet temple, surrounded by forest, and do as the sadhu said. Knowing my faithful sadhu was sitting outside the main gate made me feel safe and protected, and I let myself go deep into meditation.

On the seventh day, the sadhu, made a little fire puja, and covered my face in ash. "Tonight, your mumma will come. You must sleep on your right side and close your right nostril with your little finger." He demonstrated the position to me.

Excited, I cycled home and prepared for my big night. But my Mumma didn't come. I was disappointed but I carried on my ritual.

The next night, when I fell asleep I entered a dream-like state—and I met my beautiful mumma.

I was in a big room, sitting before a stage, in the first row, waiting for The Boss to appear. When I turned around, I saw my mumma and her friend, Pat, having a drink at the bar. I waved but she didn't wave back. She moved towards the big double doors at the side so I got up and followed her through. The room we entered was blindingly bright, as if neon strips were all over the ceiling and walls. On the left was a staircase. Pat, who in the real world was still alive, was walking down the stairs and she told me, "This is not my place."

I looked ahead and saw my mumma standing at the end of the room, gazing in a shining wall mirror. I called her and we walked towards each other. She was beautiful and happy. I had never seen her so peaceful. It filled me with joy. As she walked towards me, her form gradually dissolved into clear, bright light. "You are doing wonderful things. I hope you get your reward," she whispered as her now almost-transparent form stood in front of me.

"I will, Mumma," I replied and I wrapped my arms around her. "I love you, Mumma," I whispered and she melted into me.

"The Boss is coming!" I heard a voice shouting from the other room and ran back into the hall to take my seat.

Suddenly, everything disappeared. I was lying in my bed in bliss with my mumma's presence all around.

I sat with that sensation until I felt a pull to go to Karnapa Temple where I finished my last two days of tapas and said 'thank you' to the sadhu.

Reassured that there is something after death, and with my mumma's backing and The Boss's guidance, I felt compelled to do a ngödro, the key to the door of tantra. This consists of the four Tibetan Buddhist preliminary practices for the purification of lifetimes of misdeeds and the collection of merits. It consists of 111,111 of each of the following:

1. Prostrations to reduce pride and ego-clinging;

2. Recitations of Vajrasattva 100-syllable mantra for purification;

3. Mandala offerings to accumulate merit;

4. Guru Yoga practice, to join your Buddha-nature with the guru's Buddha-nature.

I had been putting this off for a long time, and now I had no time to waste. I started right there in my tiny apartment, with prostration. I put a pillow on the floor for my knees and, cushioning my hands with a pair of old socks, began; up and down, up and down.

Once I got over the pain, I started to love the prostrations. At first, I could only manage 20 in the morning and 20 in the evening, but it wasn't long before I was doing 1,000 every morning before breakfast. It would take me three hours and a lot of water but it was great.

So much stuff I wanted to put right and purify came to my mind. Naughty things I did as a kid, people I'd hurt and who hurt me, all the shoplifting and stealing, all the drugs and alcohol with which I'd abused my body, even stuff I hadn't thought about for years seemed to fly at me as I went up and down. I was cleaning out a filthy closet, confessing, regretting and purifying each past action as it came to mind. I started listening to myself in a different way as my faith and devotion got stronger.

After three hardcore months, I finished all 111,111 of those beautiful prostrations and knew I had to go back to Tibet. But this time to the holy centre of the world, Mount Kailash. I'd been told that one kora there could wipe out the sins of a lifetime, and one hundred and eight could bring you to nirvana and wipe the slate clean for *all* one's lifetimes. I was afraid that, with my dodgy leg, I wouldn't be able to manage 108 koras but that was a powerful incentive. Either way, it sounded like the perfect place to do part two of my ngöndro, recitations of the Vajrasattva 100-syllable mantra for purification.

4. The Center Of The Universe: 2007

From India, I could only get a one-month Chinese visa, and the month would start to tick down from the date it was issued. Plus, if I entered Tibet from Nepal, my Chinese visa would be replaced with a Tibet pass lasting just seven or 21 days (depending on what you paid). But, from Thailand, I could get a three-month Chinese visa, which I felt was long enough for Tibet to be mine.

Before I left, I had an audience with The Boss to receive his blessing, and went to the Dalai Lama's office to stock up with red cords, and herbal pills that he'd blessed. Sucking the pills brings reassurance and balance, and increases the power of your compassion.

I flew to Chengdu via Bangkok, booked a Tibet tour and waited five days for my Tibet pass, to enable me to fly to Lhasa.

I was elated to be back under that clear blue sky, surrounded by the Himalayas. It felt like home.

On my first day, I walked to the main square, did kora around Jokhang Temple, ate a bowl of thukpa and went to the tour shop. "I want to go to Mount Kailash," I told the heavily made-up woman behind the counter.

"We have a tour going in a few days with three people on it. That leaves room for one more. Maybe you should ask them if you can join?" she smiled, showing me her lipstick-marked teeth.

"How do I find them?" I asked, excited that everything was going smoothly.

"Leave your guesthouse details here and I'll pass them on when they come back to pay."

Eager to resolve the issue, I set about calling into guesthouses and restaurants, approaching each group of tourists with, "Hi, are you going to Mount Kailash?" I nearly didn't ask the woman on crutches I saw in the street, as she seemed an unlikely prospect. To my amazement, especially since she was only the fourth person I asked, she answered in a heavy accent, "Yes. I've booked a tour with two friends."

"I can't believe I found you!" I said, thinking that if she could do it on the kora on crutches, I could do it with my bad leg. "Could I join your tour group, please?"

"I need to check with the others. Have dinner with us tonight," she smiled sweetly. We made the arrangements and she hopped off.

The three of them were already tucking into their thukpa when I arrived. They introduced themselves as Anna, from Belgium, and Bob and Karen, from Australia. "We can't see a problem with you joining the tour with us," Anna told me in heavily-accented English.

"I only need a lift to Kailash—I'm going to stay there to do meditation practice—but I'll pay my fourth of the full cost," I told them as I picked up the menu.

"You won't be able to leave the tour, because the tour leader will be holding your Tibet pass," Bob said. His skinny body looked like it needed another bowl of soup.

"I have many Tibet passes," I replied showing him $100 bills, and we all laughed.

"Will you be OK, on crutches?" I asked Anna, wondering if she realised how arduous the trek would be.

"Oh yes. I've been like this for years. My leg was amputated." She pulled up her jeans to show me her solar-panelled electric leg.

"This is going to be some funny trek," I said, showing her my deformed leg in return, and wondering what disabilities the Aussies might have.

As soon as I finished my soup, I went back to the tour shop. "I found them. Please book me on their tour. But I need to be on a separate Tibet pass because I'm not coming back with them. I'll stay there," I said to Lipstick Teeth, discreetly passing her $50.

"OK. I can take care of that," she replied, slipping the note into her purse.

A few days later, we stood around a battered old jeep waiting for the driver. "Do you think this will make the ride?" Bob asked, kicking the tire.

"One way to find out," I laughed as I opened the back door for Anna and put her leg on the roof, for her, so it could recharge in the sun. "You three can get cosy in the back. I'll get in with the luggage." I wanted to continue part two of my ngödro, the Vajrasattva purification practice with 100-syllable mantra.

With the guide sitting beside the driver, we took off in what would be home for the next five days. I made a comfortable meditation seat out of the luggage, and sat back with my mala in my hand, looking out the window as the jeep rattled past snow-capped mountains against a cloudless sky. They loomed over me like a watchful god as waterfalls gently trickled down, washing my bullshit thoughts into the vast valleys below.

We drove throughout the days and slept in dirty, damp rooms, with thukpa and momos as our main diet.

Eventually, we arrived at Lake Manosaravar, 14,947 feet above sea level, stretched out before my eyes in all her beauty. If it weren't for the majestic Himalayan, snow-capped mountains surrounding her, I would not have been able to identify where her fresh water ended and the sky began. In the distance, I got my first glimpse of Mount Kailash. I sat on a rock gazing across the beautiful lake. Never before had a mountain made me feel so alive and connected to the planet.

In the tent where we had rented beds for the night, I ate a bowl of thukpa, slept content, and woke just as the sun started to rise over distant snow-clad Kailash. Wanting to purify myself before the kora, I did yoga at the edge of the lake and then plunged in, with the grazing yaks looking at me in disbelief. After three prostrations to Kailash, I immersed my whole body in the clean, glacial freshwater.

Revitalised—and almost frozen—I ran out, jumped around and vigorously rubbed my body to get my blood moving. I felt cleansed and ready to unite with the magnificent Kailash.

After a few more hours in the bumpy jeep, we reached Darshen, the nearest town to Kailash. "This has to be the dirtiest town I have ever seen," Karen said.

"You've not been to India, I take it." It didn't look too bad to me.

"No." She walked off, leaving us to unload the battered ol' jeep. When she returned, she looked horrified. "There's no toilet or running water, and everybody's going for a shit in the street." She was almost crying.

"There's human, yak, dog and horse shit everywhere, and it stinks," Bob joined in.

"One night, dudes. You can do it," I told them.

Our guesthouse was nice and friendly, and our host served us chow mein before we hit the sack ready for an early morning start.

"You're leaving your bag here?" Bob said as we got ready to leave Shitsville.

"Yes. I want the freedom to enjoy the hike." I threw my yoga mat over my shoulder.

"You're going to freeze," Karen said, observing that I was only dressed in combats trouser, jumper and trainers.

"I have faith in the blessings. I'll be fine."

"But you're going to stay up there? And you don't have a cooker or food?" Argh! Their default was to focus on the negative.

"I'll be fine. There will always be something." I was sure of that.

"Let's go. It's a 20km trek today," our guide told us, and we were off.

The rocky road had no trees, no chai shops and no restaurants. My leg was getting sore, and I struggled to keep up with the group, whose only concern was the destination. "It's going to be a long day and I want to take it slow and embrace it all. Please, you go on ahead," I told them.

"Will you be OK alone?" Karen asked, alarmed.

"Yes. I have the guru's blessing and I want to give out these blessing cords and pills from His Holiness, the Dalai Lama, to Tibetans I meet on the way."

Alone and going at my own pace, I fell into a beautiful, carefree trance as I walked through the magical landscape. It was untouched, natural and full of the colours of the rainbow. I passed many other pilgrims, some in groups, some on horseback or yaks, all chanting, singing, or prostrating themselves around the mountain. It was a world of love and worship and I felt free and alive.

And then I came upon the most beautiful sight of my life: Mount Kailash, the spiritual centre of the world. Its towering mass of black rock, speckled in pure white snow, sang to me as it stood more than 22,000 feet high, dominating the space around it.

Deeply moved, I continued walking and chanting until I saw the welcoming sight of the orange brick walls, Tibet-style windows and flat roof of beautiful Dirapek Monastery, built on the side of a hill.

I excitedly waded across the Lha-Chu River to reach it, only to be faced with 15 to 20 steep steps up to its entrance. Before I could tackle them in the oxygen-less environment, I had to sit on the bottom step to catch my breath. I was mesmerised by my view of the north face of Kailash, with three lesser mountains standing firm to protect it; Chenresig in the centre, Vajrapani to the west and Manjushri to the east.

Eventually, I hobbled up the steps to the top and opened the monastery's big wooden doors. As I entered, damp cold air filled my lungs and the first thing I saw in the dim light was a framed photo of The Boss on the altar. I was so overcome I could not breathe or talk and I fell to the floor in floods of tears. I was sure the photo was laughing at me.

A monk came to see what was going on and was surprised to see me lying there on the floor, crying like a child. I mimed that I wanted to sleep here and he pointed to a building back down the stairs.

After some time, I hobbled down and, to my surprise, found a guesthouse. It had a row of five rooms and a shop selling instant dried noodles, biscuits and candles. To the side was a restaurant, where I was delighted to spot a potbellied stove with a kettle on top. I rushed over to warm my hands, only slightly fazed by the dried animal carcass hanging from the ceiling.

Looking at me with wide-open brown eyes were two rosy-cheeked young Tibetan women, sitting on a rug-covered bench at a table. I don't think they had seen a white woman before. They were dressed in dark blue chupas, Tibetan traditional dresses made from yak wool. These full-length, sleeveless V-necked dresses tie around the middle, and are worn under a beautiful rainbow-striped apron and over a silk shirt.

"I need a room for a few nights," I mimed but, as most visitors just passed through, they could not work out what I was asking, though we managed to exchange names. Tenzin left to talk to the head monk while Drolma sat me down with a cup of hot water and investigated me from a safe distance.

Tenzin came back with a big smile on her face and took my hand to show me my room. It was a small, square room, a table beneath its one window and a door that didn't lock. Against the back wall was a mattress-less wooden cot with a thick carpet for a blanket.

"Toilet?" I mimed.

She pointed to the river. "I guess that cuts out the middle man," I thought.

Drolma came in with a hot water thermos and a bag of tsampa, the Tibetan staple food, made from barley flour. You mix it with hot water or butter tea to form a gooey biscuit or porridge, and enjoy it with dried yak meat. That explained the corpse hanging in the restaurant.

With tsampa and instant noodles from the guesthouse shop, I had food, I had a place to sleep and I had Kailash. The stars were so close I felt I could almost touch them and I knew I would sleep peacefully under their light.

In the morning, after defrosting the floor with candles, I did yoga and then moved outside to start my Vajrasattva practice. Sitting on a rock, where the previous incarnation of The Boss had sat, the defilements in me melted along with the snow on the north face of Mount Kailash.

Midday took me into Milarepa's cave. Milarepa (1052-1135) was from the Gungthang province of Western Tibet, close to Nepal. He was only seven when his father died and relatives took over his father's property, and mistreated the bereaved family. Embittered, his mother sent Milarepa to train in black magic, to wreak revenge on those who had destroyed her life. She was given her wish, as Milarepa proved adept at the practices he was taught, and unleashed a tide of destruction, killing many. But he came to regret his actions and looked for help to shed the bad karma he had acquired during his vengeful adolescence.

He first attached himself to the Nyingmapa Lama Rontgen, who observed that Milarepa had a karmic connection to Marpa The Translator and sent him to learn with him. Marpa was a teacher credited with the transmission of many Vajrayana teachings from India, including the teachings of Mahamudra. Being aware that Milarepa had, first of all, to purify himself of the negative karma he had accumulated, Marpa exposed him to an arduous apprenticeship. Among other trials, Milarepa had to build towers out of rocks to Marpa's specifications, with his bare hands —only to be ordered to tear them down again. Finally, Marpa gave Milarepa complete transmissions of all the teachings.

Practising these teachings for many years, in isolated mountain retreats, Milarepa attained enlightenment. He gained fame for his incredible perseverance in practice and his spontaneous songs of realisation. Of his many students, Gampopa became his main lineage holder, and this began the Kagyu lineage, one of the four main schools of Tibetan Buddhism.

Hearing about this great saint gave me faith that I too could purify my past and reach enlightenment. Maybe not in this lifetime but at least I could start.

After ten days of being at high altitude at the monastery, my body was getting weak and I was drying up. I had to put water into my eyes so I could blink, my lips were one massive cold sore, my skin was sagging and my poo was white from eating only tsampa and instant noodles. The vision of the Buddha and deities I'd hoped I might get at Kailash was being replaced by deep-fried chips and ice cream!

Then one day, my mumma appeared in the sky. "You silly cow! You ain't no Tibetan. Get yourself down and get something to eat!" Well, that told me.

I decided to leave the next day and head to Zuthul Puk, the next monastery on the kora, which was over the 5,650-meter Dolma La pass, to see if the food was different there. My leg was still swollen, and ached every time I thought about the pass, so I hired a horse and guide. Sitting high on a horse, with my guide leading us through beautiful, rugged, snow-encrusted mountains, I continued to do my practice to the sound of snow being crushed beneath his boots.

As we turned a corner, a rock wall filled my vision, kissing the cloudless sapphire sky. We had reached the Dolma La. "How does the horse get up there?" I asked my guide with a mind full of doubt. He just tipped his hat at me and continued walking. It was fantastic to see how the horse carefully and precisely manoeuvred over the rocky path. She had definitely done this before! My confidence restored, I relaxed and enjoyed the ride.

At the top, I jumped from my horse onto the icy snow, and hugged and kissed her goodbye, to the musical sound of fluttering prayer flags. I picked my way over slushy rubble past the lake to the tent to see what food there was, and was delighted— not— to see there were instant noodles or... more instant noodles.

Alone again, with no guide or horse, I was on top of the world in both senses of the phrase. Until a couple appeared wearing identical everything:

trousers; jumpers; boots; gloves; coats; hats; backpacks; and walking sticks. "Where's your group?" the guy asked in a strong Italian accent.

"What group?" Does he think I'm in a band?!

"Tour group?"

"No group. I left the tour weeks ago so I could stay up here and practice alone."

"Not possible." He looked at me as if I was mad. "Where's your bag?"

"I didn't bring a bag; just my yoga mat. I wanted to be free."

"Not possible," he informed me again.

"So where's your food and camping equipment?" the woman chipped in.

"My food's in that tent," and I headed off to buy a pot of noodles.

"My first English-speaking humans in weeks, and *this* is the conversation?" I thought. "I'm better off with the mountains." I sat down with my plastic pot of 'noodles again', looked over at the symmetrical couple, and saw they were making asparagus risotto on a gas cooker. No wonder they couldn't believe I only had a yoga mat. There was no way *I* was gonna be hefting bags of food and heavy equipment up the mountains.

Investigating a commotion nearby, I learned that an elderly Indian woman had just died. "It was her wish to die here next to Shiva and it happened. I'm so happy," her son told me, as her body was wrapped in a blanket, to be taken back to Darshen on horseback. Hindus believe that Mount Kailash is the abode of Shiva and some go there to die. Others die while on pilgrimage because their bodies can't manage the altitude. So I heard of a few deaths when I was there, but I was not worried: to die at Kailash would be fantastic.

To reach Zuthul Puk monastery, I had to take up the challenge of the strenuous walk down through the rugged landscape that got wilder and wilder. With my mala in hand and my mantra in my heart, I scampered over giant boulders on my hands and knees, and sometimes my bum, as my knee was fucked. I was exhausted but exhilarated when I arrived and happy to sit with its hanging yak corpse while warming my body next to its potbellied stove.

After a morning spent meditating in its cave, I decided I wanted to go back down. A beautiful six-hour scramble and bum-bump through rock formations and waterfalls brought me back to stinky Darshen, for a hot shower and a change of diet.

I went to the guesthouse I'd stayed in before, where I'd left my backpack, and had my fill of egg and chips; the meal my mumma always use to make me. Replete, I realised that only my stomach had brought me down and now I wanted to go back up. But I was just too tired so decided to go back to Nepal instead.

I handed myself in to the Chinese police as I didn't have a Tibet pass that would enable me to leave. I was ready for whatever was going to happen to me. "So you're the girl. We knew you were up there, but we also knew you would be back down," said the officer at the desk.

"Yeah, I was hungry," I laughed.

"We let you go this time" he told me, though he looked none too pleased.

They sold me a Tibet pass, the first one I had ever seen, which permitted me to hitch back to Nepal. The next day I went to the jeep stop. "I'm looking for a ride to Nepal," I said to the drivers and guides.

"There's an Indian couple that has space in their jeep. You should ask them."

I found an Indian couple in the only decent restaurant in Shitsville and asked if they were the ones. To my delight, they confirmed it and I asked if I could hitch a ride. "Where's your jeep?" The man's confusion showed on his face.

"I left it weeks ago so I could stay here to do practice."

"Wow! You went up the mountain?" The woman chipped in, in amazement.

"Yes, I was up there for nearly three weeks."

"You must be a goddess," and she touched my feet.

"Goddess, no, but crazy, maybe," I laughed.

"We were too frightened to go up," she told me, introducing herself as Anita and her husband as Sunny and inviting me to share their dinner. I tucked into all the delights on their table as I told them of my arduous journey around the sacred Kailash.

As we headed back to Nepal, they left the goddess alone in the back with the luggage, continuing her practice. It took us five days of rough-riding through rocky roads, rivers, and waterfalls, and sleeping in grubby guest houses, to get to Nepal. It was a beautiful journey. Anita and Sunny were happy to have the protection of a goddess and I was happy for the ride and to finish part two of the ngödro.

To complete part three, mandala offering, I went to the main seat of my precious guru, in Sikkim. I spent a month sitting comfortably in the shrine room, piling little heaps of rice and coloured crystals onto a brass plate to form a mandala that symbolised the universe. I offered it to the altar then wiped it clean and did it again, over and over until I reached my target of 111,111.

Feeling immensely grateful, I set off to do part four, Guru Yoga, under the sacred tree in Bodhgaya.

5. Dogs And Gods: 2004-2020

Bodhgaya didn't seem so horrifying this time. Maybe I had become used to the filth and poverty, or perhaps some dharma was starting to penetrate my heart. Either way, I saw things differently, felt more positive and saw beauty in everything, even myself!

I moved into a family-run guesthouse just off the main road. My basic room had an uncomfortable wooden bed that was home to termites, whose midnight feasts kept me awake. Hanging from the ceiling above this sad excuse for a bed, with its paper-thin mattress and greyish-white sheet, was a corroded, noisy old fan. On the back of the door were a few rusty nails with plastic clothes hangers. A plastic table and chair, and a grubby attached bathroom, completed the facilities. Luxury…not! The best things about the room were its view of The Boss' monastery, and its location just a five-minute walk from the sacred Bodhi tree.

It was all I needed. I quickly settled down to Guru Yoga practice and finishing my ngöndro during the annual prayer festival The Boss was presiding over.

I managed to find a space on the grass just to the side of The Boss' throne. Radiant, he was sitting under the sacred Bodhi tree, where Buddha attained enlightenment.

During the prayers, a group of monks handed out butter tea, served from enormous kettles, and warm bread, all paid for by sponsors. The butter tea was like a heart attack in a cup but welcoming after sitting still for hours in the frosty mornings. I liked to dip the bread into it and turn my mouth, that was dry from all the chanting, warm, soggy and buttery.

One day, as I sat on the grass near the tree, enjoying the puja's ambience and my view of the beautiful face of The Boss, a pregnant, tan-coloured dog sat next to me. I gave her my tea and bread and she lay beside me appreciatively until I left.

I was so grateful for her love, cuddles and company that I started to take her food every day. When she saw me coming, she would howl, sing and wag her tail, then sit with me until I left. I had a friend. I loved her and named her Honey.

When her six babies were born, I helped her make a cosy house inside an old tree trunk in the middle kora. Together, we pulled out all the old rotten wood until the trunk was big enough for her to get in and out. Then I filled it with straw and a couple of soft cushions. When Honey kissed me I knew she liked it, so I went and got her babies.

That tree was soon to become the maternity ward for many dogs.

One day, to my horror, I noticed that one puppy's skin had become scaly and scabby, with little open wounds filled with white dots. I had never seen this before and didn't know what to do or where to go for help. "Why doesn't somebody do something to help these suffering animals?" I asked the universe, not realising that that someone was going to be me.

"There a vet in town," a local boy who'd been watching told me, and he took me there. I walked into a small, windowless room, stepped over a few medicine boxes on the floor, and stood in front of an overweight man behind a desk in disarray.

"Please can you come and check the puppies at the temple," I asked, but he was reluctant to get out of his chair. "I can pay." That got him up. He picked up some medicine and we went back to the temple.

"It's mange. The white dots are maggots. They're eating the puppies alive," he said.

He injected the puppies with Ivermectin and soon dead maggots were falling out of the holes they had made. He removed the rest with tweezers and cleaned the puppy's wounds, leaving me with Topicure Ayurvedic gel to apply twice a day.

After just a week or two their fur was already growing back. Seeing that mange and maggot wounds could be cured so easily, I bought the necessary medicine, made myself a medical kit, and started to treat all the temple dogs and any other suffering dog I saw on my walks around town.

It wasn't long before I was going into the villages to treat dogs there too, making friends with the locals and beggars. My nursing background came in handy and I also started to treat the dogs for other problems besides mange. Although most of the time it was guesswork, that was better than *no* work. Later came Google: every answer I needed was right there on my phone, and I managed to do most of the treatments.

I made many dog friends and, as I got to know their unique personalities, names naturally started manifesting. I started falling in love with them and them with me. Watching their antics brought me so much happiness.

They would sit in the pujas, follow gurus around and lie down right in front of the shrines. I felt sure these dogs were monks and nuns that had broken their vows, or done something else negative, and so had to complete a life in the animal realm to purify their karma. But they had accumulated enough merit to be able to hear the dharma and be around the precious gurus.

They became like gurus to me. They taught me: how to be accepted into a pack by letting the alpha be the alpha; to back down in a fight and be submissive because you don't have to win; to return to playing with an opponent once a fight was over; how to express my true feelings and show someone I'm happy to see them or when I want to be left alone. And the best thing they taught me was unconditional love.

It was hard work, the conditions were challenging and it was often difficult to find the medicine I needed, but I did the best I could with the resources I could find, including my inheritance from my mumma.

It was amazing to watch the dogs flourish, and run around playing, with healthy coats. When they saw me coming, they would sing, howl and jump up, with their tails wagging so fast they would go around in circles, like the dogs were helicopters about to take off. I would see my mumma dancing and singing in every one of them.

Local people saw this love and happiness between us and started to want some of it. They became more loving towards the dogs and took to asking my advice. "What can I feed the dogs outside my house?" "Is it OK to pet them?" "Can you give me a puppy?" I was often called or tracked down to treat a sick dog or make homes for the mummies and puppies and it wasn't long before the locals dubbed me The Dog Lady, Dog Doctor, or Mamma Kutta (Dog Mother).

Outside my guesthouse one day, I noticed that a dog I called Princess had something hanging from her bum area. It was as big as my fist and full of puss and blood that was dripping from maggot-infested wounds in it. I had no idea what it could be. It was way beyond my capacity and I was clueless.

I was sitting on the road with Princess, in distress, when a voice interrupted my mantra. "Do you know Katy?" I looked up to see a western guy standing over me.

"No." I didn't have time to help him find his friend: my Princess was sick.

"She's an Australian vet, in town for the prayer festival."

"Oh my God! What does she look like?" I was on my feet so fast I nearly knocked him over.

"She's medium-built, with a blonde ponytail and wears a beige hat with flowers on the side," he told me.

It was puja lunchtime so I hunted through the restaurants until I found her. "Please, can you come and check a dog for me?" I begged, with tears in my eyes, which overflowed with relief when she nodded a yes.

"It's Transmissible Venereal Tumour, or TVT, a sexually transmitted cancer," she told me as she checked Princess.

"Can it be treated?" It sounded horrific.

"Yes. She needs to be desexed and then given chemotherapy. Vincristine sulphate once weekly for three to six weeks," she told me in a professional manner.

"Can you do it?" I pleaded, looking into her blue eyes.

"I have to leave but, if you can organise everything, I'll arrange for a vet to come and bring a surgical kit."

I felt completely out of my depth but that didn't stop me jumping into action. First, we needed to raise money for medicine, vet expenses and a space for a temporary hospital. The prayer festival was on, and over 100.000 people from all over the world were chanting prayers about love, compassion and peace in a marquee outside The Boss' monastery. During one of the breaks, I grabbed the microphone and made an announcement to the crowd, "Please help us to save the suffering street dogs. You pray here all day about love and compassion. Now is the time to put it into action. Right now, right here. We need money. Please help us with donations."

For two days, Katy and I stood outside the café, collecting money. We managed to collect around $1,000, which was more than enough to cover Princess' medicine and surgery.

Now we needed a building for a temporary hospital. Next to my guesthouse, a new guesthouse was being constructed. So far, just the brick structure was up. I rented three rooms on the ground floor.

Next was medicine. I bought what I could from the local medical store but the vincristine was not available. Finally, after some research and begging, I got a phial from an animal shelter out of town.

Staff. I found three animal lovers willing to volunteer, which was not easy in Bodhgaya. Most people come just to sit in the temple all day, chase gurus or sit in restaurants talking about gurus and their practice. They did not have time or focus for anything else, especially touching a dirty street dog. A guest house provided a room and food for the vet and his assistant, at a discounted rate.

Food. A friend had a restaurant where he cooked meat bones and rice for dogs that were undergoing surgery.

Since we had everything, we decided to make the most of it by sterilising a few females as well as Princess.

Before Katy left for Delhi, she walked me around the makeshift hospital, and briefed me on the procedure. I was now in charge and I was shitting myself. What if something went wrong and I hurt the dogs or even killed them? I had to put my nerves aside and keep squashing the negative thoughts that popped into my mind.

When the big day came, I was up at four, excited and afraid for Princess. I did some yoga and prayed to the Buddha for guidance, and by six I felt confident of my abilities to run this show.

I went to the makeshift hospital next door to meet the three volunteers, and found them waiting for me, which I took as a good sign. I prepared them for the day. "This room is for pre-surgery, where the dogs will wait. We need to cover the floor with cardboard and straw, so they feel comfortable and warm," I told them as we walked along the corridor of our hospital. "This room is for the surgery." I had already cleaned it and installed a clean table with a stick for a drip stand. "And this is the recovery room: we need to put more straw down. We'll fill these empty plastic bottles with hot water to keep the dogs warm after surgery, and I've also bought blankets. All clear?" Everyone nodded.

A group hug and we were off to get straw and cardboard, then catch Princess and four other females.

Catching them was surprisingly easy because the dogs knew us. They were happy to come and play, wagging their tails as they followed us back to the hospital. We played with them and petted them in the pre-surgery room, while we waited for the vet to arrive from Varanasi.

After an hour, the novelty wore off for the dogs. They started to howl, chew the doors and fight each other. It was getting stressful and I was relieved when my phone broke into song at noon. The vet had finally arrived at my guesthouse. I directed him to the back where we were, feeling relieved that an experienced person had arrived.

"I'll get lunch and a shower and be ready in less than an hour. By that time, the surgical kit will be sterilised, and we can start. I just did 70 dogs a day in Varanasi. I'm the best," he told us, running his fingers through his greasy black hair and wiping his hands down his jeans.

We continued to do our best to entertain the five dogs, keeping their mind off food and water because they were fasting. All they wanted to do was get out and we were getting frustrated and stressed by the time the vet returned.

I was concerned to see that he was in the same dirty clothes, and his hair was hanging over his face. "I need more light," he said as he moved the table to the window, not caring that the dog's temperature would drop during surgery and it was freezing outside. "Sedate the first dog," he said to his assistant who didn't look old enough to be out of school, let alone sedate a dog.

I didn't notice him wash his hands once or sterilise the table, and I could not feel or see any compassion in him for the dogs. I was starting to get worried about hygiene and infections. Then I heard a deep "Hoooowwwwwlllll!" from Princess and ran into the surgery room. She had come round from the anaesthetic and was distressed at being restrained. Despite her being conscious, the vet was continuing with his work and was about to cut her open.

"Stop!" I screamed, throwing myself over Princess. "Get out of here. You will not touch any one of these dogs!" The volunteers helped me get Princess off the table as the vet went outside with his assistant running behind.

Once I'd cooled down, I went to see the vet, who was sitting on the step of my guesthouse. "Please don't send me away. It will damage my reputation," he begged.

"You only care about your reputation. You can fuck off!" I gave him the money for a taxi home to Ranchi and released the five dogs.

Meanwhile, one of the volunteers had phoned Katy, who was at a conference in Delhi with another vet, Dr Dee. Dr Dee had an animal shelter in Sikkim, called SARAH (Sikkim Anti-Rabies and Animal Health Division). When she told them what had happened, they were horrified and they caught a night train to Bodhgaya, so we could start again the next day.

Early morning the next day, we went through the same routine of catching the dogs, bringing them to the hospital and trying to entertain them while waiting for Katy and Dr Dee's train to arrive. It wasn't long before two highly qualified vets walked through the door, all supportive smiles.

Seeing us huddled up with the dogs trying to keep them calm, Katy introduced us all to Dr Dee and then said, "You go and have breakfast."

"We can manage from here," Dr Dee said. I hugged them both. I knew it would be OK now and I put yesterday's experience behind me.

A full day of surgery was successfully undertaken, with love and kindness towards the six dogs. Four females and two males had been desexed and Princess went on to recover completely from TVT.

We decided to get a private audience with The Boss to show him photos of what we had spent the donated money on, and ask for help to start an annual project, which we called ABC (Animal Birth Control). "We will discuss with the committee," he responded in his hypnotic voice.

A few days later, I was in the garden with one of my favourite dogs, Ginger Spice, and her three puppies, next to the steps leading into the Mahabodhi Temple's main shrine room. I saw The Boss coming down the steps so I quickly held up the puppies. "Please help us. You're the only one. Please," I spoke for the puppies in a baby voice as he walked past. He looked over and smiled.

It wasn't long before the monastery's committee agreed to host an annual animal camp. I needed professional training quickly so Dr Dee invited me to her animal shelter to train as a paraveterinary worker.

In partnership with the magnificent team from Sikkim, Vets beyond Borders and the Brigitte Bardot Foundation, we started an annual 10-day animal camp in Bodhgaya, in the field just behind The Boss' monastery. It filled me with particular joy whenever The Boss popped in to say 'hi' or bless a sick animal or even when he simply walked by. It was magnificent to be close to him in such an informal way.

In fact, the whole camp is magnificent. At the main gate, there is an outpatient station for any injured animals. A mobile clinic goes around the villages to treat any sick animal. An education program goes to the schools to teach children how to be kind to animals.

Working with a professional and loving team each year, I learned more medical procedures and became increasingly comfortable in my role. By now, we're like a family and the whole camp glides along like a well-oiled train, getting bigger and better each year.

The catching team are amazing: it is beautiful to watch those boys in action. They go out in the truck at about five am, collecting street dogs. They catch them either by hand or with a net, which is not easy because the dogs often run away and hide at sight of them, and sometimes they bite. But these amazing boys always manage to bring a truckload of dogs back to the camp for desexing.

After breakfast, they take the recovered dogs back to where they caught them, and catch more for the afternoon or the next day's surgery.

In the afternoons, I usually go out to catch dogs with TVT and other health problems. We work hard over long days, but the results are gratifying.

Each year, around 350 dogs are desexed, and more than 1,000 animals get the healthcare they so desperately need. It's hard to believe that all this manifested from my little hospital for Princess in a half-built guest house. To walk around the town and see the healthy and recovered dogs and animals is a blessing; my mumma's blessing.

Each winter, monks and high lamas come to Bodhgaya from all over the world. It is an open buffet of teachings, pujas, blessings, empowerments and transmission. You'd need to split yourself into pieces if you wanted to attend it all. With my ngödro complete, I had a better understanding of the practices and felt ready to join the tantric teachings. But I was still struggling to fit in with the other students so, instead, I spent my free time taking care of the dogs.

During this time, I kept bumping into the humble monk whose teachings I had attended in the Himalayas, and we would smile and say 'Hi'. After he'd departed, this monk started to appear in my dreams most nights. I felt like I knew him and we needed to talk, so I went back to the Himalayas to see if I could get a private audience.

Arriving back in the fresh air of the Himalayas, I got a cheap room and went to the monastery where his little damp room was. Having climbed the steep hill, I stopped to get my breath on the terrace outside the monastery. "I need to talk to the rinpoche," I said to a monk who was passing by.

"Just knock on the door," he told me.

"Really?" Surprised it could be that easy, I knocked nervously on the metal door.

"Come in." His deep voice rang out.

Uncertainly, I entered the small kitchen that led to his living room and walked through the arch. Sitting crossed-legged on his bench, gazing peacefully, was the humble monk from my dreams. His presence was warm and welcoming and I felt myself relax. I made three prostrations, offered a katha and sat down in front of him.

"How are you?" He sound genuinely interested, which gave me the confidence to talk to him as a friend.

"I'm fine, just confused as to why are you always in my dreams."

"This is our karmic connection," he told me.

"I know we have some connection and I want to be here, but I feel excluded; as if I don't belong. I'm not comfortable here." I was holding back tears.

"Just try. Next week, I start a three-month teaching programme."

Oh wow! My heart skipped a beat. The guru had just invited me to join his class. Then I *did* belong and I *was* worthy of the teachings. I almost cried.

I floated out of that little room and back to town to look for an apartment for three months.

I attended every class. His limitless wisdom sang to me and filled my heart with happiness as it trained me in the tools I needed. Gradually, I began to love everyone and everything around me. Instead of seeing the negative side of any situation, I focussed on the positive.

He knew precisely what I needed to grow spiritually and became the assassin of my ego. No matter how well I disguised any negative emotion that I had hidden deep inside, he managed to bring it to the surface and either mirror it, address it in his group teachings, raise it in a private audience or model a better way through his own actions. It was often brutally painful and I would want to run away, but I knew he was showing me my faults and flaws, what I needed to work on for my spiritual growth, and how to benefit others.

The Me that had travelled the world alone for 20 years had a big ego. It was strong and always liked to be right so would sometimes argue back. But he never rejected me. He was always there, whether my mind was ugly or blissful. His primary purpose was to bring me to enlightenment, no matter what it took or how many lifetimes.

I devoted my life to him, the Buddha, the dharma, and the sangha and began to divide my time between Bodhgaya and the dogs, and, when the rinpoche was teaching, the Himalayas. I attended every class I could.

After a few years, the rinpoche asked me to help run his centre in the Himalayas. In truth, I was reluctant to take on this responsibility and commitment, but I knew I had to do it not only to help him, my saviour, but to also interact more with human beings and try to love them as unconditionally as I loved the dogs. So I agreed.

It was another example of the guru knowing what would be the best practice for me. It was not easy dealing with so many students, all caught up in their own emotions and afflictions. I had to develop patience, tolerance and loving-kindness—fast! I had to put their needs before mine so that no one would feel rejected, lost or unworthy, like I did when I first came to dharma.

The transformation I was experiencing was a miracle and I felt the need to share it with my friends still suffering back in the UK, so I organised a one-month UK teaching tour for the rinpoche.

It was an enormous success and loads of people asked me to bring the rinpoche again. Looking at their shining, happy faces, I knew I had to do it and it became an annual summer event.

On the 7th July 2013, an unknown terrorist planted ten bombs in and around the Mahabodhi Temple complex in Bodhgaya, and the explosion injured five people. In response, security was stepped up. The government bulldozed the market area outside the temple complex and replaced it with a giant wall. Bored, armed police and army officers stood around the little town, on the lookout for further attacks.

To enter the temple, you now had to pass two security checkpoints, be searched and have your bag X-rayed. No mobile phone was allowed, in case it was a disguise for a bomb detonator. Although there was an office outside where you could leave your phone in a deposit box, there were more phones than boxes and the queues were so long that no one wanted to waste their time in them. Instead, they tried to sneak them in, hiding them mainly in their shoes since that was the only place the police would not touch.

The queues to enter became long and tedious, and there were often disputes as monks, nuns and lay practitioners with dead flowers on a plastic plate to offer to a statue, fought, screamed, shouted, pushed and shove their way to the security checkpoint. There was no love and compassion in those queues.

While searching you, the policewomen would often have a feel of your tits and fanny. They were so bored that they would have competitions to see who could find the most phones, when they found one, there would be a big drama as you were reprimanded and sent away.

Because I treated the sick temple dogs, I had an official pass from the temple management, enabling me to avoid all this drama and skip the line with my phone safely in my pocket.

High officials of the district often came to see the Mahabodhi Temple's facelifts and check the security, and one of these officials did not like street dogs. He ordered that they be removed from the temple grounds in any way possible. He did not care how.

The management did not know what to do, so asked me if could hide them when he came. Foolishly, I agreed, not realising how challenging it would be.

Before his next visit, it took me and two friends, two days to construct an iron cage in a gated area at the back of the temple. Then at five am on the day he was due to visit, I went to the temple with food to entice the dogs to follow me to the gated area. By about 10 am, I had gathered around 30 dogs and settled them down with a big dinner, and was waiting there with them.

At two pm, the official in question came into the temple to do kora. To my horror, he strayed from the kora path over to the gate behind which the dogs and I were hiding. I felt sure he would find us but the dogs were all quiet, and we lay calmly until he'd moved away.

As soon as he left the temple, I was notified that I could let the dogs free. I opened the gate and they drifted into the temple complex.

On his next three visits that season, I hid them at The Boss's monastery, 15 minutes' drive away. This was even more challenging and stressful. I organised a few volunteers, including a driver, to help me dismantle the iron cage at the temple, load it into a pickup truck, take it to The Boss's monastery and reassemble it on his monastery grounds. The day before his visit, I cooked up loads of food and the driver took the pickup truck to a welder to get a cage built onto the back, for transporting the dogs.

In the early morning on the day of his arrival, we started our Save The Temple Dogs mission. It took three runs to catch around 30 dogs, loading 10 at a time into the truck, then transport them to the monastery and unload them into the cage.

To keep them calm, I fed and watered them while waiting for the phone call that would let me know he had left the temple. Then we loaded the dogs back into the truck ten at a time and took them back to the temple.

The dogs were not happy with this at all, and used to cry and fight each other. Not knowing where they were going made them afraid and being cramped together in a cage all day distressed them. One would start howling and it would start the others off. It was stressful for them and for me.

Then, the last time I hid them, the temple guards would not let me return them to the temple. I had to release them onto the street outside the temple and walk them through the main gate.

Feeling let down, I refused to do it again. These days, security guards chase the dogs out of the temple for these official visits. I don't like to see this brutality so I stay away on his visits. I concentrate on healthcare for the street dogs, and the annual animal camp.

~ ~ ~

I'd began to get hot and sweaty during meditation. I thought it was a sign of progress until I realised I hadn't had a period for months. So this was menopause. I had heard so many horror stories about this body change and counted my blessings that, for me, it was mild.

It was immensely freeing not to have the surprise of blood dripping out of me and ruining my pants, the mood swings, stomach cramps and thoughts about having a baby. I had my certificate of middle age. However, it did have a significant effect on my mental state. I would get bouts of depression and paranoia. I also put on weight and started to feel dumpy, ugly and unfeminine. So I started a casual love affair with a younger man, Freddie. He was tall, fit and handsome, and I thought it would boost my deflating ego.

But sitting in the temple one day, I saw him walking around the outer kora with a younger woman, and something told me she was not just a friend. "Are you having sex with her?" I asked later that day, when we were sitting in a teaching.

"Yeah, of course I am," he replied, well chuffed with himself, with no clue that I was heartbroken.

I became depressed and tried my best not to be in the same place as them because, when I saw them together, I would feel rejected and stupid. I tried meditation and yoga and went to many teachings, but nothing was shifting my pain. I decided the answer was to get laid—and I knew the man to do it with.

"I need to have sex. Can you do it?" I asked Mark, a friend of mine that tried to shag every woman in town.

"Sure. When?" He was a bit taken back but ready for action.

"Now," I demanded.

"OK, I'll come to your room in five minutes."

We started a fling that helped me feel less rejected and ugly, but it still crushed me to see the other one walking around this small town, with his new younger trophy on his arm.

One day, as I sat in my usual spot in the temple, Mark appeared with two plastic cups of chai and sat next to me. "My girlfriend's coming for Christmas, so I'm not sure what we should do," he said as he sipped his hot tea.

"You have a girlfriend?" I couldn't believe it.

"She'll only be here for a few weeks," like I was to wait!

"We need to finish," I told him. I didn't want the complication.

Now I had two men I didn't want to see walking around this tiny town with their girlfriends, all loved-up. It was impossible not to bump into them. I was devastated and felt fat, ugly and rejected.

Trying to pretend it didn't matter to me, I went on a mission to get myself a new boyfriend. "Come to my room," I told my young Tibetan friend, who was in town for the teachings.

He obliged and we got straight down to business. As I lay in his arms afterwards, he whispered, "My wife mustn't find out."

"What wife?" He had never mentioned a wife to me before. Shocked, I asked him to leave.

I now felt like a total tramp and was fed up with the whole dating game.

On New Year's Eve, I sat at the feet of the Buddha statue in the temple and made a New Year's resolution of celibacy.

I found it difficult at first because I still had strong sexual desire, but it diminished over time and it has become one of the best decisions of my life. I feel free when I check out a member of the opposite sex not as a partner but as a friend. Without the distraction of spending time with my current man, and all the emotions that a sexual relationship creates, I have more mental space to focus on dharma. Instead of love and sex, I devote my life and my time to the dog project, The Boss and the rinpoche.

6. Lockdown: 2020

I was in Bodhgaya when I first heard about this coronavirus killing people in China, then moving to Europe; but I carried on with life and caring for the dogs.

Then one day, I woke to find all the schools closed and international flights cancelled; and I knew our lockdown was coming.

I didn't think Bodhgaya would be the best place in which to get locked down, or sick, for many reasons. The summer heat was the main one; no health care, a close second. So I bought my tickets out (Gaya to Delhi to Goa) and the next day I went to the airport.

As I watched the flights on the board change from scheduled to cancelled, I held on tight to my ticket and prayed. Not until the plane took off, with me aboard, did I believe I was going anywhere.

I spent the night in Delhi, went through the same anxiety with my Goa flight—and arrived safely two days before the first curfew.

It was great to see the ocean from my taxi and I couldn't wait to get in it, walk along the soft yellow sand and inhale the fresh salt air. I had been longing for a holiday for months.

I spent my first night in a beach hut, but I needed a room with a kitchen: lockdown was coming, and I would need to cook.

The following day, I went out hunting and was disappointed that none of the beach huts contained more than a bed: none had cooking facilities. I walked along the beach road to see if I could find anything there.

Not having much luck, I went to see Johnny at his restaurant and to have a lunch break. I had met him many times and knew he had his fingers in a lot of pies on this beach, plus, going by the size of his increasing stomach, I knew he must be eating them as well.

"Johnny," I shouted out as I entered his resort. It was lovely to see his familiar, chubby face.

"Welcome back." He offered me his hand with a warm smile and pulled me over to sit with him at a table.

"I need an apartment with a kitchen close to the beach for a local price."

"I have something for you. Meet here tonight at seven." He smiled, patted my hand and was off.

Feeling somewhat sorted, I ordered an extra spicy curry with rice and relaxed.

At seven, I went back to meet Johnny and he took me on his scooter to show me my new home, a two-storey house in a great location, next to the shops on the beach road and backing onto the river, with a big, lush garden full of banana and coconut trees.

Johnny led me to the back and up an outside tiled staircase to the top floor where we entered the apartment, via a communal balcony, into a big room with a bed, wardrobe, table and bathroom. This room led into a fully-equipped kitchen, with a second, private balcony overlooking the river. There were two other apartments, one next door and one underneath, but they were empty. I was the only guest.

I liked it a lot: no roadside noise and no drunk or stoned neighbours disturbing me with their parties and dope fumes. I moved in the next day.

I turned the private back balcony into a practice space, complete with a shrine and crystals, and the front one into a dining area, stocking the kitchen with pulses and the fridge with veg.

Then came the announcement of the first curfew. I knew there would be more to come, and I would not be able to get out for a while, so I went to see Johnny at his resort, 15 minutes' walk away, to get extra bedding.

"You're on your own here. I have my own family to look after, so don't come here if you get sick," he said as he handed me the bedding.

I was shocked our friendship could vanish so quickly but, when I called a few western friends who lived in Goa, I got a similar response. I was on my own. Frightened, I went to the local doctor to buy medicine I might need if I got sick from the virus. I managed to say, "Can I get a packet of antibiotic, paracetamol and vitamins?" before I burst out crying.

"Why are you crying?" She was a cuddly, short woman of about 40, with gold-rimmed glasses.

"I'm alone here, and I'm afraid." I was shaking.

"You are not alone. I will help you." The care in her voice made me cry even more.

She gave me her number and, feeling less alone and a little better, I went to the beach to swim. As I floated in the water, I felt relaxed, calm and remembered the teachings of the Buddha:

All compounded things are impermanent.

All dualistic emotions are painful.

All phenomena are empty and void of self.

Nirvana is true peace.

In Buddhism, there are many teachings on the death moment. Buddhism teaches that, at death, you are simply changing form, like changing hotels. The consciousness, or mind, continues. Why then was I letting my emotions drag me into paranoia and fear?

When I stayed in the present moment, I felt good. So I decided to focus on the breath.

Breathe in "I'm alive. I'm happy."

Breathe out fear and sorrow.

Lockdown one, for three weeks, arrived and I was ready. My fridge and tiny freezer were full of vegetables and fruits. I had lots of dried food and bottles of drinking water. I set up my back balcony for a Tonglen meditation retreat, exchanging myself with others.

Breathe in the suffering of the world.

Breathe out healing, love, peace, and happiness.

Except—this was not going so well. I was not feeling much love, peace or happiness. For the first time since I started to travel, my freedom to move as I pleased was gone. My future was cancelled and unsure. I was back to sitting and watching, like when I was a disabled child... but this time I was watching my mind.

In my deepest loneliness, I felt stripped of everything I ever knew or identified myself with and was full of anguish and fear. Emotions buried inside me were coming up and flying at me. Maybe I should fly back to the UK? But if I'm going to die, would I want to die there? No, I want to die in India near my gurus.

My mind was overloaded so I moved to my front balcony, where the sun was shining. I was reading when a man came up my steps. "Can I help you?" I asked, not knowing who he was.

He held his palm out in front of my face as he walked past me to switch on the electricity to pump the water from the well. I watched him go back down the stairs to the house next door, where a woman who was gardening started shouting at him in konkani. Konkani is spoken in a screeching tone that rises at the last symbol. When shouted, it sounds like a load of cats having a standoff. It went right up my spine.

I was soon to learn that this rude man was the owner of the house. Johnny rented from him and sublet to me. He lived next door with his wife, two girls of around 13 and 10, and their precious boy of six. I named him Cunty and his wife Bitchy since, unfortunately, they were the worst people in Goa. I usually found Goans friendly and relaxed but lockdown brought out the worst in some people, I guess.

Several times a day, Cunty would come up to my part of the house to turn on or off the water pump, fix something on the roof or pick mangos from the tree. One morning when he came to switch the pump on, I tried to offer to switch the pump off to save him coming back up. "Hi, I ca..." Before I got any further, he moved to push me in the face. Luckily, I moved back in time. "What the fuck's the matter with you?!" I asked in shock. Without even looking at me, he went back down the stairs.

Bitchy never spoke to, or looked at, me, and the kids just stayed away. The only time they spoke was to complain about something I had done or not done, or just because they objected to me breathing.

Cunty did repair work every day that involved lots of banging about, chopping trees, burning wood and shouting at his family members. Meanwhile Bitchy did gardening, with the little boy running behind her, whining. She had also started cooking on an open fire under my back balcony and the smoke billowing in prevented me from sitting there.

They wanted me out but, because of lockdown, no guesthouses were taking new people. The situation was uncomfortable and I started to feel lonely, rejected and depressed.

After three weeks, when the lockdown eased and we could go out from seven am to nine am for shopping, I would sneak out, walk the isolated beach at sunrise, and find some comfort in the warm water.

One day, Cunty had three fires burning all around my part of the house and was banging nonstop at the concrete path to make a hole. I could hardly breathe and the noise was giving me a headache. At breaking point and fearing that, if I did not go out, I would badly beat up that cunt, I called the police. "Please, sir, listen to this noise. I need to get out or I'm going to go mad." I held the phone over the balcony.

"OK, madam. You go out but don't get caught," the officer replied.

I walked past Cunty, banging away at the concrete, opened the garden gate and ran across the road, cutting through the closed resort opposite and onto the beach. I stood there in shock, not because I was out but because so were many others. The beach had bodies all over it, sunbathing, swimming, surfing, walking. There were even children playing with inflatables in the water. It was as if I had entered a different world just by walking through that resort gate. Two minutes from my hell was heaven.

"Every day it's like this," a waiter at the resort told me.

"But it's lockdown." I was stunned.

"Not on the beach and the sunny restaurant is also open for food and drinks." I ran into the water giggling like a child and splashed my fears and frustration away.

I talked to the foreigners lying on the sand but most of them seemed to have got drunk and stoned at the first curfew and hadn't sobered up since. I might have snuck out for a solo swim but they were holding secret forest parties, sharing spliffs and having casual sex with each other. They didn't seem to know or care about what was going on and clearly had no respect for the virus, the precautions, the risk of infecting others, India or its laws.

"Those rules are for Indians," one guy told me.

"Goa's a green zone so we can do as we please," another said.

These people seemed to be in a completely different reality to mine and I just couldn't relate to them. I had lost a few friends to the virus and was getting calls from people in Bodhgaya that were starving. And what about my precious dogs? I felt distressed and isolated.

Then I realised that my judging mind was at play so I decided to do my own thing and leave them to do theirs.

At one end of the beach was the start of the forest, where multi-coloured boulders and rocks surrounded a beautiful oasis of calm, clear water. I would often see fish and dolphins jumping. Huge trees and plants of various shades of green and yellow stuck out between the boulders, and monkeys swung from branch to branch while eagles flew above. And of course, there were doggies.

I would float on that calm water and watch the beauty of this continuous show. Peace and gratitude would fill my body and it would be a nice break from my anxiety about 'corona', as we called it at first; a time for some normality.

One day, returning from the beach, I found Cunty covering the outside of my apartment in blue plastic. Goans do this to prepare for the rainy season. "Cyclone coming," he told me. My room was now dark and hot.

The cyclone's rain and strong winds lasted three days and destroyed some of the village and beach, including my roof. Now I had a water feature in my kitchen, as rain poured down the wall like a waterfall and splashed onto the floor. On the first night, I tried to fix it myself. I climbed a rusty ladder onto the roof and covered what I could with some of the plastic Cunty had left lying around outside my door, weighing it down with rocks. It didn't help: the water feature just got more elaborate.

"Please, can you fix my roof?" I asked him the following day, when he came up to pump the water.

"No materials. All shops are closed," he replied.

"Can't you do something? It's dangerous." I was worried about the electricity and also getting sick. He just walked off and it took all my inner strength not to push him down the stairs.

I fixed it as best I could and put towels and buckets around. When it stopped raining, I went to try and find a new place but, still, no one was taking new guests.

I decided to try and make friends with them and create harmony but they were not interested. They just wanted me out. But I had nowhere to go.

Some dharma friends in north Goa told me a friend of ours had made it to the Himalayas. We discussed travelling together and started organising the paperwork in line with the requirements of the travel restrictions.

We were only allowed one check-in bag so I sewed two rice sacks together to make one big sack. I put my backpack, trolley wheels and yoga mat inside to keep it all COVID-19 free. I downloaded the tracking app and waited for the COVID-19 e-pass which would enable me to cross into different Indian states. Then I could buy my travel tickets. My future was looking brighter.

After another day of abuse from the Cunty family, with no friends or sober people to talk to, and with the full moon rattling me, I decided to leave without the e-pass. Yes, it was risky but anything had to be better than staying in that house one more day. So I booked tickets for the next day: Goa to Delhi; sleep one night in Delhi airport; Delhi to Dharamsala.

I didn't sleep that night. Fear of the trip made me shake uncontrollably. I felt like I would explode. I had to keep catching my breath, getting up and walk around. I had never felt anything like it before.

In the morning, I did yoga and meditation to calm myself and went to the gate to get a taxi to the airport. Bitchy was there as I put my luggage in the car and it was the first time I saw her smile.

The drive to the airport was smooth, but I was still shaking and my stomach kept turning over. I felt sick. Dark thought were passing through my aching head. What am I doing? Will I get to Dharamsala? Will I get the virus? Will I get stuck in Delhi?

At the airport, everyone was in masks and disposable gloves and walking around like zombies in a mass of confusion. I floated along with them. A man sprayed my rice sack with disinfectant and directed me to join the socially-distanced queue. I stood behind a green line on the floor. Each time the person in front of me moved forward, I kicked my rice sack and moved my shaking body along, feeling like I was in some kind of horror movie.

I reached the entrance and showed my ticket and passport to a camera, an officer behind a plastic riot shield checked my temperature, and I was finally allowed to enter the airport.

There were no trolleys so I struggled with my rice sack to the check-in desk, threw it on the scales, checked in and headed to the security check. Again, there were social-distancing lines on the floor. I moved towards the X-ray machine, put my electronics into a plastic box that got pushed along with a stick, and went for my body check. The police officer stood arm's length from me behind a curtain, zapped me over with her metal detector and stamped my boarding pass, and I was through.

COVID-19 felt real, and my anxiety and shaking worsened as I walked to the departure gate. Black eyes, wide with fear, peered at me from behind masks.

I sat on a chair in a room full of tension until it was time to board. Social-distancing my way onto the aircraft, I was handed a plastic shield to cover my face and a small bottle of water.

I sat back in my socially-distanced seat and tried to relax, but I was still shaking inside and was starting to feel sick. It was one of the saddest things I had ever seen or experienced.

At the baggage carousel in Delhi, I could feel the tension, including in my own body. I nearly lost control of my legs so I sat against a wall.

We were all each other's enemies.

I started to cry and couldn't stop, and then the shaking started again. I was beginning to feel I had made a mistake, and there was nothing I could do about it.

I got out my yoga mat and lay down to relax but air-conditioning was making it too cold. Even with all my clothes on, and the rice sack pulled over me, I still couldn't warm up or even stop shaking. I lay under the bright strip lighting, trembling, feeling sick and anxious, and struggling to breathe. I stuffed earplugs into my ears to drown out the farting, snoring and loud chatting into phones. It didn't work. Again, I thought I was going to explode.

Suddenly I shifted from thinking to awareness. I was watching myself lying there, shaking. Everything around me was a display; an illusion. Nothing was real. I was an actress playing my role. I lay there in a dream-like state until it was time to check in for my Dharamsala flight.

I still felt distant from my body as I watched it repack its backpack, put it back into the rice sack with the wheeled trolley and yoga mat, leave Delhi arrivals and enter Delhi departures. The guards were kind and helpful, which enhanced my dream-like state as I followed the same procedure as in Goa, physically-distancing myself to the check-in counter.

"You are not a resident of Himachal Pradesh, so you cannot board this flight," the lady behind the desk said as she waved over her supervisor.

"I am a resident," I said and showed her my permit and other papers.

"But you were not born there," she insisted.

After examining my papers, the self-important supervisor directed me out of the line to a help desk. "I'll make some calls." He picked up the phone. After five minutes, he returned the phone to its cradle and smiled at me triumphantly. "No!" Passing me back my papers, he walked off.

My body froze and my dream-like state vanished as my mind went racing everywhere. "Now what will I do? I don't want to be stuck in Delhi. Why did I leave the paradise of Goa?" Goa now indeed felt like a paradise that I desperately wanted to go back to.

I managed to buy a new ticket for Goa, leaving the following day, and organised a night in a five-star hotel, with a car to and from the airport. I waited just inside the door of the airport for the car, which turned out to be spotless, with the smiling, calm driver sitting safely inside a plastic, tent-like shield. Sitting in the back, I started to feel myself relax.

The hotel was gleaming with cleanliness, and friendly staff showed me to my room, which helped me relax further. After a hot shower and hot food, I managed to sleep until my alarm went off.

I did yoga to ground myself and meditation to chill myself out, then went back to brave the airport.

Having gone through the whole physical-distancing procedure again, I finally sat down on an empty Goa-bound plane.

At Goa airport, I counted my blessings and embraced my second chance as I collected my rice sack and walked out the exit gate.

I now had two choices. I could do a COVID-19 test and stay in government quarantine until the results came back, or I could do 14 days of self-quarantine at home. I didn't want to hand my freedom over to the government, as I could imagine all kinds of problems and it costing me lots of money, so I joined the line for home quarantine. I had a temperature check, gave my name, address and phone number, had a get-out-of-quarantine date stamped on my hand, and I was out.

I jumped into a taxi, the driver of which was not wrapped in a protective tent as in Delhi, and headed to the beach. I wound down the window, breathed in the fresh air while looking at the green palm trees, and relaxed.

It was time to stop trying to get somewhere and just enjoy being here. I needed to accept the universe's flow and stay in the present moment, where everything is fresh, new and blissful, increase my equanimity, decrease my judging mind and stop following my emotions. Now was the perfect time to apply all the Buddha's teachings that I had received, and to be the light for others.

I still hadn't found anywhere to stay so I sat in the back of the taxi, continuing to search the Internet but finding nothing. I phoned Johnny, who told me my old place did not want me back. No surprise there! Just as I was starting to get anxious, someone sent me an ad for a beautiful one-bedroom apartment.

"When is the apartment available, please?" I asked the voice at the end of the phone.

"Now."

"I'm coming. I'll be there in 30 minutes." I asked the taxi to go directly there.

"Where have you come from?" the owner asked me, noticing I'd arrived in an airport taxi.

"Palolem," the neighbouring beach. I was too scared to say I had just come from Delhi.

"OK." He knew I was lying but didn't seem to care. He was just happy to have a renter. He gave me a discount without argument, lent me a bicycle, provided me with vegetables and fruit and sent me a hot thali. I was blessed.

The apartment was new, modern, fully furnished, and set back from the road on the top floor of a two-storey building. There was a lounge, with a dining table, a sofa and glass doors overlooking the rice fields. The bedroom had a huge double bed, a wardrobe, and air-conditioning. The kitchen had a fridge, cooker and a water filter, and the bathroom had a hot shower. Every window had green vegetation outside. I could not believe my luck. I had never had such a beautiful, luxurious home and I quickly got down to cleaning it.

In the morning, I went out to get some basic needs for my two weeks' quarantine and found an open shop where I bought two big bags of supplies. On my way back, I noticed a man and a woman dressed in moon suits, masks and gloves outside my old place.

"What are you doing?" I asked.

"Looking for Miss Gardiner," the woman answered.

"That's me."

"You are in quarantine. Why are you outside?" She was cross.

"I'm sorry, I needed food." I showed her my shopping bags. "I will not come out again, I promise." I was afraid they would take me away to the government quarantine. "I live in a different place but do not know the address." I gave them directions to a nearby restaurant. "Call me once you reach the restaurant and I will come and fetch you."

I rushed home and awaited their call. When they called, I went to the restaurant one minute walk away, to meet them.

"You are out again," she said, more sternly than before.

"But I had to come to get you. I'm sorry." I was almost in tears from the fear of being put in government quarantine. She eased off and we walked at a social distance to my place.

The whole village was coming out to see what was going on, with two moon suits and a white foreigner walking down the road. When a woman grabbed her two children and ran into the house, I started to feel nervous. I had heard horror stories of villagers getting together to get quarantined people out of the neighbourhood. I thought I was going to be stoned or beaten or worse.

"Come in," I offered when we reached my apartment.

"No need," she said and stuck a big 'In quarantine' sticker, stating my out-date, on my door.

"You're doing the health check here?" I was confused.

"No need," she said, and they walked off.

My immediate neighbour had two children, and I was sure she wouldn't want a quarantined foreigner from Delhi next door, so I thought it would be best to come clean with my landlord. I phoned the building manager, Rappy, and explained my situation. "Don't worry. Just remove the sticker and go out," he laughed.

I did not do that, but I started to feel more relaxed and was brave enough to look over my balcony at my neighbours in the garden below. To my relief, they smiled and waved. I walked around my luxury apartment, giving thanks to the universe that I had made it back safe.

Alone in quarantine, I felt grateful for my experience in Delhi. It had been one of the most terrifying yet enlightening experiences of my life. My darkest moments of uncertainty, fear and loneliness had been the start of a complete turnaround. It taught me to accept, and surrender to the present moment.

As my quarantine end-date approached, I was excited about getting on my bicycle and going to the beach. I was unsure whether I was allowed out as I hadn't seen or heard anything from the moon suits since they had put the sticker on my door. But when my release date arrived I decided just to go.

I put some biscuits for the dogs in my bicycle basket and cycled along the main beach road. Fuck, it was depressing! The street was empty and everything was closed and covered in blue plastic. The silence was so eerie I was starting to get freaked out, so I started singing *This little light of mine I'm gonna let it shine*, and I got louder and louder as I threw biscuits to the tail-wagging dogs. Locals started to come out of their homes and I continued to sing, smile and wave while throwing out the biscuits.

I parked up and took a walk along the beach and breathed in the mighty monsoon that was churning the sea into constantly-crashing high waves.

Reaching the beautiful oasis of the rock beach, I sat on the highest rock, feeling the power and vibrations of the ocean as its waves crashed beneath me. "I wish I could do that with my constant flow of thoughts," I said to the spray of water. "I feel so lost, lonely and friendless. Most of the other foreigners are constantly drunk, stoned or hungover, and living messy lives: the type of life I left behind and don't want to enter again. I feel like I'm swimming upstream. Please don't let this loneliness drag me back to that." I started to cry, let it out and couldn't stop. "All my efforts, achievements and attainments have vanished into space. I'm no longer The Dog Lady or the guru's helper. There's no planning, no organising, no tickets, no travel, no life, nothing. I feel stripped naked."

Then, through the ocean on the strong wind, came the rinpoche's voice, "Me. Me. Me. I. I, I. You are not your thoughts. You are not your emotions." My tears of sadness turned to tears of laughter. All my attachments to the mind-created past and future fell away, and I finally settled into the present moment. As consciousness itself emerged, the sad, desperate feeling, which after all had never been concrete or tangible, dissolved and I felt as free and light as the eagles flying above me in the cloudy monsoon sky.

I, me, my life, the rock, the ocean, the waves and everything around me became one, in timeless space.

When I got off the rock, I walked into my new beginning, no longer lonely, just alone with the freedom to be whatever I wanted to be.

Tara Gardiner

Epilogue

I have travelled the world and experienced life to the full, and there is not much I haven't done or seen. Life was a party, and I was the party. All day and all night, with a drug and alcohol-infused body, I would be on the move, constantly searching for the next fleeting thrill to replace the last. I could never get enough; because, deep down, I was never truly happy.

Short-lived happiness was OK while it was happening but, when it was gone, there was an empty void inside that I tried to fill with more debauchery. Eventually, I started to get bored with the travelling scene. Everything begun to look the same, and it was becoming exhausting finding my way around a new culture, language and customs, while always on the lookout for a better deal or some sucker to pay for me.

When I found yoga, I didn't realise it would have such a transforming impact and would lead me through the best journey of my life. I have learned to find stillness, to look deep inside myself for buried triggers and habitual patterns that spark my negative emotions and reactions, and to transform them. It's not about what happens to you: it's about how you react to it. Everything depends on our mind's projections and reactions, so it's up to me if I want to be happy, sad, positive, negative or chase after my thoughts and emotions.

You are your own master: don't let your ego fuck it up.

I am now dancing in the light, swimming in the ocean of knowledge, and hiking the trail that takes me to sit on the highest mountain and enjoy the view.

If you have never travelled in the way I have, I want to let you know one thing. You can be high up in the Himalayas, on a beautiful beach, in a concrete jungle or in a cardboard box. As long as you allow yourself time and patience to stay in the present moment with the breath, and travel inside yourself, you are going to have the most beautiful journey, the journey of a lifetime.

I wrote part one of this book in 2002, in my jungle house in Thailand and part two during the 2019 lockdown, in Goa. I wrote it to help others and hope that whoever reads it gets something out of it.

Writing my life story has been purifying and uplifting. I now like the naughty part of me, and I'm less righteous with the clean part of me. I've have managed to blend them to make a better me; the person I have always wanted to be.

For as long as space endures,
And for as long as living beings remain,
Until then, may I too abide,
To dispel the misery of the world.

~ Shantideva ~

GLOSSARY

A

Aarti - A Hindu ceremony in which brass candelabras, with wicks soaked in ghee, are lit and offered up to one or more deities and the departing sun.

Acid - Lysergic acid diethylamide or LSD, a hallucinogenic drug.

Afro - a hairstyle in which naturally tightly-curled hair is styled to stand out all round the head.

Asado - Barbecue. (Argentina).

Ashram - A centre for spiritual learning and religious practice.

Ayurvedic – Pertaining to Ayurveda, the traditional Hindu system of medicine.

B

Babylon - Police. (Jamaican slang).

Backpackers – Backpackers' hostel. (Abbreviation).

Banter - Playful and friendly exchange of teasing remarks

Blessing - Spiritual protection.

Blow - Cocaine.

Blowing - Having taken, or taking, lots of cocaine.

Blow job - The act of oral sex performed on a man.

Bodhicitta - Enlightenment-mind - A mind that strives towards awakening, empathy and compassion for the benefit of all sentient beings.

Bodhisattva - In Mahayana Buddhism, A person who is able to reach nirvana but delays doing so through compassion to stay in samsara to benefit suffering beings.

Bombed - High on drugs.

Boombaclart - A Jamaican insult. (Literally, arse cloth).

Booze - Alcoholic drink.

Buiti achuluruni – welcome (Garifuna)

Bula - Hello or love. (Fijian).

Butter lamp - A brass lamp that holds butter and a wick for making offerings of light to a holy object, often used as a focus for meditation.

Butter tea - Tibetan tea made with yak butter and salt.

B-52 - A layered shot composed of coffee liqueur, Irish cream, and Grand Marnier.

C

Camper - Campervan. (Abbreviation).

Cannabis - Refers to three plants with psychoactive properties (Cannabis Sativa, Cannabis Indica, and Cannabis Ruderallis). The flowers and leaves are dried and smoked.

Cash-in-hand - Cash payment for work (which enables the worker to avoid declaring the income for tax).

Chai - Boiled milk, sugar, and tea.

Chenresig, Vajrapani and Manjushri - Great Bodhisattvas of Mahayana Buddhism symbolizing respectively the compassion, power, and wisdom of the Buddhas.

Crack - Cocaine cooked into pure solid rocks.

Cutlet - Fried vegetable patty.

D

Downs/downers - Drugs that calm you down or put you to sleep.

Dreadlocks/Dreads - Hairstyle of African origin involving locking or braiding to form rope-like strands.

Drum - Home. (London slang).

Djellaba - A long loose-fitting unisex robe.

Dumb waiter - A small lift to move things from one level of a building to another.

Dunny - Toilet. (Australian slang).

E

E - Ecstasy.

Ecstasy - A synthetic, psychoactive drug.

Eightfold path - A summary of the path of Buddhist practices leading to liberation from samsara. The practices are: right view; right intention; right speech; right action; right livelihood; right effort; right mindfulness; and right concentration.

Empowerment - Within Buddhism, a ritual performed by a qualified Buddhist master to enable a student to begin a specific tantric practice.

F

Fags - Cigarettes. (UK slang). Gay men. (Derogatory).

Fallen off the back of a lorry - Stolen.

Farang - A foreigner. (Thai).

Four noble truths - The first teaching given by the Buddha: suffering; the cause of suffering; the cessation of suffering; and the path that leads to the cessation of suffering.

Fiddle - To falsify figures or data. (Typically to steal).

Fleece - To trick or cheat someone for money or belongings.

Frappé - A Greek iced coffee drink.

Full-body prostration - A gesture of reverence used in Buddhist practice, which involves putting the hands together in prayer and touching the forehead (body), throat (speech), and heart (mind), followed by bending the knees to lie flat on the floor, with the hands together in prayer, beyond the head.

G

Ganesha, Ganesh or Ganapati - The elephant-headed Hindu god of beginnings. He is traditionally worshipped before any major enterprise and is the patron of intellectuals, bankers, and authors.

Geoglyph - A large design or motif produced on the ground.

Ghat - A flight of steps leading down to a river (Hindi).

Gobsmacked – Surprised. (UK slang).

Goon - Flagon, two litres of wine in a box (Australian slang).

Green card - Card proving permanent residency status for the USA.

Guru - Teacher. Literally, one who dispels the darkness. From gu - darkness, ru - light.

H

Hand-me-downs - Secondhand items (often clothes), often passed from an older child to a younger within a family.

Hash - Cannabis compressed into a solid block.

Have a puff - Take a draw on a joint.

Hit - A blast of a drug.

Hit on - Attempt to seduce.

High five - A hand gesture whereby two people each raise one hand, about head-high, and clap their palms together.

Hook up - Meet and have sex.

I

Ivermectin - A medication used to treat parasitic infections, such as mites, demodectic mange, scabies, ear mites, intestinal parasites, hookworm, roundworm and capillaria.

J

John - A prostitute's customer.

K

Kagyu - One of the four main lineages of Tibetan Buddhism.

Kasbah - Fortress (Arabic).

Kathoey - An identity used by some people in Thailand. Some people who describe themselves as kathoey might be described as transgender women in English. Others might be described as effeminate gay men.

Katha - A traditional ceremonial scarf that, when offered to a Tibetan Buddhist guru, symbolises purity, goodwill, auspiciousness, compassion and sincerity of one's offering. The tradition of offering katha also aims to ensure that everyone can afford to offer something.

Knackered - Very tired. (UK slang).

Knacker's yard - Scrap metal yard. Also graveyard.

Kora - A pilgrimage or meditation that involves walking clockwise around a holy site (Tibetan).

L

Ladyboy - An identity used by some people in Thailand. Some people who describe themselves as ladyboys might be described as transgender women in English. Others might be described as effeminate gay men.

Lakshmi or Laksmi - The Hindu goddess of wealth, good fortune, youth, and beauty.

Lego - A brand of children's plastic building bricks.

Long Island Iced Tea - A cocktail, made with vodka, rum, gin, tequila, triple sec and sour mix, shaken and poured over a glass full of ice, with a splash of coke.

LSD - Lysergic acid diethylamide, a hallucinogenic drug.

M

Mahamudra - The union of all apparent dualities.

Mala - Prayer beads, usually consisting of 108 beads on a string, for counting mantra.

Malaka - To masturbate. An insult, often used affectionately (Greek).

Mandala - A geometric configuration of symbols.

Mantra - A sound, word or phrase repeated to aid concentration while praying or meditating.

Mashed - Highly intoxicated.

Middle - Drugs that stabilise you from an 'up' or a 'down'.

Monosodium glutamate - A flavour enhancer commonly added to Chinese food, canned vegetables, soups, and processed meats.

Momo - Tibetan (and Nepalese) savoury steamed or fried filled dumpling.

Muezzin - A man who calls Muslims to prayer from the minaret of a mosque.

Mull up - Roll a spliff. (Australian).

Mzungu - A white person. (East African).

N

Nigga - A form of address used non-pejoratively within black communities.

NVQ - National Vocational Qualification, accreditation of a work-based form of training in the UK.

O

OD - Overdose. (Abbreviation)

Off one's tits or face - Highly intoxicated.

Out of it - Drunk or stoned.

P

Peeps - People. (UK slang).

Piña colada - A cocktail, made with rum, coconut milk and pineapple juice.

Pitcher - A jug of beer, usually three or four pints.

Pokey - Gambling slot machine. (Australian slang).

Prostrations - A gesture of reverence used in Buddhist practice, which involves putting the hands together in prayer and touching the forehead (body), throat (speech), and heart (mind), before kneeling and touching the forehead to the floor.

Prayer-wheel - A cylindrical wheel on a spindle, made from metal, wood, stone, leather or coarse cotton, used in Tibetan Buddhist practice. A mantra is written on the outside, and often also placed inside. Spinning a prayer-wheel clockwise is believed to achieve the same meritorious effect as reciting the prayers. Rows of prayer-wheels are found in temples and hand-held ones are also available.

Prostration board - A board for performing full-body prostrations.

Psychedelic - Pertaining to the psychedelic drug subculture of the 1960s. Psychedelic art and music reflect the altered consciousness achieved by taking drugs such as LSD.

Puff - Hashish, or a draw on a joint.

Pulled - found a sexual partner.

Puja - Hindu prayer ritual.

Q

Quid - British pound. (Slang).

R

Rass - Arse (Jamaican slang).

Rastafari - Religious and political movement, begun in Jamaica in the 1930s.

Rastafarian/Rasta - A follower (often dreadlocked) of the Rastafari movement.

Rebirthing - An alternative therapy technique used to resolve negative experiences from birth or childhood.

Reincarnation - A new existence after death. A key belief within Buddhism is that beings' consciousnesses are reincarnated in a new form in an endless cycle (saṃsāra), which is unsatisfactory and painful (dukkha). The cycle stops only if enlightenment (moksha) is achieved by insight and the extinguishing of craving.

Riad - A traditional house built around a central courtyard. Such a house converted into a hotel. (Moroccan).

S

Sadhu - Religious ascetic, mendicant or holy person.

Sakyamuni - One of the titles of the Buddha, deriving from his birthplace of Sakya.

Salt pans/flats - expanses of ground covered with salt and minerals, formed by evaporation.

Samadhi - The highest mental concentration state that a person can achieve while still bound to the body, uniting them with the highest reality.

Samosa - Deep-fried vegetable/meat/fish pastry.

Samsāra - The Buddhist cycle of death and rebirth.

Sangha - Spiritual community.

Sarong - A long piece of cloth worn wrapped around the body.

Sawadee Ka - Hello. (Thai).

Score - Buy drugs.

Shag - Have sex (with).

Sheila - A woman. (Australian slang).

Shim - A transwoman or transvestite.

Shiva - One of the principle deities of Hinduism.

Shot - A measure of sprit, or mixed, alcoholic drink, intended to be drunk quickly in one go.

Skin up - Roll a cigarette containing drugs.

Skinny dipping - Swimming naked.

Slums - Rundown housing.

Spark up - To light (e.g. a spliff).

Spliff - Rolled-up cigarette containing either hash or weed.

Springbok - Medium sized antelope found in southern and South West Africa.

Squat - Unlawfully occupy an uninhabited building.

Stoned - intoxicated by drugs.

Stupa - A form of Buddhist architecture that is generally considered to be place of burial, or a receptacle for, religious objects

T

Tabs - Dried drops of liquid LSD on blotting paper, which can be swallowed to bring on a psychedelic trip.

Tag along - Follow the crowd.

Tapas - Ascetic Hindu practice, voluntarily carried out to achieve spiritual power or purification.

Thames - London's principal river.

Thangka - A Tibetan Buddhist painting on cotton, or silk appliqué, usually depicting a Buddhist deity, scene or mandala.

The bollocks - Literally, the testicles. Colloquially, the best.

Toyboy - A younger male lover. (Derogatory).

Transmission - Oral transmissions are passed down from master to student to create an auspicious connection with a sacred text, which gives the student permission to study that text

Trip - A psychedelic "journey" that can last for several hours after taking a hallucinogenic drug, such as LSD.

Tots - Second-hand stuff, usually clothes. (London slang).

U

Ups/uppers - Drugs that give you energy.

Ute - Pickup truck. (Australian).

V

Vajrayana - The tantric tradition of Buddhism.

W

Walkabout - A traditional journey, usually on foot, taken by Aboriginals.

Weed - Cannabis in the form of dried flowers and leaves.

Wrap - A paper fold to form an envelope, typically used to refer to such an envelope containing illegal drugs.

Y

Yaba - Methamphetamine and caffeine tablets smoked in a pipe or cigarette.

About the Author

Tara Gardiner wanders around India, going where the wind takes her, and everything she owns, still fits in a backpack

To contact me and read more stories

visit my website

https://taragardiner.org

Printed in Great Britain
by Amazon